# Policy Analysis for
# the Real World

. F

# Policy Analysis
# for the
# Real World

BRIAN W. HOGWOOD
and
LEWIS A. GUNN

OXFORD UNIVERSITY PRESS

Oxford University Press, Walton Street, Oxford OX2 6DP

Oxford New York
Athens Auckland Bangkok Bombay
Calcutta Cape Town Dar es Salaam Delhi
Florence Hong Kong Istanbul Karachi
Kuala Lumpur Madras Madrid Melbourne
Mexico City Nairobi Paris Singapore
Taipei Tokyo Toronto
and associated companies in
Berlin Ibadan

Oxford is a trade mark of Oxford University Press

Published in the United States by
Oxford University Press Inc., New York

British Library Cataloguing in Publication Data
Data available

Library of Congress Cataloging in Publication Data
Hogwood, Brian W.
Policy analysis for the real world.
Bibliography: p.
Includes index.
1. Policy sciences.   2. Political planning—
Great Britain.   I. Gunn, Lewis A.   II. Title.
H97.H625   1984   361.6'1'0941   84-16645
ISBN 0-19-876184-8✓

11 13 15 17 19 20 18 16 14 12

Printed in Great Britain
on acid-free paper by
Biddles Ltd
Guildford and King's Lynn

# Preface

As teachers of policy analysis to both conventional students and practitioners of policy in Britain, we were struck when we developed courses from the early 1970s onwards by the acute shortage of published material derived from or relevant to, the British scene. That problem is less serious today and several useful British texts have appeared in recent years (see e.g. Jenkins, 1978; Pollitt *et al.*, 1979; Carley, 1980; Ashford, 1981; Burch and Wood, 1983). But for each such reference in the typical reading list there are still several which require of the British student an unusual knowledge of, or willingness to be instructed in, the intricacies of ward politics in San Francisco, say, or the finer points of bureaucratic procedure in Washington DC. Clearly, then, the problem of generating suitable and readily available teaching material for British courses has not yet been overcome. Although our primary interest was in producing policy analysis materials for British students, our experience has made us aware of the limitations of much American literature for *American* students since it offers as generic truths what are merely contingencies. While the illustrations used in this book are mostly British, we feel that our general framework will be of interest to American students, particularly those who have previously thought of policy analysis as merely American politics rehashed, or as arcane mathematical techniques.

A good policy analysis teaching course must make students aware of the repertoire of techniques available for assisting analysts and decision-makers at various stages of the policy process. However, much of the literature about particular techniques concentrates on technical points and assumes that the 'optimal' decision will automatically be taken and enforced by a single, authoritative decision-maker. This literature fails to discuss the use and limits of policy analysis techniques in real-world political settings. Accordingly, there is a need for materials which stress the *consumption* of analysis as well as the techniques for generating it.

Obviously, no one book on policy analysis can cover in detail the whole range of theories, techniques, and policy contexts which the policy analyst might face. What we have attempted to provide in this book is a framework which is at the same time self-contained but into which additional material can readily be 'plugged'. We provide guidance in each chapter about how particular techniques or other themes can be further explored and we hope that this book provides a critical frame of mind in which to conduct such exploration. In our view, it is the absence of such a framework which leaves many policy analysis students perhaps knowledgeable but unsure what their knowledge signifies.

Much of the material in this book has appeared in a series of teaching modules prepared as part of a Policy Analysis Teaching Project funded by the Nuffield Foundation. We would like to thank those who have commented on those modules. Chapter 13 draws heavily on work conducted jointly by Brian Hogwood and Guy Peters. Above all, we would like to thank students at Strathclyde over the years, who have helped to teach us most of what we know about trying to teach policy analysis.

Brian W. Hogwood
Lewis A. Gunn
University of Strathclyde,
November 1983.

# Contents

## Part II Analysis in the Policy Process

# Part I
# An Approach to
# Policy Analysis

# 1

# A Framework for Analysis

## 1.1 The intellectual framework of the book

There is considerable room for disagreement about what constitutes 'policy analysis'. The distinction between *description* (how policies *are* made) and *prescription* (how policies *should* be made) is necessary, but it can be taken too far and we do not believe that either can be excluded from teaching and, especially, training in policy analysis. Our own position is closest to that of Harold Lasswell (1970) in his concern for both 'knowledge of' and 'knowledge in' policy-making. If forced to indicate a priority, however, we would have to say that in our eyes the defining characteristic of policy analysis, as well as its novelty and value, lies in its prescriptive aspect. It was the applied, socially relevant, multi-disciplinary, integrative, and problem-directed nature of policy analysis which attracted us, as it did many other social scientists in the United States and Britain in the 1960s and 1970s. That bias towards prescriptive analysis—towards the analysis of the 'improvement' of policy processes and policies themselves—certainly influences the policy approach adopted throughout this book. However, our focus on prescriptive analysis is concerned with enabling students to *analyse prescriptions* rather than presenting any single 'correct way' to make policy of our own design.

The intellectual framework of this book, which is the basis of the chapters in Part II, can be described as a 'mixed framework'. Below we try to spell out the assumptions of the framework as well as what it does not assume.

## 1.1.1 A FRAMEWORK FOR BOTH DESCRIPTION AND PRESCRIPTION

The first sense in which the framework is 'mixed' is that it can be used as a framework for both description and prescription. Like many other analysts, we find it useful to analyse the policy process in terms of a number of stages through which an issue may pass. We list below the stages which we find useful for the purposes of presenting the analysis which can be brought to bear on an issue, recognizing that these are not definitive (and that from time to time we adjust this list ourselves):

(1) Deciding to decide (issue search or agenda-setting)
(2) Deciding how to decide (or issue filtration)
(3) Issue definition
(4) Forecasting
(5) Setting objectives and priorities
(6) Options analysis
(7) Policy implementation, monitoring, and control
(8) Evaluation and review
(9) Policy maintenance, succession, or termination

It should be stressed that this list is not intended as a straightforward description of what actually happens to every issue; rather, it is a framework for organizing our understanding of what happens—and does not happen (see chapter 4). The policy process applied to any given issue in practice may be truncated (e.g. the option selected may be to do nothing). The dividing lines between the various activities are artificial and policy-makers are unlikely to perform them consciously or in the implied 'logical' order. To take two examples, it is sometimes only at the implementation stage that questions are raised about the objectives the programme is expected to achieve, and one lesson often learned at the evaluation stage is that the logically prior activity of defining the problem to which the programme is addressed has never been undertaken or, perhaps, consensus about the nature of the problem was assumed where none existed. Despite these limitations, students, including those who are themselves practitioners, find this set of stages valuable as a means of organizing what they already know about how policies are made.

Turning to the prescriptive aspects of the model, this framework provides an aid to understanding how different kind of analysis can be brought to bear at different stages of the policy process. It should be stressed that what is being advocated here is not a simple-minded: carry out analysis relevant to stage 1; complete stage 1; carry out analysis relevant to stage 2; complete stage 2, etc. There are two important reasons why this would be inappropriate. (1) First, the framework stresses the importance of analysing the implications of each stage *in advance* of actually carrying it out. Pressman and Wildavsky (1973) drew our attention to the importance of taking possible problems of implementation into account when designing a policy (see also Wolman, 1981). Hogwood and Peters (1983) stress the importance of taking into account the possibility of future policy replacement or termination at the time of selection of the initial policy. To leave analysis until the process has reached the stage where the analysis is 'relevant' would in many cases be useless, since the analysis, or the options suggested by it, may be precluded by decisions taken at earlier stages of the process. For example, improvements in 'implementation' might imply changing the policy already decided on. It may be impossible to evaluate a programme properly if provision for evaluation was not built in to the programme design. It may be difficult or impossible to terminate or replace a programme if this possibility was not taken into account when the policy was originally formulated. (2) The second reason why it would be misleading to view analysis in terms of a straight-forward sequence through each stage is that the processes of analysis will frequently be iterative: e.g. some initial prior definition of an issue is necessary to conduct initial issue search; more careful issue definition later may lead to further issue search; issue search and issue definition often involve forecasting, etc.

## 1.1.1 SELECTION OF APPROPRIATE MODE OF ANALYSIS

The second major sense in which the framework could be said to be 'mixed' is that it does not conform to either of the stereotype extremes of the synoptic rational–comprehensive model or the incremental 'muddling through' approach (see chapter 4). Our approach is not so much a 'middle' way as a recognition that the appropriate mode of analysis and decision-making will vary according to the issue and the issue context. It is thus a contingent approach, which recognizes both the resource limitations which preclude in-depth analysis of all issues, and political factors which sometimes makes attempts at 'objective' analysis irrelevant. Our framework stresses the consideration and explicit selection of the appropriate mode or modes of analysis at an early stage of the policy process, preferably on the basis of explicit criteria. For a few issues this will entail detailed and expensive analysis drawing on a range of sophisticated quantitative techniques; for others, it will indicate the need for a politician to take a quick decision on the basis of limited information.

The overall emphasis in the framework lies more towards 'rationality' approaches, though towards the rationality of Simon's prescriptive model rather than the straw-man 'rational–comprehensive' model set up by Lindblom (see chapter 4). This emphasis is reflected in the contingent approach in our framework already referred to. Following Dror (1968), our approach is also 'economically rational' in the sense that we argue that analysis should be conducted only to the extent that it is likely to produce benefits through better informed decision-making at least commensurate with the cost of analysis. Again following Dror, we include an important role for qualitative judgement in analysis, and would go further to argue that political debate can itself be an appropriate form of 'analysis'.

## 1.1.3 TECHNIQUES AND PROCESS

This leads us to the final major sense in which our framework is 'mixed': it is concerned both with the application of techniques and with political process. Indeed, what should distinguish policy analysis from, say, 'management sciences' is precisely this emphasis on the use of analysis in political settings. The political and institutional setting will help to determine whether particular techniques or procedures will 'take' and will affect how the results of analysis are 'consumed' by decision-makers; emphasis on particular techniques may in turn have (often implicit) implications for political process (e.g. the degree of central direction in the political system). The use of techniques in policy analysis is rarely 'value free'. Many techniques have unstated but built-in assumptions about values. In other cases a particular technique may be used for political purposes to advance a case or protect an organization from outside interference rather than for genuinely analytical purposes. Some processes are inherently value laden: issue definition, which we argue should take place at an early stage of analysis, is often a highly political, rather than merely technical, activity, which shapes all the subsequent stages of analysis.

The role of policy analysis, as we see it, is not to replace but to supplement political advocacy. As Wildavsky (1980) has argued:

The purpose of policy analysis is not to eliminate advocacy but to raise the level of argument among contending interests . . . The end result, hopefully, would be higher quality debate and perhaps eventually public choice among better known alternatives.

Our framework does not assume (as arguably many other models of decision-making do) that there is only one policy actor who may be interested in commissioning or consuming analysis. This implies that the 'appropriate' mode of analysis may vary from actor to actor, and that critiques of technical analysis may enter into political debate. Access to policy analysis can itself become a political resource with an uneven distribution. This book should help to provide a training in such 'counter-analysis'.

It should be clear that our framework provides no quick 'policy' analysis fix' to the complex, often intractable problems of a developed industrialized society nor a neat method for marrying analytical techniques to democratic or participatory processes. It offers no general 'right way' to make decisions, nor does it provide a clear pointer to the substantive content of decisions. What we hope the framework does provide is a structured opportunity to explore issues which requires readers to face up to the need to make an explicit decision at each stage about how to analyse an issue.

## 1.2 Analysis in the policy process

Bearing these considerations in mind, we outline briefly below the relevance of analysis to each of the stages listed in section 1.1. Each chapter in Part II of the book will explore a stage in detail.

### 1.2.1 DECIDING TO DECIDE (ISSUE SEARCH OR AGENDA-SETTING)

This involves the identification and anticipation of problems or opportunities which suggest the need to consider action. One of the least explored aspects of real-life policy-making in Britain is how certain issues get on political 'agendas' for discussion and action while others do not. It is difficult to feel that we perform this crucial activity of what is sometimes called 'problem search' or, as we prefer, 'issue search' in a sufficiently informed or forward-looking manner. Some problems and opportunities are unforeseeable, but others might be identified at an earlier stage through improved methods of scanning the agency's 'horizon' for advance indicators. Relevant approaches include the development of 'social indicators' and various types of needs-analyses, demand forecasts, technological forecasts, etc.

### 1.2.2 DECIDING HOW TO DECIDE (OR ISSUE FILTRATION)

Once a problem or opportunity has been identified and a decision is thought necessary, the question arises of how the decision should be made: should the issue be left to normal political and administrative processes or should it be selected for more fundamental and 'objective' analysis? This stage is often neglected in actual policy-making, but one approach is known as 'issue filtration'; this entails making a conscious choice on the basis of explicit criteria of which issues should be handled by the scarce analytical capacity available to an organization.

## 1.2.3 ISSUE DEFINITION

Once a problem or policy issue has been identified, it normally requires some further definition. This may be done in highly subjective political terms, or it may be done with an element of 'objective' analysis. Often what is defined as 'a problem' is really a combination of problems and the various strands need to be separated and identified. Where possible, problems (and opportunities) can be measured as well as identified and there are often advantages in quantification. It is not enough, however, to identify that a problem or opportunity exists; we must also attempt to explain how it has arisen and what combinations of causes and effects appear to be at work. It may be possible to identify a syndrome among the symptoms, but in any case we should try to avoid confusing symptoms with causes. The issue definition adopted is crucial in shaping the remaining stages of the policy process. Often it is impossible to come up with an unambiguous definition, but this does not preclude a role for thought and analysis.

## 1.2.4 FORECASTING

It is often possible and necessary to forecast how a situation will develop. It may also be useful to speculate about alternative possible futures, given different assumptions about the development of both problems and policies. It is important to have an appreciation of the theoretical and practical advantages and limitations of the wide veriety of techniques from modelling to subjective judgement.

## 1.2.5 SETTING OBJECTIVES AND PRIORITIES

The explicit setting of objectives is often avoided or at least 'fudged' in policy-making. A more analytical approach would encourage two questions: what are we trying to do, and how will we know when we have done it? Since there is usually a gap between the expected and the desired futures it is necessary to identify the important constraints and limiting factors. In large, multi-purpose organizations or programmes there may also be a need to examine the relative priorities of various objectives competing for limited resources.

## 1.2.6 OPTIONS ANALYSIS

There are usually several possible routes in attempting to achieve any given policy objective (or set of objectives). One criticism of actual policy-making is that typically only those options which have backers within the organization will be considered and that more independent analysis would help to identify a wider range. In appraising and comparing options, too, the emphasis may be upon advocacy or upon the sort of analysis provided, for example, by cost-effectiveness studies, cost–benefit analysis, decision analysis, PAR (programme analysis and review), etc.

## 1.2.7 POLICY IMPLEMENTATION, MONITORING, AND CONTROL

When a 'preferred option' emerges from the previous stage, it is usually necessary to formulate and communicate the resulting policy and to engage in more detailed design of associated programmes. Implementation must be seen as part of the policy process, since the interaction between policy-making and policy implementation is often very complex. For effective policy implementation it is essential that potential problems are considered in advance of implementation itself and that appropriate procedures (e.g. for securing inter-organizational clearances) should be designed into the programme. Once a policy, and its component programmes, are under way, some attempt is usually made to monitor its progress and to check whether actual performance is living up to earlier expectations. In practice, such monitoring may be very unstructured and unspecific or it may be much more rigorous and analytical. More analytical approaches involve comparing actual progress against the detailed schedule and plans drawn up at earlier stages; i.e. prior specification of a programme in operational detail is a prerequisite of control. Where analysis demonstrates that the programme is not proceeding according to the plan, remedial action may be necessary— for example, by allocating more resources to lagging programme elements.

## 1.2.8 EVALUATION AND REVIEW

At certain points (either predetermined or not), more fundamental reviews may be made of the policy. These will involve asking whether the policy has been successful in achieving the *outcomes* desired (in

contrast to securing the desired *outputs*, which is the focus of implementation, monitoring, and control). The possibility of carrying out
such an evaluation will depend on a prior specification of what the
desired outcomes are and of designing the programme in such a way as
to enable one or more evaluation techniques to be employed; otherwise it may be difficult or impossible to determine whether the policy
is 'working' as intended. The evaluation should extend to considerations
of whether there are now strong contenders for resources elsewhere
in the organization and whether the present policy still merits priority
or should be downgraded, even terminated.

### 1.2.9 POLICY MAINTENANCE, POLICY SUCCESSION AND POLICY TERMINATION

The results of evaluation and review are not self-executing. It is often
difficult to replace or terminate a policy even if an explicit 'decision'
has been made to do so. The chances of a successful succession or
termination are enhanced if the possibility of replacing or terminating
the policy at some future date was 'designed in' to the initial policy.
Although no simple techniques are available to resolve these problems,
it is worth considering the possibilities and limitations of sunset laws,
organizational design (e.g. matrix organizations), and the use of units
skilled in redeploying resources.

## 1.3 Relationships between the stages

We have presented an overview of the framework in this introductory
chapter because it is useful to know from the start how each stage of
analysis relates to the other. Although we consider it useful for purposes
of exposition to analyse each stage in turn, it has to be borne in mind
that these stages are not completely self-contained: the policy process
will frequently 'loop' between stages (e.g. issue search and issue definition) as analysis proceeds. Further, some techniques (e.g. social indicators) are potentially relevant to more than one stage in the policy
process. Such 'cross-walks' to other stages will be highlighted in the
individual chapters.

Before attempting to tackle the role of analysis in individual stages
of the policy process, it would help if we had a clear idea of what is
meant by the terms 'policy' and 'policy analysis' and why there has
been an upsurge in interest in a policy focus on the activities of government. These themes are now tackled in chapters 2 and 3. Chapter 4

level, it will quickly become evident that the everyday language of policy 'fields' and 'areas' suggests a degree of boundary definition and self-containment which simply does not hold up when we attempt, for example, to draw sharp dividing lines between economic, foreign, and defence policies.

### 2.2.2 POLICY AS AN EXPRESSION OF GENERAL PURPOSE OR DESIRED STATE OF AFFAIRS

Among other statements of Conservative 'policy', the *Conservative Manifesto 1983* included this passage on inflation:

In the next Parliament, we shall endeavour to bring inflation lower still. Our ultimate goal should be a society with stable prices.

This is a fairly typical statement of 'policy' in that it expresses the broad purposes (or 'ends') of governmental activity in one field and also describes the state of affairs which would prevail on achievement of those purposes.

It is, of course, easy at a polemical level to criticize such statements. at a more analytical level it can be suggested that they often sent the 'rhetoric' rather than the 'reality' of policy. Chapter 9 eal with some of the more technical problems of identifying ves' and relating them to observed practice. These problems are ored even by academic commentators. For example, one basic on the economics of social policy (Le Grand and Robinson, ts off each chapter by describing 'society's objective'. Thus, bjective in tackling the regional problem is described as ance'. Apart from the question of whether 'society' as such bjectives and, if so, whether these are concerned with ch as 'balance', this perspective ignores who (if anyone) objectives of policy or, indeed, whether analysis starting tion of objectives is a useful approach to explaining ally evolve.

hand, as we shall see in section 2.3, many writers anything meriting the title of policy must contain rposiveness (in much the same way as those organi- o build into the definition of 'formal organizations' e underlying goal or objective). There is a danger n this approach and we shall return to the dis- at several points in this book (see especially oment, we would simply point out that the

deals with models of policy-making and is designed to assist readers to spell out the assumptions of the explicit or implicit models assumed by analysts or practitioners of public policy.

# 2

# Analysing Public Policy

## 2.1 Is there anything new about policy analysis?

Policy analysis is both old and new. It is old because it draws on disciplines which have been analysing the activities of government for decades and on techniques which have been developed for decision-making outside government. It is new because there has undoubtedly been an increased interest over the past twenty years in the *analysis of policy* as a focus (as opposed to specific disciplinary or professional focuses). This increased interest has been accompanied both by grandiose claims for how 'policy science' can improve the decision-making capacity and the outputs of government, and by imitative relabelling as 'public policy' of traditional courses in government or public administration. A study of the origins of this interest can help us to understand the current status of policy studies and policy analysis, and the prospects for the future. We discuss the development of this 'policy orientation' in chapter 3.

To speak of an 'orientation' is to suggest a tendency rather than an organized movement, and this seems appropriate, since many people have come to the analysis of policy from many points of departure and for many different reasons. If this diversity has produced some richness it has also produced a good deal of confusion, not least in the different usages of basic terms. The word 'policy' is indeed one in everyday use, both among academics and practitioners, but it is used in a variety of different ways. This chapter will therefore begin with a discussion of usages and chapter 3 will go on from there to look at the origins of the policy orientation, the current status of policy analysis, and the prospects for its development.

## 2.2 Different uses of the word 'policy'

A useful and simple exercise, which a student can easily undertake for himself, is to explore the variety of different ways in which the word 'policy' is used by going through a quality newspaper over a period of a week or so and noting how often it occurs and in how many different contexts. The student might then be asked to attempt a categorization of these usages. One possible scheme for categorization is suggeste[d] below.

### 2.2.1 'POLICY' AS A LABEL FOR A FIELD OF ACTIVITY

The most commonly encountered usage is in the context statements about a government's 'economic policy' or its 's or 'foreign policy'. Within these broad labels there may b references to the government's policy towards natio say, or to housing policy, or to policy regarding So being described here appears to be 'fields' of g and involvement.

A more abstract but useful concept is th concept can be used to illustrate the wa typically tends to become more 'crowde more governmental interventions and in among them. Thus, much of the hi maintenance policy has involved f margins of social policy. By the volved in virtually every potent It could be argued that futu largely involve the integrat of anomalies created by past interventions (see Adams, 1975, 220). the degree of crow recreation a relat involvement, a

While the and involv one, it c and po aspiration a between policy 'intent' of policy-makers is not always reflected in their policy's 'content'. Also the 'rational' case for clearly defined objectives at an early stage in the policy-making process may blind us to the occasional reality of objectives which are invented retrospectively as a means of 'rationalizing' what has gone before.

### 2.2.3 POLICY AS SPECIFIC PROPOSALS

Those perusing newspapers for usages of the term 'policy' will often find statements of specific actions which political organizations (interest groups, parties, the Cabinet itself) would like to see undertaken by government. Here is an example from the *Conservative Manifesto 1983*:

We shall give union members the right to:
hold ballots for the election of governing bodies of trade unions;
decide periodically whether their unions should have party political funds.
We shall also curb the legal immunity of unions to call strikes without the prior approval of those concerned through a fair and secret ballot.

Such proposals may be *ad hoc*, or may have to be related to other proposals, or may represent the 'means' of achieving the larger 'ends' or purposes discussed at 2.2.2 above.

### 2.2.4 POLICY AS DECISIONS OF GOVERNMENT

The case-study approach which has often been favoured by political scientists tends to focus on particular 'decisions', typically those arising from 'moments of choice' in some famous (and therefore atypical?) episode such as the Suez Crisis. Policy analysts are as susceptible as anyone else to the fascination of such crucial decisions, but they should, perhaps, take a larger view of policy-making in the sense, first, of looking for broader patterns of related decisions and, secondly, of taking into account a longer time-span which should certainly extend to what happens *after* the 'moment of choice' and to questions of implementation and actual outcomes.

The probability of a 'decision' by government becoming embodied in legislation or otherwise receiving formal authorization will vary according to the political structure: majority party governments in Britain can normally count on more-or-less automatic ratification by Parliament, whereas the President of the United States, whatever his party or the composition of Congress, has to fight to mobilize support for his 'decisions'.

## 2.2.5 POLICY AS FORMAL AUTHORIZATION

When it is said of government that is 'has a policy' on a particular topic, the reference is sometimes to the specific Act of Parliament or statutory instrument which permits or requires an activity to take place. Or it may be said when legislation is enacted that the policy has been carried out or implemented. This can be misleading, however, since all that has happened at this stage is that a bit of paper has been signed. Funds still have to be spent and, perhaps, staff hired before any of the activities envisaged in the Act can take place. This is not to argue that the passage of legislation is unimportant; it is an important legitimating stage in the policy process. But it does not tell us what happened afterwards. In 1974, for example, the Control of Pollution Act was passed, but its enactment coincided with a major cutback in expenditure, and important sections of the Act have not been implemented to this day.

## 2.2.6 POLICY AS A PROGRAMME

Less familiar to British students than to Americans, who use the term as a matter of course, is the idea of a programme—a defined and relatively specific sphere of government activity involving a particular package of legislation, organization and resources. Thus we can talk of a school meals programme, which involves a specific piece of legislation, various resources, and the manpower to deliver the programme. Government housing policy (policy as label) can be said to consist of a number of programmes such as the provision of subsidized council houses, a housing improvement programme, an option mortgage programme, and so on. Programmes are usually seen as being the means by which governments pursue their broader purposes or ends (see 2.2.2 above). This may often be so, but there are other cases where programmes—especially poorly defined programmes—develop objectives of their own. Some of the Community Development Projects of the 1970s may be cases in point.

## 2.2.7 POLICY AS OUTPUT

Here policy is seen as what government actually delivers as opposed to what it has promised or has authorized through legislation. Such outputs can take many forms—the payment of cash benefits, the delivery of goods or services, the enforcement of rules, the invocation of symbols or the collection of taxes. The form of outputs varies between policy areas.

It is sometimes difficult to decide what the final 'output' of government policy is in a particular area. In the health service, for example, there is a tendency to describe such items as more funds, more trained staff, and more beds as the outputs of a policy intended to improve the quality of medical care. In fact, these are necessary but not sufficient conditions of improved medical care: they should be regarded as important contributory factors to the desired output, but not the output itself. They could perhaps be described as 'intermediate outputs' rather than the final or 'ultimate' output.

Outputs in practice may not conform to stated intentions. For example, the last Labour government established under the Community Land Act a programme to bring land into community ownership. However, with the exception of Wales, very little land was taken into public ownership, mainly because local authorities were not interested in implementing the Act. This calls into question the extent to which it is meaningful to talk of bringing land into public ownership as 'policy' when this was not in fact happening.

## 2.2.8 POLICY AS OUTCOME

Another way of looking at policy is in terms of its outcome, that is, in terms of what is actually achieved. This distinction between outputs (the activities of government at the point of delivery) and outcomes (the impact of these activities) is often slurred over, and is sometimes difficult to make in practice, but it is an important one. Thinking of policy in terms of outcomes may enable us to make some assessment of whether the stated purpose of a policy appears to be what the policy is actually achieving. For example, if it was found that the effect of policies labelled as regional policies was to subsidize declining firms, then one might feel entitled to describe the policy as a 'social policy' rather than a 'resource-mobilizing' or 'economic' policy.

Focusing on the impact of policies also serves as a reminder that policy delivery and impact are rarely a matter of a straight-line relationship between a single policy instrument or organization interacting with its environment to produce a clear-cut impact. There are frequently several organizations operating in the same policy area which impact on the same targets, thus producing further interaction effects. The overall outcome will be the product of the outputs of these organizations and their effect on the environment and on one another. This *product* of the impact need not necessarily reflect the sum of the purposes of the organizations concerned or of the original decision-makers. Some aspects of the impact may be entirely unintended. A good example of this is the evolution of the 'poverty trap' in Britain as a result of the separate development of the personal taxation system and of a large number of policy instruments designed to assist the poor.

Definitions of policy in terms of outcomes may therefore at times seem rather perverse ones (e.g. 'poverty maintenance' policy rather than 'income maintenance' policy) but, if so, they draw attention to the need to re-evaluate policy in terms of the other meanings of policy considered above. For example, is the problem the stated objectives, the process by which decisions are made, the arrangement of policy instruments and funds into particular programmes, or the way in which responsibility for delivery policies is allocated among different organizations?

### 2.2.9 POLICY AS A THEORY OR MODEL

All policies involve assumptions about what governments can do and what the consequences of their actions will be. These assumptions are rarely spelt out, but policies nevertheless do imply a theory (or model) of cause and effect. At its simplest this theory takes the form 'if X, then Y will follow'. An example of policy as theory where the assumptions were to some extent spelt out comes from the Queen's Speech on 15 May 1979:

By reducing the burden of direct taxation and restricting the claims of the public sector on the nation's resources they will start to restore incentives, encourage efficiency and create a climate in which commerce and industry can flourish. In this way they will lay a secure basis for investment, productivity and increased employment in all parts of the UK.

If we think of policy in terms of the simple 'if X, then Y' theory, we can see that failure of a policy can arise either from the Government's failure to do X in full or because X fails to have the consequences expected according to the theory. In practice, the causal chains involved in policy as theory are normally much more complex. We shall return to this theme in chapter 11. One of the tasks of the policy analyst is to try to tease out the theories underlying policies and examine the internal consistency of the resulting model and the apparent validity of its assumptions.

### 2.2.10 POLICY AS PROCESS

The aspect of policy which the student reading a newspaper for a week or two would be least likely to identify is that it involves a process over a much longer period of time. Many of the nine usages listed above could be compared to still photographs—the statement of an objective, the moment of decision, a Bill becomes an Act, and so on. What we need, however, is the equivalent of a film which will allow us to study the unfolding over time of the complexities of the policy-making process. At section 2.4 below and in greater length in Part II, we shall try to develop this processual approach to the study of public policy and to an understanding of the contributions which might be made by policy analysis. First, however, we must turn from commentary on other people's usages to the more difficult task of offering our own definition of public policy.

## 2.3 Defining public policy

Just as there are many everyday usages of the term, so there are many academic definitions of 'policy'. Some excellent reviews and critiques of these definitions have been published (e.g. Heclo, 1972). Here we shall work towards our own definition by identifying some of the elements and distinctions which we regard as important in seeking to characterize 'public policy'.

### 2.3.1 POLICY IS TO BE DISTINGUISHED FROM 'DECISION'

As noted at 2.2.4 above, the distinction between 'policy' and 'decision' is often overlooked in everyday usage. Our view of the distinction is that:

(a) Policy is larger than decision. A policy usually involves a series of more specific decisions, sometimes in a 'rational' sequence (e.g. deciding there is a problem; deciding to do something about it; deciding the best way of proceeding; deciding to legislate; etc.) Even when the sequence is more erratic, a policy is typically generated by interactions among many, more or less consciously related, decisions.

(b) While one decision in the sequence may be seen as crucial—often the 'moment of choice' when one option is chosen from several contenders—an understanding of the larger policy requires some study of decisions both preceding and following the so-called 'crucial' episode. For example, how (and by whom) were the options defined in the first place? When the preferred option had been defined and set in motion did unforeseen problems at the implementation stage produce significant changes?

(c) The concept of 'decision' is often associated with that of a 'decision-maker'. The latter may be seen as an individual or a group or a particular organization. Again, however, the study of a 'policy' usually involves tracing multiple interactions among many individuals, many groups, and many organizations. The whole concept of 'decision-makers' may occasionally be challenged, when it seems that events and the larger environment have forced a particular policy direction upon the agencies of government.

## 2.3.2 POLICY IS LESS READILY DISTINGUISHABLE FROM 'ADMINISTRATION'

If some distinctions (such as that between policy and decision) are commonly overlooked, other distinctions are often made which we would regard as less than convincing. An example is that distinction which used to be made—at least for public consumption—by Administrative Class civil servants between 'policy' and 'administration' and, more recently, between both and 'management'. Desmond Keeling (1972) has given a lucid account of the classical Whitehall argument that administrators should only advise ministers on the crucial questions of policy, including questions of basic objectives and priorities, the overall balance between competing claims upon resources, and broad strategies for achieving the Government's stated aims. Once policy was made, administrators would have considerable discretion within the policy's broad framework, especially in making the important, precedent-setting decisions which, in turn, provided guidelines or 'decision rules' for officials at less exalted 'management' levels.

The classical view is open to challenge, however, since the 'trickle-down' model of policy-making, with objectives stated at a high level and implementation proceeding through layers of increasingly routine and detailed decision-making, tends to be less common in practice than the theory would suggest. A so-called policy is often the cumulative outcome of many operational decisions or responses to problems first perceived at relatively low levels of the organization. Especially in highly technical areas, quite junior personnel with specialist skills may have disproportionate influence in policy determination. The famous definition of the Old Administrative Class civil servant as 'the lieutenant of policy and the field-marshal of techniques' (including managerial techniques) perhaps belonged to a simpler age, if indeed it ever applied.

## 2.3.3 POLICY INVOLVES BEHAVIOUR AS WELL AS INTENTIONS

In analysing the development of any public policy it is an obvious first step to attempt to define what appear to have been the policy-maker's intentions. As the analysis proceeds, however, it often proves difficult to reconcile observed behaviour with stated intentions. This may be because public statements were always an inaccurate guide to actual motives, or because original and sincere intentions were forgotten or subtly altered over time, or because later events led to unstated (perhaps even unrecognized) shifts in required 'coping' behaviour. Whatever the reason, the study of policy cannot ignore the behaviour of those who formulate, implement, and respond to it.

## 2.3.4 POLICY INVOLVES INACTION AS WELL AS ACTION

Policy behaviour includes involuntary failures to act and deliberate decisions not to act. Such 'non-decisions' include circumstances in which a person or group, consciously or unconsciously, creates or re-inforces barriers to the public airing of policy conflicts (Bachrach and Baratz, 1962). We consider the importance of agenda-setting in shaping the policy process in chapter 5.

As Heclo (1972) suggests, 'A policy can consist of what is not being done.' He does not give an example, but one might be the sharply varying use which has been made by governments of their long-standing powers to dissuade firms from locating in, say, South-East England and to persuade them to locate in Scotland or North-East England. Some-times little or no use has been made of such statutory powers and this inaction can be seen as an aspect of location-of-industry policy. If Parliament enacts a law—such as the Litter Act—but provides insuf-ficient resources and generally does little to enforce it, then we are entitled to say that the Government's policy is not to implement its own law. Policy as inaction is, however, much more difficult to pin down and analyse than policy as action. Is it too cynical to suggest that compulsory wearing of car seatbelts may soon provide us with an interesting case-study of the balance between action and inaction?

## 2.3.5 POLICIES HAVE OUTCOMES WHICH MAY OR MAY NOT HAVE BEEN FORESEEN

The differences between intentions, outputs and outcomes have already been discussed at 2.2.7 and 2.2.8 above, but the positive importance of these concepts is worth re-emphasizing. To quote Heclo (1972) again:

'The term policy needs to be able to embrace both what is intended and what occurs as a result of the intention; any use which excluded unintended results . . . would surely be impoverished.'

### 2.3.6 POLICY IS A PURPOSIVE COURSE OF ACTION BUT PURPOSES MAY BE DEFINED RETROSPECTIVELY

Most writers on public policy build into their definitions the necessity for any policy to have some explicit or implicit purpose or objectives. For example, Anderson (1975, 3) provides as a definition of policy: 'A purposive course of action followed by an actor or set of actors in dealing with a problem or matter of concern'. In most cases, it is reasonable to assume the existence of a prior objective although, as already noted, the objective may change or be partly ignored as time passes. In a sense it is true to say—indeed it may even be a truism—that a wholly purposeless policy is a contradiction in terms. Sometimes, however, purposes are defined retrospectively in order to suggest a clearer strategic sense or a greater degree of foresight about outcomes than actually prevailed at earlier stages of the policy-making process. Purposes, in other words, may be invented *ex post facto* in order to rationalize past actions rather than formulated *ex ante* as a rational guide to future action. Politicians, like army generals, sometimes act from a need to be seen to act or from instinct: this need not be a bad thing and, in any case, reasoning (and reasons) can be left to auto-biographies written in retirement.

### 2.3.7 POLICY ARISES FROM A PROCESS OVER TIME

This only sums up much of what has been argued above and in section 2.2. We shall attempt in later chapters to indicate our perception of that process and of the various sub-processes which it subsumes.

### 2.3.8 POLICY INVOLVES INTRA- AND INTER-ORGANIZATIONAL RELATIONSHIPS

Decisions (see 2.3.1 above) may be taken by single organizations, even by individual actors; but policies typically involve the interplay of many actors and organizations and the working out of complex relation-ships between them. There is no sharp distinction between policy analysis and organizational (including inter-organizational) analysis and the latter has many insights to offer the former. When we move from description to prescription, moreover, we shall often be reminded that policies conceived of in the abstract or which assume a single policy actor may fail to be successful in a real-world organizational and political setting and that techniques which work in one organization may not be readily transferable to another.

## 2.3.9 PUBLIC POLICY INVOLVES A KEY, BUT NOT EXCLUSIVE, ROLE FOR PUBLIC AGENCIES

The blurring of the distinction between the 'public' and 'private' sectors has been much discussed in recent years (see, for example, Barker, 1982; Dahl, 1970), especially with the visible proliferation of quasi-public and quasi-private agencies (the so-called 'quangos'). It follows that it has become more difficult to draw any sharp distinctions between public policy and, say, business policy. Few public policies, at least few domestic (as opposed to foreign and defence) policies, involve the participation of governmental agencies alone, even when a very broad definition is given to 'governmental'. How, then, do we recognize a 'public policy'? At the very least it must have been processed, even if only authorized or ratified, by public agencies. The policy may not have been significantly developed by government but it must at least have been partly developed *within* the framework of government.

## 2.3.10 POLICY IS SUBJECTIVELY DEFINED

The confidence with which we often speak of policy fields, processes, participants, purposes, and outcomes may suggest that these are self-defining or objectively knowable phenomena. Usually, of course, they are not. It is the individual observer who perceives boundaries, processes (including inaction as well as action), the influences and relationships of various participants, 'real' as opposed to stated goals, and the impact (or non-impact) of policies. He can only perceive them subjectively and his perception may differ from that of another, equally detached and rigorous, observer of the same events. The danger may be even greater in policy analysis than in other areas of social science because as Allison (1971) suggests, we all tend to view policies and policy-making through our own 'concepfual lens'. We shall return to this theme in chapter 4 on 'Models'.

## 2.3.11 TOWARDS A DEFINITION OF PUBLIC POLICY

Let us try to summarize the discussion in section 2.3. Any public policy is subjectively defined by an observer as being such and is usually perceived as comprising a series of patterns of related decisions to which many circumstances and personal, group, and organizational influences have contributed. The policy-making process involves many sub-processes and may extend over a considerable period of time. The aims or purposes underlying a policy are usually identifiable at a relatively early stage in the process but these may change over time and, in some cases, may be defined only retrospectively. The outcomes of policies require to be studied and, where appropriate, compared and contrasted with the policy-makers' intentions. Accidental or deliberate inaction may contribute to a policy outcome. The study of policy requires an understanding of behaviour, especially behaviour involving interaction within and among organizational memberships. For a policy to be regarded as a 'public policy' it must to some degree have been generated or at least processed within the framework of governmental procedures, influences and organizations.

## 2.4 Analysing public policy in terms of a process

Our emphasis upon studying policy in terms of a process will have been clear from chapter 1 and from the first three sections of this chapter. The framework outlined in chapter 1 has the following stages:

(1) Deciding to decide (issue search or agenda-setting)
(2) Deciding how to decide (or issue filtration)
(3) Issue definition
(4) Forecasting
(5) Setting objectives and priorities
(6) Options analysis
(7) Policy implementation, monitoring, and control
(8) Evaluation and review
(9) Policy maintenance, succession, or termination.

Although first versions of this framework go back over seventeen years (Gunn, 1966), no particular originality is claimed for it. Most attempts to depict the policy process have to include some, at least, of the same stages. The example in Figure 2.1 is derived from Rose (1973). The use of a process framework has both advantages and limitations. Some of the advantages we would claim are as follows.

First, any process framework is *dynamic*. The analogy has already been drawn with the continuous film approach rather than the still photographs offered by too many case-studies of the 'moment of choice' variety. As well as forward movements, the opportunity for feedback can be seen at many points in the process, as when experience

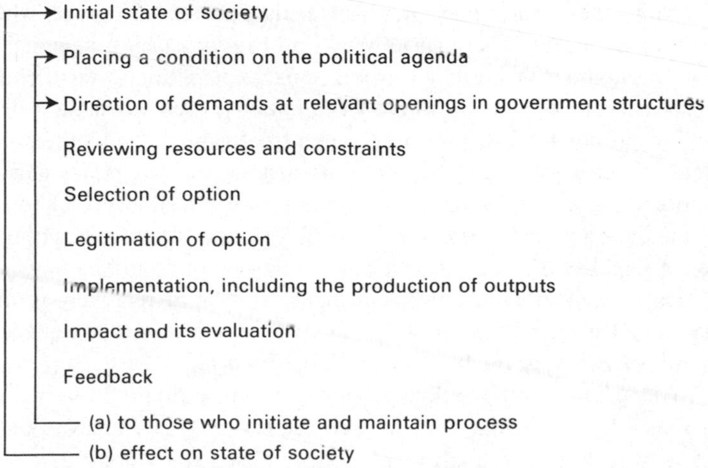

> Initial state of society

> Placing a condition on the political agenda

> Direction of demands at relevant openings in government structures

Reviewing resources and constraints

Selection of option

Legitimation of option

Implementation, including the production of outputs

Impact and its evaluation

Feedback

(a) to those who initiate and maintain process
(b) effect on state of society

FIG. 2.1. Stages in the policy process

gathered during the implementation stage results in the problem being redefined or when monitoring of existing programmes leads to modification of previously stated objectives.

Secondly, as with the political system models to which they are closely related, process frameworks do lend themselves to the identification and study of *interactions*, not only among the various stages in the process but also among various participating organizations and between organizations and the larger social and economic environment (see Easton, 1979).

Thirdly, it is an advantage of a process framework that it is *flexible*, in the sense that it enables us to systematize existing knowledge without precluding the integrating of future insights (about stages, influences, interactions, etc.) to the framework.

The process approach also has its limitations and dangers, however, and we can briefly indicate some of these.

First, the *status* of any model or framework has to be made clear. In chapter 4 we shall discuss the distinctions between ideal-type, descriptive, and prescriptive models.

Secondly, there is the danger that a framework may degenerate into a strait-jacket: that is, a particular conceptualization of the policy process derived from past research may lead us to the *imposition* upon future events of an explanatory scheme which is inappropriate or misleading.

Thirdly, there is the associated danger that the use of a model with a clearly defined sequence of stages may lead to *rationalization*, which we use in this context to mean 'giving a rational explanation or justification of past acts' (*The Penguin English Dictionary*), even when the acts in question do not lend themselves to such treatment. Viewing the policy process in terms of stages may seem to suggest that any policy episode is more or less self-contained and comprises a neat cycle of initial, intermediate and culminating events. In practice, of course, policy is often a seamless web involving a bewildering mesh of interactions and ramifications. Also much of government consists of relatively routine ('maintenance') activities in which few policy initiatives take place or else happen in a very incremental and disjointed way.

Provided that these possible dangers are kept in mind, however, our experience has been that students can use the process framework as at least a 'way into' the analysis of policy. Post-experience trainees, in particular, seem to find the model valuable as a means both of articulating what they already know about how policies are made and as an aid to thinking more clearly about how their own and their employers' policy-making and administrative procedures might be improved (leaving aside, for the moment, what 'improvement' might involve).

## 2.5 Different uses of the term 'policy analysis'

Terms such as 'policy analysis', 'policy sciences', and 'policy studies' are used by various authors in different ways, at times interchangeably, at times in an attempt to impose a particular meaning on a specific term (see Gunn, 1976 and 1980; Gordon, Lewis and Young, 1977; Rhodes, 1979a, 23–8).

This could readily be established by quoting the different ways in which various authors have used the term policy analysis (see Gunn, 1980)..However, a more fruitful way to proceed is to suggest a possible classification of approaches to the analysis of public policy. In practice, of course, more than one approach may be used in a particular study, perhaps with the analyst being unaware that he is moving from one to the other.

### 2.5.1 STUDIES OF POLICY CONTENT

These have been a particular feature of the study of social policy and administration in Britain. The focus is on the origins, intentions and operation of specific policies in areas such as housing, education, health, and social services (Gordon *et al.*, 1977, 28). Such studies may help to inform policy-makers as well as students, but their aim is primarily descriptive, though the analysis in some cases may be at a highly abstract level.

### 2.5.2 STUDIES OF POLICY PROCESS

The concern here is with how policies are actually made in terms of the actions taken by various actors at each stage. This can consist of individual case studies or attempts to devise generalizable but largely descriptive propositions about the nature of public policy-making.

### 2.5.3 STUDIES OF POLICY OUTPUTS

These typically seek to establish the determinants of the pattern of distribution of expenditure or other indicators of policy outputs. Such studies often involve complex statistical analysis with a number of variables relating to economic, social, and political characteristics of local authorities. (In Britain, the seminal work is Boaden, 1971; for a useful overview, see Newton and Sharpe, 1977.)

### 2.5.4 EVALUATION STUDIES

These seek to assess specific policies in terms of the extent to which their outcomes have achieved the objectives of the policy. In contrast to the United States, relatively few formal evaluation studies are conducted in the United Kingdom. Evaluation studies can perform a descriptive purpose by improving our understanding of the factors which shape policy, as well as providing information which can be used in future policy-making (see chapter 12).

### 2.5.5 INFORMATION FOR POLICY-MAKING

This refers to the collection and analysis of data with the specific purpose of aiding a policy decision or advising on the implications of alternative policies. Such work may be conducted within universities, independent policy institutions, commissions or committees of inquiry, or (the most frequent location in Britain) within government organizations themselves. Such analysis differs from 'content' studies in that it is explicitly designed to contribute to policy-making.

### 2.5.6 PROCESS ADVOCACY

The analyst is here concerned not simply to understand the policy-making process but to change it—usually in terms of somehow making it more 'rational'. This often involves putting a high value upon particular approaches, procedures, and techniques. The emphasis is less upon what any particular policy should be than with *how* policies ought to be made.

### 2.5.7 POLICY ADVOCACY

This involves the use of analysis in making an argument for a particular policy. It may be worth distinguishing between (a) the analyst as political actor and (b) the political actor as analyst. Both roles are controversial. Thomas Dye (1972) is critical of academic analysts who involve themselves in the policy process to the extent of becoming 'policy advocates', since they do so at the expense of scholarly standards of objectivity and detachment. When, on the other hand, political actors such as ministers and senior civil servants set themselves up as analysts (or as eager consumers of analysis) both the quality of the resulting analysis and its motivation are often questioned. The suspicion lingers that politicians and their advisers are interested only in analytical findings which will serve to support positions they wish to adopt or to vindicate positions already adopted.

### 2.5.8 THE ANALYSIS OF ANALYSIS

A secondary industry has grown up recently in the form of critical appraisal of the assumptions, methodology, and validity of policy analysis, especially 2.5.5–2.5.7 above (see for example, Tribe, 1972). The extent to which 'facts' and 'values' can be separated in analysis is one topic which has been discussed at length (see 7.7). There is also the problem of distinguishing between analysis as description and analysis as prescription. While types 1–7 above do not fit neatly into an ordered spectrum, we can see that they range from basically descriptive activities at 2.5.1–2.5.4 to prescriptive activities at 2.5.5–2.5.7. This distinction and the ·relationship between various types of analysis are illustrated in Fig. 2.2 (cf. Gordon *et al.*, 1977).

### 2.5.9 THE ROLES OF DIFFERENT TYPES OF ANALYSIS

Our view is that there is a place for most of the types of analysis outlined above. We accept Lasswell's depiction of the policy sciences as being legitimately concerned with both 'knowledge *of* the policy process' and 'knowledge *in* the policy process' (Lasswell, 1970). The teaching of policy analysis, whether to conventional students or to practitioners, must seek to develop both types of knowledge. The argument for descrip-

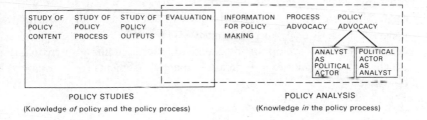

FIG. 2.2. Types of public policy-making

tive and explanatory studies, apart from their intrinsic interest, is that they help the analyst to appreciate the complexity of, and constraints upon, any more prescriptive ventures. What you would change you must first understand. The analyst must also develop a critical faculty about his or her own assumptions and methods and we regard the 'analysis of analysis' (at 2.5.8 above) as an important part of his or her training.

One final point about nomenclature. The term 'policy studies' is normally used to indicate an essentially descriptive or explanatory set of concerns (see 2.5.1–2.5.4 above). The term 'policy analysis' is often, but by no means always, reserved for prescriptive activities (knowledge in rather than of the policy process, or 2.5.4–2.5.7 above). The term 'policy sciences' is used by some writers as a synonym for (prescriptive) policy analysis and by others to encompass both policy studies and policy analysis. We have a mild preference for using 'policy studies' for descriptive accounts and 'policy analysis' for prescriptive exercises, with 'policy sciences' as an umbrella phrase to cover both types of undertaking.

## 2.6 The characteristics of policy analysis

One characteristic of writers on policy analysis is their delight in listing the characteristics of policy analysis; see, for example, Rhodes (1979a), 27), Dror (1968, 241–4), and almost every article in the inaugural issue of *Policy Sciences* (Spring, 1970). A fairly standard listing would include the following claims for policy analysis.

*Applied rather than pure.* Policy studies and, specifically, policy analysis (as defined in 2.5 above) are applied rather than pure, problem-oriented rather than problem-blind, prescriptive as well as descriptive.

*Inter-disciplinary as well as multi-disciplinary.* Policy analysis is not a single discipline but nor should it represent a loose assembly of disciplines. If it is to deal with real, many-sided problems (such as urban decline), it must develop an integrated or interdisciplinary approach, which will combine in a synergistic manner elements from many disciplines.

*Politically sensitive planning.* Many policy analysts have argued for more 'rational' approaches to policy-making. We shall leave to later chapters the discussion of what such approaches might involve. Typically, however, there is concern with developing some sophisticated indicators of social conditions and problems, better forecasts, hierarchies of objectives, improved definition and appraisal of options, and so on. To this extent, there is an obvious overlap between policy analysis and policy planning. But there is a welcome awareness that analysts have to be trained in the political skills as well as in planning techniques and approaches. The trained analyst (whether undergraduate or post-experience) should emerge with a heightened awareness and understanding of, and sympathy for, the essentially political nature of the policy process. This is not only an intellectual necessity since, in severely practical terms, any analyst must understand the complexities and constraints of the political system if his recommendations are to have any impact.

*Client-oriented.* There is some disagreement about the extent to which policy analysts ought to be available for hire to whichever patron can afford them. One view is that the analyst—especially if operating from a base in higher education—should address himself to a wider constituency and operate as an agent of social change with a commitment to the amelioration of society. Our own view is that policy analysts as individuals need feel under no obligation to accept commissions from governmental or other agencies, but that there is something unconvincing about policy analysis which is conducted without even a potential client in mind.

## 2.7 Use with caution

It should be clear from this chapter that for all the emphasis on precision of some policy analysis techniques, the terminology of public policy covers a wide variety of concerns and activities. We have not sought in this chapter to enforce a particular restricted meaning of these terms, though we have offered our own definition of public policy which we hope encapsulates all the characteristics of public policy. Similarly, we have not attempted to suggest that only particular types of analysis of public policy are valid. The key lessons which should emerge from this terminological tour are that it should always be made clear in which of the many possible senses of 'policy' the word is being used and that the student or practitioner should always be clear in his or her mind what type of analysis he or she is conducting.

# 3

# The Policy Orientation

## 3.1 Origins of the policy orientation

It is possible to exaggerate the novelty of the relatively recent upsurge of interest in the policy orientation. After all, social scientists have been providing inputs to public policy-making for many decades, and the publication of Lerner and Lasswell's *Policy Sciences* (1951) marked an upsurge of interest in policy-focused analysis. However, it was only in the 1960s that there was a sustained increase in interest in the United States, echoed in the late 1960s and 1970s by a corresponding, if more limited, movement in Britain.

The origins of this increased interest in the policy orientation lie both on the 'demand' side (perceived inadequacies in government and in existing policy responses to chronic problems) and on the 'supply' side (dissatisfactions and developments in academic disciplines).

### 3.1.1 THE DEMAND FOR ANALYSIS

On the demand side, many social problems began to receive more attention in the 1960s in the United States than had been the case in the relatively complacent Eisenhower years. The 'New Frontier' and 'Great Society' programmes reflected a greater willingness on the part of federal government to intervene, particularly to remedy the problems of poverty. As these programmes developed, however, it became clear that there were few simple or 'common-sense' answers to the complex and interacting problems of modern urban society. Indeed, it often appeared difficult to diagnose and define just what these problems were. The nature of such problems is dynamic in any case:

policy-makers have to operate in conditions of rapid and accelerating change caused, at least in part, by changing technology and other circumstances largely outside their control.

In the United States there was a general view that techniques and personnel from business management (for example, McNamara at Defense) and insights from academic analysis could contribute towards resolving these problems and to greater effectiveness in government. This was accompanied by a willingness (at a time of economic growth) to commit substantial funds both to new programmes and to associated research and analysis. In the 1980s, a greater degree of scepticism prevails in the United States (not least among social scientists) about the extent to which business techniques and social science insights can ensure the success of complex programmes of social intervention. The absence of economic growth has also reduced funding for programmes and analysis both.

In the United Kingdom, the 'rediscovery of poverty' in the mid-1960s and growing awareness of urban and regional decline provided a reminder that Britain's much more extensive post-war welfare legislation had not solved our social and economic problems. The early 1960s saw the growth of a 'planning mood', reflected in the Plowden Report (1961), the 1961 White Paper on the nationalized industries, incomes policy, health services planning, manpower programmes, and much else. The Plowden Report, in particular, marked the beginning of official interest in more systematic methods of ordering priorities and relating expenditure to resources.

The 1960s also saw, in Britain, a much greater willingness to question the effectiveness and efficiency of public institutions such as the civil service. There were all too many examples of inadequate responses to problems, resulting from lack of foresight, failures to define objectives, limited and inadequately prepared options, weak implementation, and very little provision for monitoring and review of policies. Everyone will have their own examples, but most lists would include the Concorde fiasco, the still-running Channel Tunnel and Third London Airport sagas, forecasting blunders (road transport, prison population, etc.), the chronic non-planning of higher education, and failure to tackle the disposal of nuclear waste until it became a polemical political issue.

Such a record might have seemed to make Britain ripe for the types of policy analysis input sought (although not always utilized) in the United States. But while British governments (especially Conservative governments) have been prepared to consider the application of business techniques, they have been much more sceptical about the potential value of policy-focused analysis derived from the social sciences (with the partial exception of economic analysis). To a much greater extent than in the USA, where there has been a mixture of demand and supply factors, the development of the policy sciences in Britain has been 'supply led'. (For a discussion of differences in government attitudes to social science in Britain and the USA, see Sharpe, 1975.)

### 3.1.2 DISSATISFACTIONS WITH THE SOCIAL SCIENCES

Turning, then, to the supply side, there has been over the past twenty-five years a spasmodic dissatisfaction in some academic circles with the very limited practical contribution to problem-solving made by the social sciences. Research and teaching have often been seen as 'over-academic', inward-looking, concerned with methodology rather than substance, and irrelevant to real social problems. Given the segmented nature of the social sciences, much of this discontent has surfaced within particular disciplines.

(1) *Political Science*. In the United States in particular, political science has been seen as straining after ever higher levels of generalization (as in systems theory) at the cost of remoteness from 'real' problems; or over-concerned with its 'scientific' status, so that only those topics which are quantifiable have been seen as suited to research (sometimes resulting in highly sophisticated answers to deeply uninteresting questions); or engaging in empty exercises in comparative government; and so on. Within the American Political Science Association (APSA) there was a backlash in the 1960s about the lack of any significant contribution to (or even interest in) the practice of government and the solution of problems such as poverty, racial conflict, or urban decline. In other words, political science was 'problem blind'. Since then, the public policy focus within APSA has grown substantially (Hansen, 1983). In Britain political science only partly absorbed the 'behavioural revolution' and a more common criticism, also levelled at public administration as a subject, was of its excessively institutional focus, sometimes resulting in prescriptions for institutional change which displayed a lack of awareness of underlying process and the distribution of power.

(2) *Public Administration*. Public administration in Britain in the

past has suffered from being an off-shoot of political science alone, rather than the multidisciplinary subject taught in American universities (often with a strong 'management' bias). In the early post-war years, British public administration was often dismissed as being concerned with 'statutes and sewers', with structures rather than processes, with procedures rather than behaviour, and with specific decisions (in such few case-studies as existed) rather than policy-making. Much of this characterization was overstated but there was some truth in it. For a more discriminating and balanced critique see Stewart (1974).

(3) *Economics*. Like political science, economics has often seemed over-concerned with its claims to 'scientific' status and with abstract model-building. It has also threatened on occasion to fragment into many sub-disciplines and, until recently, attempts develop more integrated and policy-oriented approaches—such as 'economics of public policy'—have had relatively low esteem in the profession. Economists are sometimes seen as being happily ignorant of other social science disciplines (such as political science) which might alert them to the complexities of real-world policy formulation and implementation. As we shall argue (in chapter 13), prescriptions by economists often fail to distinguish between circumstances where the Government would be entering a new field of activity and those where they are seeking to replace an existing policy.

(4) *Management Studies*. Management studies have often been, in Britain, a synonym for 'business studies' and some business schools have been too ready to assume that their offerings would apply to the public sector. The political setting has sometimes been neglected and, although there has been a concern with 'problem-solving', insufficient attention has been given to how problems arise and are processed within the 'political-management system' (Stewart, 1974) of central and local government. Many business lecturers have themselves criticized the tendency to deal with 'techniques' at the expense of any understanding of underlying processes and behaviour. Particularly at senior levels, the manager's need is for integrative studies, some of which are now emerging under the label of 'business policy'. We would argue that in the British context these should overlap significantly with studies of public policy.

The above characterizations of particular disciplines are not meant to be comprehensive or balanced, but anyone who has attended conferences in the various social science disciplines over the past ten or twenty years will probably have heard some such criticisms voiced. A less obvious, but potentially more significant, development has been the impatience expressed in some circles with the sanctity of 'disciplines' as such. Many single disciplines are historical accidents but they become self-perpetuating, since academics have the vice of wanting to teach what they were taught as students. The danger is that many political scientists or economists end up speaking only to one another and to their captive students, and seem to have little to say to practitioners in business and government. Sometimes the problems which academics identify have little to do with problems as identified by practitioners, and vice versa. Part of the modern history of policy studies has been an attempt to develop both a more applied and a more inter-disciplinary approach to research, teaching and training, though a high degree of fragmentation continues to exist within policy studies (see Hogwood, 1984).

## 3.2 The current status of policy analysis

The differing status of policy analysis in the United States and the United Kingdom provides an interesting reflection both of the contrasting political structures (see Jordan, 1981) and of the status of the social sciences more broadly in the two countries (see Sharpe, 1975).

The would-be policy analyst in Britain may look with envy at the openings for policy analysis provided by the 'multiple crack' of federalism. State and local governments, as well as the Federal Government in Washington all provide openings for policy analysts, either full-time or commissioned to conduct specific research. In Washington analysts move between Federal departments and agencies, research institutes, and the staff of Congressional offices, committees and individual Congressmen. The Policy Studies Organization publishes directories listing individuals interested in analysis, policy research centres, and universities offering policy analysis teaching programmes. However, the corollary of multiple openings for the consumption of analysis is that there is a much lower chance of one analyst working for any given sponsor seeing his analysis incorporated in an authoritative decision than would be the case if his analysis was accepted by a government department in Britain.

Potential openings for analysis will not necessarily ensure that analytical techniques 'take', as the fate of attempts to introduce into the Federal Government techniques of Planning, Programming, Budgeting Systems (PPBS), Management by Objectives (MbO), and Zero Based Budgeting (ZBB) all show (see Wildavsky, 1975, 1980; Rose, 1976b). While much policy analysis in the United States tries to tackle difficult problems in a thoughtful way, there has been a partial tendency for analysis to regress to tackling limited, pre-defined, almost technical problems (see Rhodes, 1979a).

While British social scientists may sometimes look at policy analysis in the United States through rose-tinted glasses—exaggerating its initial impact and ignoring both subsequent disillusionment and the poor quality of much work—there is no doubt that the scale of the 'policy analysis industry' and the opportunities for consumption of its product are much larger in the United States than in Britain. In a review of Aaron Wildavsky's *The Art and Craft of Policy Analysis* (1980), Rudolf Klein (1980) recalled attending a seminar arranged seven or eight years previously by the US Embassy in London to introduce leading American policy analysts to a group of British academics and civil servants. Those who attended the seminar would agree with Klein that there was a good deal of scepticism as well as interest in the audience. To quote his account of British reactions:

Why set up special university institutions to practice and teach policy analysis—as Wildavsky had done at Berkeley—when we, in Britain, were already doing so without attaching fashionable new labels to these traditional activities? Why invent a new discipline when British academics and civil servants were already involved in the business of analysing social and other problems and providing solutions to policymakers?

He goes on to argue that:

This dismissive reaction proved prophetic. In the event, policy analysis as a distinct discipline—involving political scientists and economists among others—has not caught on in Britain. Policy analysis is not taught in British Universities, at least by that name; policy analysts are not a recognised category in the civil service, as in the United States. The loss, I suspect, is Britain's.

Some aspects of Klein's summation appear overstated. For example, several British universities are now offering classes and, in some cases, courses in public policy. Proposals to offer degrees in policy studies are coming forward in growing numbers from the colleges and polytechnics. The Civil Service College has introduced policy components to several of its training programmes and short courses on policy analysis have been organized for senior civil servants at Sunningdale. Individual government departments are also showing an interest in including a policy component in their training. In local government and NHS circles, too, policy analysis has attracted some interest and support, at least in terms of training and consultancy, and indeed local and health authorities appear more open than central government to considering the potential value of a policy analysis approach.

These reservations having been made, however, it is difficult to refute Rudolf Klein's argument that in Britain we do not take 'policy analysis seriously as an activity in its own right'. One symptom is that few, if any, of the graduates of British public policy courses would choose to call themselves 'policy analysts', even if they had completed a curriculum identical to that taught at Berkeley. Another is that it would do them little good anyway, since (as Klein says) the civil service does not recognize any such professional group and the only recruitment of policy analysts as such is by a handful of individual local and health authorities.

The relatively closed nature of British decision-making, with Whitehall departments and interest groups bargaining and exchanging information with relatively little 'interference' from outside influences, including Parliament, reduces the potential entry points for policy analysis. In addition, few British ministers or MPs see social science inputs as having much value in the policy process, and those who do tend to 'regard themselves as their own social scientists' (Sharpe, 1975, 25). British civil servants, too, Sharpe saw as having 'a much stronger sense of self-sufficiency' than their American counterparts, no doubt helped by the absence of checks and balances, such as the necessity to explain and justify policies to powerful committees of the legislature.

When we move to the fate of policy planning and other policy-focused techniques within British government, we also find a failure of such techniques to 'take' on a systematic basis within Whitehall. Programme Analysis and Review (PAR) was formally abandoned in 1979 after gradually evaporating over the years (see Gray and Jenkins, 1983). Policy planning units within government departments have failed to provide a systematic analytical input to decision-making (see Macdonald and Fry, 1980; Prince, 1983). Such policy planning elements as were ever embodied in the PESC approach to public expenditure decision-making have been eroded in a climate of inflation and lack of economic growth. The Central Policy Review Staff (CPRS), after performing various roles at different stages of its existence, was abolished by Mrs Thatcher in 1983, symbolizing her government's greater concern with cost savings than with a sometimes provocative source of policy analysis input (see Plowden, 1981).

The picture may be less bleak in British local government, despite the failure of 'corporate planning' to live up to some of the more inflated claims made for it. For example, in several of the larger local authorities, policy planners have found a home and a power base in the Executive Office (along with finance, research and intelligence, and other 'staff' functions) or in some other form of close association with the Chief Executive. Faced with the entrenched influence and autonomy of the professionally-staffed line departments of the local authority, any Chief Executive has to develop his own organizational resources, and a wide-ranging policy planning unit or department can be one such resource.

### 3.3 The enemy within?: prospects for policy analysis

These factors, which have helped to shape the development of policy analysis, have to be taken into account in assessing the future prospects for the policy orientation. Perhaps the first point to make is that the factors which were important in sparking off the initial interest in the policy orientation are at least as valid as ever. Both American and British societies face a wide range of problems, and it is increasingly being argued that many of these problems stem from inadequacies in previous government involvement. The ending of the assumption of economic growth has removed a solvent for the easy treatment of social problems and makes it imperative that more thoughtful analysis is used to ensure a more effective use of limited resources (though it also obliges the policy analyst to justify the resources consumed by analysis).

The political structure of British government will continue to make the penetration of analytical approaches into Whitehall a slow and partial process, with frequent setbacks. In the medium term, policy analysis approaches are likely to make more headway in local, health and other authorities and in 'counter-analysis' by organizations not fully integrated into the Whitehall 'policy communities' of civil servants and interest groups (though such outside organizations will rarely have the resources to employ the more expensive analytical techniques).

If policy analysis outside Whitehall is shown to be effective (particularly if it is used in the preparation of ammunition to fire at Whitehall departments) then Whitehall interest in policy analysis may be awakened.

However, the relative failure of policy analysis to penetrate Whitehall is also a reflection of the 'cultural disdain' in which it is held: policy analysis lacks credibility in British government. Any claims to a unique and potentially valuable contribution to policy-making are regarded much more sceptically in Britain than appears to be the case in the USA. British resistance to policy analysis often seems to reflect a more basic refusal to accept its legitimacy.

Such scepticism is nourished, of course, by some of the wilder claims made for policy analysis, especially its alleged ability to offer value-free, scientifically validated, rational solutions. This 'life, the universe and everything' approach to selling policy analysis will always provoke scepticism and consumer resistance, and too often sounds like self-pleading for jobs for the (policy analysis) boys. True friends of policy analysis would do better to admit that it is a very long way from what Meltsner (1976) terms 'an adequate base of knowledge and associated theoretical paradigms', and that, in the absence of an objectively knowable public interest, analysts are not immune from introducing their own highly subjective views to the definition of problems, identification of goals, and evaluation of programmes.

Arguably a more serious potential undermining of the policy orientation has been the result of its recent fashionability. Traditional courses on British government institutions and public administration have in some cases been tarted up as 'new' courses on 'decision-making' and 'implementation', without losing their original limited disciplinary focus. As Rhodes (1979a, 23) has remarked, 'The trouble with products emblazoned with the slogan "new" is that, under the packaging, the product is remarkably similar to earlier products.' Our own strongly held view is that the teaching of public policy and policy analysis courses can make a very valuable contribution both to academic degrees and vocational training, but that the job is only worth undertaking if it is done thoughtfully and thoroughly, and that an excessive growth of merely relabelled courses will devalue the standing of policy analysis.

The reaction to the difficulties outlined in this chapter should not be one of weary despair but one of healthy scepticism, which is aware at the same time of the limitations but also of the possibilities of policy analysis. We must give thought to the selection of issues for analysis and to the significantly different contributions which analysis can hope to make in different policy areas. For example, analysis may have little to offer policy debate on a topic as value-laden as the abortion laws, but it could probably raise the level of debate on alternative weapon systems, say, or on how to gain more from spending on road safety. In chapter 6, we will be presenting the concept of 'issue filtration', by which policy-makers (or students in exercises) can filter out issues which appear (a) to require, and (b) to lend themselves to further analysis.

If policy analysts are to win recognition and influence in the policy process, they must first apply some of their powers of reasoning and discrimination to the selection of issues for analysis. Where policy areas and issues are well chosen, it should be possible to demonstrate that the analyst (or the career administrator trained in analysis) has a modest, but genuine, contribution to make to the policy process.

# 4

# Models of Policy-Making

## 4.1 Types and uses of models

We are all model builders, in the sense that we need to see some sort of pattern in the world around us and tend to interpret events in terms of that perceived pattern. We *create* 'reality' rather than simply observe it. As Graham Allison (1971) suggests, we carry around 'bundles of related assumptions' or 'basic frames of references' in terms of which we ask and answer such questions as: What happened? Why did it happen? What will happen next? Such descriptive, explanatory and predictive models are, in Allison's phrase, the 'conceptual lenses' through which we view our world and try to make sense of it. In these respects, practical men such as politicians and administrators are as much prisoners of theory as any academic social scientist. Keynes's remark about economics can be generalized to all aspects of public policy:

Practical men, who believe themselves to be quite exempt from any intellectual influences, are usually the slaves of some defunct economist. [1936, ch. 24.]

The academic social scientists should, however, be more self-aware and, one would hope, more capable of making such elusive but essential distinctions as that between, say, descriptive and prescriptive models.

The simplest definition of a model is that it is 'A representation of something else, designed for a specific purpose' (Bullock and Stallybrass, 1977). The purpose may be as simple as providing a visual reminder: for example, a former pilot may keep a model aircraft on his desk. A more elaborate model could be used to simulate the aeroplane's performance under varied conditions in a wind-tunnel. Such a model can assist in hypothesizing and experimentation ('if we give Concorde a droop-snout will lift be increased at slow speeds?'). Models need not be physical, however, and modern aircraft designers work mainly with mathematical models in which variables and their relationships are represented in abstract or symbolic terms. The purposes of such abstract model-building remain those of representation, simulation, explanation, prediction, experimentation, and hypothesis-testing.

These essentially *descriptive* models can be derived from complex social phenomena as well as from material objects. Thus a model of the working of the economy will seek to represent the interactions of such variables as investment, consumption, employment and the movement of prices. The more complex the phenomena to be represented, the greater will be the tendency towards selectivity, simplification and generalization in the making of models. Provided that simplification does not involve gross distortion, such models can assist description, explanation, and understanding.

Clues to another use of the term 'model' are to be found in colloquial languages, as when one hears of a 'model husband' or 'model village'. The reference here is to what is desirable or to be emulated. Such models are normative, or *prescriptive* rather than descriptive. They raise questions about what *ought* to be rather than what *is*.

Finally, there is a much less readily comprehensible use of the term 'model' which involves the exploration of concepts. These include the development of *ideal types* or mental constructs dealing with entities which nowhere exist in real life but which can help us to understand and explain real phenomena and to formulate or refine statements of what is desired. Examples from the natural sciences include the friction-less engine and the perfect vacuum. In social sciences there are such familiar examples as 'charismatic authority' (Weber, in Shils and Finch, 1949), 'perfect competition' in economics, and 'pure rationality' in decision-making (Simon, 1947).

One of the traditional ways of introducing students to policy analysis is to compare the 'rational' approach of Herbert Simon with the 'incremental' approach of Charles Lindblom. However, this simple comparison obscures the different fuctions which models are called upon to perform by these writers. We therefore explore their models (and others) in terms of whether they are ideal types, descriptive or prescriptive. This classification is itself an ideal-type one, and it is not how the models are always presented by the authors themselves, but it is designed to help us understand what functions models can perform.

## 4.2 Ideal-type models of 'rational' policy-making

### 4.2.1 THE STATUS OF IDEAL-TYPE MODELS

In a sense, the term 'ideal type' is unfortunate because of the everyday meaning of 'ideal' as 'highest and best conceivable' (*Chamber's Twentieth Century Dictionary*). The use of the term in social science models carries no such normative connotations. An ideal type is an exploration of an 'idea' rather than a statement of an 'ideal' in the everyday sense.

Examples will perhaps be more helpful. In teaching economics, reference is initially made to the concept of 'perfect competition' and to the manner in which prices would be determined in a totally open, free, and competitive market. This ideal type of perfect competition is not put forward as a realistic account of how prices are determined in the real world; nor is it necessarily advanced as something to be desired and attained. The analyst is concerned with prefect competition as an *idea* rather than as an *ideal*. One reason for building an ideal type of this sort is to improve our understanding of the real world, which can be described in terms of deviations from the ideal type—so that the economics teacher goes on to describe the working of the real economy in terms of imperfect competition, oligopoly, monopoly, etc.

Ideal types can also have prescriptive utility in that, having described the real world, one can then ask how satisfactory that world seems and whether there is a case for attempting to approximate, at least, to certain features of the ideal type. It is worth repeating, however, that an ideal type is not the same thing as a prescriptive model. Some economists might wish to move towards the perfectly competitive market but others would not, prescribing instead some form of regulated or planned economy.

In the context of policy analysis, the 'idea' most frequently discussed is that of 'rationality'. In constructing a 'model of rational policy-making' one is posing the question: 'How *would* policies be made if policy-makers pursued and were capable of complete rationality? Here we look briefly at the two main approaches: (1) considering values simultaneously with considering options; (2) setting out objectives at the beginning and then subsequently considering options designed to fulfil those objectives.

### 4.2.2 CONSIDERING VALUES AND OPTIONS TOGETHER

The approach of relating the consequences of all options to all values rather than pre-specifying objectives is common to a number of theories, including utility and social welfare functions in economics, and also provides theoretical underpinning to cost-benefit analysis (CBA), which is considered in chapter 10. In decision-making theory the most prominent writer to use this approach in developing an ideal-type model is Herbert Simon (1957a; also 1957b, 1960, 1983; March and Simon, 1958). As derived from Simon's writings, the main activities which would be involved in rational policy-making are roughly as follows:

(1) *Intelligence gathering*. Intelligence is here used as in the sense of 'military intelligence', namely the gathering of information prior to taking action. In a completely rational world, any policy-making agency would continually and systematically scan its horizon, seeking to identify *all* present and potential problems and opportunities relevant to its mission or interests.

(2) *Identifying all options*. Several policy responses (or 'behaviour alternatives') are usually possible when a problem or opportunity is perceived. The completely rational policy-maker would identify *all* such options and consider them in detail.

(3) *Assessing consequences of options*. In considering each policy option, it would be necessary to know what would happen if it were to be adopted. This perfect knowledge is unattainable in real life but would be essential to complete rationality (in Simon's terms, 'objective' rationality, where the reasoning is not only rational in intention but correct in the event, unlike 'subjective' rationality, where reasoning is intendedly rational but proves, with hindsight, to have been incorrect). Thus the fully rational policy-maker would identify all the costs and benefits ('consequences') of all his policy options.

(4) *Relating consequences to values*. From the preceding gathering of data about problems, options, and consequences, the rational policy-maker would now have a large amount of information, a great many facts. But facts alone are useless if they cannot be related to a set of criteria or some sort of preference-ordering procedure. Thus for Simon (1957a), 'rationality is concerned with the selection of preferred behaviour alternatives in terms of some system of values whereby the consequences of behaviour can be evaluated'.

An example may be useful at this point. Let us take the decision with which any student will soon be familiar if he has not already made it, namely the choice of a career. What would be involved in making this important choice in a completely rational manner? First, the student would have to consider *all* the career options open to him. Then he would have to explore in great detail the pros and cons of each career possibility, including such considerations ('consequences') as job security, career earnings, social status, opportunities for travel, length of vacations, and so on. But these data would be useless if the student did not know how he valued job security as against high earnings and both against, say, social status and opportunities for travel. Thus he would have to think through his value system with great thoroughness. Given both comprehensive information and a fully worked out preference-ordering set of criteria or values, a rational career choice would be possible.

(5) *Choosing preferred option.* Given full understanding of, and information about, all his problems and opportunities, all the possible policy responses, all the consequences of each and every policy option, and the criteria to be employed in valuing these consequences and thus assessing his policy options—then and only then would the policy-maker be able to arrive at a fully rational policy.

Simon sets out this way of relating values to the consequences of options because he does not find what he calls 'the means-ends' schema useful. The initial specification of objectives may foreclose unduly the courses of action that are considered and the initial focus on objectives may distract attention from the actual situation in which the decision-maker is placed.

### 4.2.3 SETTING OBJECTIVES FIRST

The alternative ideal type of rational decision-making, however, stresses the importance of specifying objectives before looking for options which might achieve them. This approach is common in much 'managerialist' writing on decision-making and it tends to be this approach which appears in prescriptions for administrative reform in the public sector. This is the approach used by Lindblom (1959) in setting up an ideal-type model of rational decision-making. Lindblom's rational policy-maker would:

(1) define and rank his governing *values*;
(2) specify *objectives* compatible with these values;
(3) identify all relevant *options* or means of achieving these objectives;

(4) calculate all the *consequences* of these options and compare them;
(5) choose the option or combination of options which would *maximize* the values earlier defined as being most important.

As well as stressing the importance of objectives in this 'rational–comprehensive model', Lindblom also places the elements of rational policy-making in a different sequence from that suggested by Simon. Most practitioners find Lindblom's version of rationality more readily comprehensible or 'commonsensical' than Simon's. Businessmen, for example, may claim to see in the Lindblomite synoptic model a rather abstract version of what ought to be involved in corporate planning. Thus a business or corporate plan should begin by identifying the values which the firm regards as of overriding importance: profit maximization, perhaps, but some weight might also be attached to 'social responsibility' or, say, to providing shareholders with a safe investment based upon diversified products and markets. These values having been clarified and ranked, the planners should go on to specify relevant objectives (rates of return to be achieved on resources employed, degrees of diversification, levels of market penetration, etc.). There are usually many different routes to achieving such objectives: not only many product/market strategies but many mixes of such strategies. In planning theory all these options would have to be identified and their consequences calculated and related back to the values earlier defined as being most important. This, after all, would only be 'good business'. It comes as a rude shock, then, to discover that Lindblom is setting up 'comprehensive rationality' not as a descriptive or prescriptive model but rather as a straw man to be pulled down!

### 4.2.4 CRITICISMS OF RATIONALITY MODELS

The most obvious criticism is that models of rational policy-making are unrealistic or impracticable. In a sense this is an unfair, even irrelevant, criticism since an ideal type is not required either to represent reality or to provide a blueprint for action. Even within its own 'unreal' terms, however, many people find it difficult to accept the assumption of perfect knowledge as an integral part of a rationality model. Surely it is enough, they argue, to require of the decision-maker that he is intendedly rational and follows rational *processes*: he should not also be required to guarantee a rational *outcome*. Another version of the same criticism would attack rationality models for being insufficiently dynamic. The decision-maker, in other words, might conceivably acquire perfect knowledge of the present (static) situation but should not be expected to have similar knowledge of an essentially unknowable future situation, in which a great many external and unpredictable factors may prevent the anticipated 'consequences' of a strategy occurring in the event.

The main intellectual difficulty with rationality models lies, however, in the part played by *values*. Surely this is the arbitrary element in any decision? Our rational student's choice of a career, for example, required him to specify and rank such values as high earnings as against job security, and so on. How can such 'value judgements' be made on anything other than a personal, intuitive or subjective basis? Ideal-type rational models are about procedures for developing an argument or taking a decision and the model does nothing to guarantee the desirability of the values fed into it or even the validity of the factual assumptions made (see Simon, 1983, 16).

Any prescriptive model derived from the ideal-type rationality model cannot be a complete substitute for political mechanisms for determining values and priorities, since the model cannot determine these but requires them to be fed in from outside. To see 'rationality' and politics as intrinsically incompatible is based on a fundamental misunderstanding of the role of values in rational models. Because the model assumes that at some stage an authoritative person or organization will inject an explicit set of values there is, however, a tendency for prescriptive models derived from the ideal-type rationality model to have centralist, technocratic connotations.

The difficulties do not end there, unfortunately, and the question arises of *whose* values should prevail. Simon does grapple with this problem and distinguishes between personal and organizational rationality, leaving us in little doubt that his concern is with what is rational for the employing organization rather than what the individual employee might see as being in his own selfish interest. There is no problem, of course, when a decision involves and affects only the individual, as in a choice of career. But let us revisit our student twenty years on in his chosen career. He is now a senior manager in a British car-making firm. He is helping to negotiate a merger with a Japanese competitor, a merger which is expected to benefit the British firm but might well threaten his own status and prospects. Here we have two competing rationalities—the manager's personal self-interest and the larger organizational interest of the firm and its shareholders. It is even more compli-

cated, however, because the British Government has reservations
about the Japanese merger and asks the firm to consider the national
interest. Whose interests should he favour in his contribution to
corporate policy-making about the proposed merger: those of the
nation, the firm's shareholders, or his own?

The public sector is particularly vulnerable to such questions about
the most appropriate scale on which to consider policy issues. A topical
example is that of expenditure cutbacks (see Glennerster, 1981). The
necessity for, and incidence of, spending cuts might be viewed from
the narrow perspective of the self-interested individual officer within a
local authority. Or he might take a slightly broader view in terms of
what would be best for his particular sub division of the department.
Or he might raise his sights to consider cutbacks in terms of the department as a whole. A more 'corporate' level of reasoning would require
him to take into account the scale and balance of spending within
the local authority as a whole. A supreme effort might even allow him
to take into account national criteria for assessing his authority's
expenditure.

A truly rational policy would be based upon the *largest* relevant
scale of values and interests. It would avoid the type of sub-optimal
policy-making which results from confusing a sub-system (such as one
department in a local authority) with a larger system (the local authority
itself). This still begs the question, however, of how values at this
largest relevant scale would be set and articulated.

## 4.3 Descriptive models of policy-making

The nature and purpose of a descriptive model seem, at first sight, to
be both more obvious and more straightforward than those of an ideal
type. Whereas the latter is a 'mental construct' or essentially artificial
exercise in reasoning, the development of a descriptive model is a very
natural human activity, since we need to see some sort of shape or
pattern in the world about us. Unfortunately, however, we do not all
see the same 'reality', especially when it comes to describing and
explaining something as complex as public policy-making. In his classic
study of the Cuban Missile Crisis, Allison (1971) shows how different
descriptive perspectives or 'conceptual lenses' lead to different interpre-
tations of events.

In terms of highly general descriptive models, Simon and Lindblom,
having set up their largely similar models of rational policy-making,

both go on to describe reality in terms of deviations from perfect rationality.

Simon appears to believe that policy-makers seek to be rational but do not succeed because of bounds or limits to their individual and collective capacities for logical, economic or maximizing behaviour. Real-life 'administrative man' (unlike 'economic man', of the older textbooks) settles instead for 'satisficing' behaviour, that is, for a level of performance which will 'get by' or meet 'reasonable' expectations. ('Satisficing' was coined to accommodate in one word both 'satisfying' and 'sufficing' behaviour.) Simon's original descriptive model is to be found in his account of 'bounded rationality' (Simon 1957a), in which he explains the combination of 'psychological' and 'organizational' deficiencies which limits our capacity for fully rational decision-making and leads us to satisfice.

Lindblom develops his arguments, partly at least, in the same way as Simon, by identifying limits to rationality in real-life policy-making. He emphasizes the 'costliness of analysis' and is particularly strong on the political environment of policy-making and the constraints of the given situation in which policy is made.

If we combine these contributions of Simon and Lindblom, then, we can identify at least five important categories of limitations to rationality in actual decision-making behaviour.

(1) *Psychological limitations.* Some obvious limits to rationality lie in the individual policy-maker's powers of cognition and calculation. Put simply, we lack the knowledge, the skills and the value-consistency which would be needed to achieve complete rationality. To return to an earlier example, why will our student not be able, in practice, to make a fully rational career choice? Because: (a) he lacks full *knowledge* of all his possible career options; (b) he lacks the *skills* to calculate all the consequences (earnings, security, etc.) of even such options as he can identify; and (c) he lacks the degree of self-knowledge, clarity, or consistency about *values* which would allow him to make use of such information as he might acquire.

(2) *Limitations arising from multiple values.* The problem of values is further exacerbated when we move from individual to collective rationality (see Simon, 1983, 84). Arrow (1954) in his 'impossibility theorem' has demonstrated that under quite plausible assumptions about the conditions that a social welfare function

should satisfy—such as that different people are to be allowed to weight their values in different ways—then no such aggregate function can exist. In other words, there is no purely 'rational' way of resolving a conflict of interest.

(3) *Organizational limitations.* Even if the individual could overcome his personal limitations as policy-maker, he would still find great obstacles put in his way because of the fact that he has to work as part of an organization (business firm, government department, local authority etc.). In the name of efficiency, for example, modern organizations tend to involve a high degree of division of labour and *specialization of function.* But this often gets in the way of what might be called the 'whole problem' approach, since different aspects of a problem are handled by organizational sub-units and co-ordination of their problem-solving efforts is usually less than perfect. The treatment of homeless people (especially the elderly homeless) is a good example. Another organizational impediment to rationality is departmentalism of *outlook.* That is, instead of taking the 'whole organization' perspective we often look at problems through narrower departmental 'spectacles'. This failure stems from a refusal to look beyond the sub-system to the larger system's requirements. Finally, organizations tend to have major deficiencies as processors of *information.* Most MIS (management information systems) studies indicate that an organization's information flows do not relate to its information needs. Organizations tend to swamp us with information we do not want but fail to provide us with information we need for policy-making, or the right information comes in an unusable form or too late to be useful (see chapter 5).

(4) *Cost limitations.* These might also be called 'resource' limitations to rationality. In other words, it costs to be rational, in terms of time, energy and money. One would have to be very confident that the benefits accruing from a more rational approach to a problem would outweigh the costs of the rational approach: if not, one would be behaving quite irrationally.

(5) *Situational limitations.* A fifth category of limitations upon rationality is situational. That is, a policy-maker does not write on a clean slate, he does not decide in a vacuum. We are all influenced by the past (e.g. by precedents), by powerful vested interests in the present, and by people's assumptions and

expectations concerning the future. A good example is budgeting. A rational approach would require a strong case to be made anew each year for any and all future expenditure. This is, of course, the theory of what is now called 'zero base budgeting' (see 10.6.6). In practice, however, the constraints of precedents, politics and expectations create a situation in which the main determinant of next year's budget is who got what and how much in last year's budget.

Lindblom goes far beyond identifying limits to rationality, however, and often seems to delight in demonstrating how real-life policy-making stands rationality on its head. If we sum up the main features of Lindblom's descriptive model as developed in his writings in the 1960s, it will be seen that what emerges is a positive theory rather than a regretful account of why fully rational policy-making is impossible (Lindblom, 1959, 1965, 1968; Hirschman and Lindblom, 1962; Braybrooke and Lindblom, 1963). The main characteristics of real-life policy-making, as seen by Lindblom, all have an internal logic. They include the following.

(1) Policy-makers often avoid thinking through or at least spelling out their objectives. This may reflect a shrewd awareness that to do so would precipitate conflict rather than agreement. It would also provide standards by which to judge performance, and why give such hostages to fortune?

(2) When it is clear that existing policies are failing to cope, the remedial action taken by legislators and administrators will tend to be 'incremental': That is, they will make relatively small adjustments to policies rather than sweeping changes. In doing so, they are moving cautiously and experimentally from a basis of what is known rather than taking a giant step into an unknown future.

(3) Policy-makers accept that few, if any, problems are ever solved once and for all time. Instead, policy-making is 'serial' (we keep coming back at problems as mistakes are corrected and new lines of attack developed).

(4) Few policies are made by individuals or even single agencies, but are instead made by the interaction of many policy influentials operating in a power network ('polycentricity').

(5) While these actors are self-interested, they are not blindly partisan and are capable of adjusting to one another, through

bargaining, negotiation, and compromise ('partisan mutual adjustment').

(6) A value is placed in most pluralist liberal democracies on 'consensus seeking', so that what emerges is not necessarily the one best policy but rather that compromise policy upon which most groups can agree.

Simon's and Lindblom's descriptive models are at a high level of generality, though it could be argued that Lindblom's model reflects special characteristics of the American political system. Each country will have its own 'policy style' with its own special characteristics (Richardson, 1982). For example, Richardson and Jordan (1979) characterize the British system as one in which Parliament plays little direct role in the policy process, with both the formulation and the implementation of policies being determined through consultations within relatively closed 'policy communities' of government departments and interest groups. Clearly it is important to have an understanding of the policy process in a particular country (and of particular policy areas within it) if we are to be able to assess whether prescriptions for change in either procedures or policy substance are likely to 'take'. However, as the debate about whether or not we have 'corporatist' policy-making in Britain illustrates (see Jordan, 1981), there may not be full agreement among political scientists about how to characterize the policy process in practice.

## 4.4 Prescriptive models of policy-making

### 4.4.1 TOWARDS GREATER RATIONALITY?

Simon's writings of the 1940s and 1950s had demonstrated the extent to which 'administrative man' fell short of rational decision-making behaviour. But should, and could, administrative man become more rational? Simon's answer to both questions is 'yes'. For his prescriptive model we must look first to his 1960 book on *The New Science of Management Decision* (which has since 1960 been published in various revised editions and with at least one change of title).

Simon distinguishes between 'programmed' and 'non-programmed' decision-making. Decisions are programmed 'to the extent that they are repetitive and routine [and] to the extent that a definite procedure has been worked out for handling them'. Decisions are non-programmed 'to the extent that they are novel [and] unstructured': the problem may not have arisen before, or its precise nature may be elusive and complex, or it may be so important 'that it deserves custom-tailored treatment'. In non-programmed decision-making, the system has no specific procedures or capacity for dealing with the situation but must instead 'fall back on whatever general capacity it has for intelligent, adaptive, problem-oriented action'. Sinon argues, however, that such general-purpose capacity is expensive to provide and maintain, so that programmed, specific procedures and criteria for decision-making should be used wherever possible.

Thus Simon looks first to improvements in programmed decisions. The new capacity for such decision-making he finds in operations research (operational research in British usage), systems analysis, and mathematical techniques such as linear and dynamic programming, game theory, probability models, etc. Such techniques have only been made 'operational', in many cases, by great advances in computer technology, allowing of much more elaborate analysis, assessment of alternatives, simulation, and modelling.

There remain many administrative problems which are not amenable to programming. But Simon argues that we have learned a good deal about 'heuristic problem solving'—that is, methods which help us to define and solve problems in the absence of scientific, objective or quantitative methods. Such problem-solving proceeds by way of search activity, abstraction, analogy; and by groping attempts to break down problems into sub-problems, and to deal with them on the basis of precedent, observation, and so on. Such decision-making is essentially a learning process but, even here, there is some scope for analysis, including computer-assisted analysis.

Simon then turns to some structural or organizational implications of 'the new science of management decision'. He describes organizations as 'three-layered cakes': (1) bottom layer—'the basic work processes' (manufacture, distribution, etc.); (2) middle layer—'programmed decision-making processes that govern day-to-day operations'; (3) 'non-programmed decision making processes that are required to design and redesign the entire system, to provide it with its basic goals and objectives, and to monitor its performance'. If more decisions could be programmed, 'top layer' management could deal in greater depth with its remaining, unpredictable, and least tractable problems.

What of the basic organizational problem of 'centralization versus decentralization'? Simon rightly says that the issue is not one of small-scale versus large-scale as competing principles of organization, but rather of defining 'optimal' scales for different types of activities. But he appears to be arguing that modern management methods both demand and facilitate larger-scale fields of operation. In his 1960 text, then, Simon would appear to be pointing us towards a centralized, technocratic, planned form of government.

However, in his 1983 book, *Reason in Human Affairs*, Simon explicitly addresses (among other topics) the role of rationality in public policy-making, and the emphasis which emerges is rather different from that in *The New Science of Management Decision*. There is still considerable stress on the way in which computer-based techniques can aid decision-making. However, Simon also stresses the limitations to expertise and the need to strengthen our understanding of political institutions, based partly on his practical experience of public policy and administration. Thus we find him arguing for adversary proceedings in cases (such as allegations of health dangers from nuclear power stations) where there is a tendency for experts to close ranks and reject the need for an impartial enquiry. He also urges a more sympathetic understanding of the role of politics and political processes:

we must recognize that certain kinds of political phenomena—the attempt to influence legislation or the administration of laws, the advocacy of special interest— are essential to the operation of political institutions in a society where there is, in fact, great diversity of interest. [Simon, 1983, 100.]

He bemoans the decline of political parties and the rise of the 'individual voter' in the United States, claiming that this has lowered the level of 'civic rationality'. Unfortunately, Simon does not develop this concept of 'civic rationality' further, but clearly we have moved a long way from the individualistic rationality of his ideal-type model. Rationality in public affairs is seen as having an important but heavily qualified role.

Reason, taken by itself, is instrumental. It can't select our final goals, nor can it mediate for us in pure conflicts over what final goal to pursue —we have to settle these issues in some other way. All reason can do is help us to reach agreed-on goals more effectively. But in this respect at least, we are getting better [Simon, 1983, 106.]

Simon is probably the most prominent, if misunderstood, name associated with advocacy of a more rational approach to policy-making, but other writers have also attempted to make a distinctive contribution. For example, Dror (1968; 1971) to some extent dissociates himself from Simon, since 'trying to point administrators towards an unachievable model of total rationality is likely to be counter-productive'. However, it is clear that Dror's approach has much more in common with Simon and the science of management decision than with Lindblom and the 'science of muddling through'.

Dror emphasizes the costliness of analysis in his 'economically rational model', which says that the various phases of pure-rationality policy-making should be developed in practice only in so far as the cost of the input into making policy-making more rational is less than the benefit of the output (in terms of the marginal improvement of the policy's quality). He is unusual in his readiness to include in both his descriptive and prescriptive models the contribution of 'extrarational' (intuitive, judgemental) processes. Finally, he is more specific than the other theorists discussed in this chapter about the necessity for 'meta-policymaking' or 'deciding how to decide'.

Dror thus sees himself as occupying a unique position which avoids the extremes of both incrementalism and rationalism. While there are some grounds for such a claim, we believe that Dror does lean towards the Simonian end of the spectrum. Much of his analysis can be seen in terms of improvments in the factual and value premises of the policy-maker as a means of pushing back the bounds of bounded rationality. His stated purpose could be that of Simon as well, namely: 'What is needed is a model which fits reality while being directed towards its improvement.'

### 4.4.2 'STILL MUDDLING, NOT YET THROUGH'

If Simon's normative model can be characterized, perhaps too glibly, as an attempt to approximate to at least some features of his rationality (or ideal-type) model, what is Lindblom's position? On the basis of his earlier writings (Lindblom, 1959, 1965; Hirschman and Lindblom, 1962; Braybrooke and Lindblom, 1963), it was often said of Lindblom that his descriptive model ('muddling through') was also his prescriptive model: what *is* was also what *ought* to be, and incrementalism and partisan mutual adjustment were not deplored but rather defended by Lindblom as the only way in which policies could and should be made in a pluralist, democratic, and liberal society.

Lindblom's 1959 essay on 'The science of muddling through'—which by 1979 had been reprinted in forty anthologies—became the target of much criticism in the 1960s and 1970s. For example, Dror (1964), while admitting the force of Lindblom's writings as description, viewed their prescriptive element as a 'dangerous over-reaction to the rational–

comprehensive model. Dror focused his attack first on incrementalism.
He saw at least three circumstances in which incrementalism would be
inadequate, namely:

(1) Present policies may be so manifestly unsatisfactory that merely
to tinker with them is pointless.

(2) The problems requiring a governmental response may be changing so fast or so fundamentally that policies based on past
experience are inadequate as a guide to future action.

(3) The means available for problem-solving may be expanding, so
that major new opportunities exist but are likely to be neglected
by incrementalists. (For example, changes in political influence,
economic capability, technology, etc, 'In military technology . . .
incremental change results in the tendency to be excellently
prepared for the last war.')

Dror then shifted his attack to the 'second key element' in Lindblom's
thinking, namely 'consensus'. There may be many circumstances where
'agreement as the criterion of good policy' is acceptable, especially
when, in times of relative stability, there is informed agreement based
on the lessons of a relevant past. But in times of rapid change such
lessons may not be relevant. For this and other reasons, 'deceived
consensus' may result. Dror also appears less than enthusiastic about
the contribution that 'participatory democracy' can make to the
solution of highly complex and technical problems.

Lindblom himself has usually been depicted as an arch-conservative
defender of the status quo, champion of market systems and dedicated
opponent of planning. At the close of the 1970s, however, Lindblom
replied to his critics and presented a rather different view of his own
position (Lindblom, 1979; see also Lindblom, 1977; Lindblom and
Cohen, 1979). While Lindblom is as scathing in 1979 as he was in 1959
about the pretensions of full-blown planning, he goes on to develop a
number of distinctions which could be read either as a clarification of
his 1959 position or (as we tend to think) the statement of a rather
different 1979 position.

First, he distinguishes between 'incremental *politics*' and 'incremental *analysis*'. Incremental politics is a 'political pattern' characterized
by 'political change by small steps'. In his earlier writings, Lindblom
had seemed more than a little complacent about this type of politics.
In 1979, Lindblom makes a significant distinction between the *theory*
and *practice* of incremental politics. The theory is still defended, but

Lindblom accepts that in practice incremental politics have been viewed by many Americans as ineffective in coping with 'big problems like environmental decay, energy shortage, inflation, and unemployment'. He makes it clear that he shares such concerns. However, he sees the problem as lying not in incremental politics *per se* but rather in particular 'structural' features of the American political system. He attacks the number of 'veto powers' in the constitution, legislature, judiciary, and business interests. These obstacles to change—even, he points out, to incremental change—also lead Lindblom to reconsider the practice of 'partisan mutual adjustment' in the United States. He admits that some interests are unrepresented or only weakly represented; there are 'disturbing tendencies towards corporatism'; the discussion of 'grand issues' is often stifled by a heavily indoctrinated 'homogeneity of opinion'; and there are too many issues on which 'though none of the participants can on their own initiate a change, many or all can veto it'.

Lindblom is not, then, the conservative he has been branded, but nor do his criticisms of incremental politics lead him to renounce the system, and he continues to deny that a centralized, planned system offers a feasible or acceptable alternative. His response is in terms of *improvements* to incremental politics including the more skilled use of incremental *analysis*.

Turning, then, from incremental politics to incremental analysis, Lindblom insists that 'incomplete' analysis is none the less a form of analysis and as such, it seems, a useful supplement to partisan advocacy and politics. He distinguishes three types of such analysis. The first two are familiar from his earlier writings.

*Simple* incremental analysis is 'Analysis that is limited to consideration of alternative policies all of which are only incrementally different from the status quo'.

*Disjointed incrementalism* emphasizes the analytical features of incrementalism as described in section 4.3, namely: analysis limited to a few familiar alternatives; analysis of policy goals intertwined with empirical aspects of the problem; analysis concerned with remedying ills rather than positive goals to be sought; a sequence of trials, errors and revised trials; analysis of only some of the important consequences of those alternatives considered; and analytical work fragmented among many partisan participants in policy-making.

The third type of 'incremental' analysis is less familiar, however, and he calls it *strategic* analysis, or 'Analysis limited to any calculated or thoughtfully chosen set of stratagems to simplify complex problems, that is, to short-cut the conventionally comprehensive "scientific" analysis'. Such 'strategems' include 'skilfully sequenced trial and error . . . limitations of analysis to only a few alternatives, routinization of decisions and focusing decision making on crises' Moreover, such analysis can be supplemented by 'broadranging, often highly speculative, and sometimes utopian thinking about directions and possible features, near and far in time' (sic: but for 'features' we should read 'futures'?). In other words, Lindblom seems prepared to find a place for 'theory' and for innovative policy analysis?

Surely this 1979 'strategic analysis' plus theoretical insights which 'liberate us from both synoptic and incremental methods of analysis' all add up to a form of modified rationality rather than Lindblom's earlier attempts to stand rationality on its head. What is in 1979 called 'grossly incomplete analysis' (i.e. the 'muddling through' of 1959 in its purest form) is no longer prescribed. Instead Lindblom tells us that 'we can aspire' to a shift along the spectrum towards synoptic analysis, although we shall always fall far short of such 'completeness'. This 1979 position of Lindblom's is still different in degree from the 'new science of management decision' of Herbert Simon, since the latter clearly aspires to move much further towards complete rationality, but are the early 1980s positions of Lindblom and Simon as different as appeared to be the case in the early 1960s?

Another writer associated with the 'pluralist' or 'incrementalist' approach to policy-making, Aaron Wildavsky, has also recently stressed that analysis has a role to play, albeit as an input to politics. In his early work (Wildavsky, 1962) he had defended the American political system, which he characterized in terms of 'coalition politics' and 'free bargaining'. The market-like nature of his view of the political process was reflected in his praise of the 'heroic feats of rational calculation performed through the interplay of interests in the American political system'. Wildavsky's reputation is largely based on his debunking of attempts to achieve rationality in government, especially through the introduction of budgeting techniques such as PPBS (see Wildavsky, 1969; 1971; 1973; 1975; Heclo and Wildavsky, 1974).

The best guide to Wildavsky's position at the end of the 1970s is The Art and Craft of Policy Analysis (1980). This immensely long book does not lend itself to brief summary, but one is left with the impression that, like Lindblom, the later Wildavsky is prepared to accept a positive, if necessarily limited, role for analysis and planning in the policy process. He tells us that as he began writing the book 'the necessity of connecting thought to action was uppermost in my mind'. He dwells on the tension between 'social interaction' (markets and politics) and 'intellectual cogitation' (planning) and argues that 'pure planning or pure politics alone are unsatisfactory as modes of making collective choices'. The task of policy analysis is to balance intellectual cogitation against social interaction to supplement but never to supplant the political process. Policy analysis is 'about improvement, about improving citizen preferences for the policies they—the people—ought to prefer'.

### 4.4.3 A MIDDLE WAY?

We have made it clear in the previous two subsections that when the later writings of Simon and Lindblom are taken into account it is a distorted caricature to cast one as the centralist technocratic rationalist and the other as the 'politics as a market' incrementalist. However, it cannot be denied that teachers have found it useful to have the 1959 Lindblom available for contrast with the 1960 Simon, since these prescriptions appear to represent opposite ends of the spectrum. Other writers can then be 'located' at various points along the spectrum. One writer, Etzioni (1967), sets out quite specifically to explore and lay claims to the middle ground between Simon and Lindblom—namely, 'Mixed scanning: a third approach to decision making'.

The term 'mixed scanning' is derived from the analogy of cameras employed in such activities as weather observation. If total information about weather patterns and trends were required, cameras would have to incorporate a capacity for scanning the total weather scene plus a capacity for the most detailed observation of each and every part of the scene. This is difficult to achieve and what we settle for is a mixed-scanning approach, in which wide-lens cameras take in a broad sweep to provide at least a rough indication of significant new developments while other cameras are focused much more narrowly on particular areas where developments are confidently expected and detailed observation therefore required.

Translated into policy-making terms, rationalism would seek detailed and comprehensive information about the whole weather scene, thus swamping the observers in largely unusable and enormously costly data. Incrementalism would focus only on those areas in which troublesome patterns had developed in the past and, perhaps, on a few adjacent areas. It would thus ignore significant weather information in unexpected areas. The mixed-scanning strategy combines a detailed examination of some sectors with a more cursory review of the wider weather scene. This feasible and economically defensible operation is seen as adequate for most purposes. Also it is flexible since the 'mix' of broad and detailed scanning can be varied depending on changing circumstances (e.g. in the hurricane season it would be advisable to increase comprehensive scanning because of the consequences of missing early signs of an unexpected hurricane formation).

The mixed-scanning approach also emphasizes the need to differentiate fundamental decisions from incremental ones. Fundamental decisions should be made by exploring as many as possible of the options open to the decision-maker, but with deliberate omission of detailed assessment so that an overview is possible. Before and after such fundamental decision-making (taken in a relatively rational or synoptic manner) there will still be wide scope for incremental decision-making—within the context set by fundamental decisions.

There are several difficulties in applying Etzioni's model to the practical concerns of decision-makers (quite apart from the fact that his original metaphor of weather satellites is inaccurate as a description of how weather satellites operate and how they fit into overall weather forecasting). In the first place, it is not clear whether the analogy between weather satellites and social problems holds up. The surface of the world is of fixed geometrical proportions which can be scanned on a simple pattern and the phenomena to which closer attention has to be paid are fairly well known. It is not clear in the same way what the layout of the social world is or what phenomena should be focused on. In his book on *Social Problems* (1976) Etzioni discussed the application of his model to urban renewal and impact statements. What he has to say about these matters contains a lot of sense (though he neglects the disadvantages of impact statements) and he is right to point to the inappropriateness of fully synoptic or fully incremental approaches; however, the analysis does not derive directly from the original mixed-scanning metaphor.

As the name implies, the 'mixed-scanning' model is of particular potential relevance to decisions about how to allocate analytical resources. However, Etzioni, while providing us with criteria about what kind of weather formations require detailed analysis, does not provide a set of criteria for determining which policy-issues should be analysed in which way (see chapter 5 on 'Issue Search', and chapter 6 on 'Issue Filtration' in this book).

## 4.5 A contingency approach to policy analysis

The framework for this book, consisting of analysis related to stages in the policy process, does not conform to the stereotyped extremes of either 'rational comprehensive' analysis or 'muddling through'. We regard such polarization as being, in the end, sterile and smacking too much of an either/or choice. Nor do we simply seek a 'middle way'. The crucial stage in our framework is the second, that of 'deciding how to decide' or issue filtration (see chapter 6). In other words, we suggest that different policy issues require different policy-making approaches.

Some issues will always require a highly political, pluralist, bargaining, and incrementalist approach. But some other issues—probably only a small minority—will both require and lend themselves to a much more planned or analytical approach. These are the issues which, having been identified at the second or 'issue-filtration' stage, should then be subjected to all the other stages, with due concern for their logical sequence (plus, of course, opportunities for feedback and interaction). At each stage—forecasting, say, or options analysis—full use should be made of any planning or managerial aids available. Following Dror (1968) our approach is 'economically rational' since we accept that analysis should be conducted only to the extent that it is likely to produce benefits commensurate with the cost of analysis.

Thus we advocate a 'contingency' approach (adjust policy-making methods to the circumstances and to the issue in question). There is no 'one best way' of making decisions, just as there is no universal prescription for 'good organization'. Among the diagnostic skills required is a very high degree of *political* sensitivity and discrimination as well as a grasp of the technical skills of planning and analysis.

## 4.6 Models in public policy and policy analysis

A policy analyst must be aware of the existence and importance of models in everyday life as well as in the literature of policy studies. He should be explicit and self-critical about the models he himself uses. As Allison (1971) says, 'the fact that alternative frames of reference . . . produce quite different explanations should encourage the analyst's self-consciousness about the nets he employs.' The 'policy frame' he adopts in defining a problem will certainly influence his solution to the problem. In forecasting, too, he will construct a theory or model of how several variables are likely to interact to bring about some future

state cf affairs. In moving from policy formulation to policy implementation he will have developed a theory of cause and effect, along
the lines that 'it we do $x$ now, $y$ will follow'.

Model-building holds its dangers and traps for the unwary. The
analyst, like any social scientist, should understand the distinctions
between ideal-type, descriptive, and prescriptive models and, even in
the heat of argument, should avoid the temptation to slip unobtrusively
from one to another. In developing any model he should realize that a
process of abstraction, selection, and simplification is going on. An
obvious danger is of over-simplification and distortion. However, as
simplifying assumptions are relaxed to make models more realistic, the
elaborate model may become too complex to understand or too clumsy
to use. A particular disciplinary background (such as economics or
psychology) will give a characteristic slant to an analyst's thinking:
hence the need for an inter-disciplinary approach (see section 3.1.2).
Above all, of course, the analyst should be aware of his own political
and ideological biases and the preconceptions, assumptions, and sheer
wishful thinking which will influence his view of 'the way things are'
and might be. A useful corrective device is occasionally to reconsider a
particular problem (or solution) in terms of a diametrically opposed
perspective to that so far employed by the analyst.

In seeking to understand the real-world policy process, the analyst
must try to identify the particular models or sets of related assumptions
which influence different policy actors. Such assumptions may, in the
analyst's eyes, be incoherent or internally inconsistent, but they will
none the less be models of policy which can influence practical action.

Whether he is operating in the academic arena or the world of policy
actors, then, the analyst has an important role to play as an exponent,
identifier, and interpreter of relevant policy models. Where different
participants in an intellectual or political debate have different frames
of reference which are implicit or ambiguous, then there will be particular problems of interpretation (cf. Rose, 1976c). Even though the
same words may be used, different 'languages' are often being spoken.
The analyst's role as interpreter can extend to identifying which values
and perceptions are shared by various models, which are genuinely
incompatible, and which, though not completely shared, are not
mutually contradictory.

When an analyst is working for a particular client, he will have the
often delicate task of clarifying and possibly questioning the assumptions and implicit models underlying the client's view of problems and

acceptable responses. Since securing and then implementing a particular policy usually involves interactions (conflict, competition, accommodation, collaboration, etc.) with other agencies, the analyst can also help his client by similar clarification of those agencies' interests, values, perceptions, and assumptions.

If he wishes his policy advice to be 'consumed', either generally or by a particular client, the analyst must give considerable thought to the language and reference points he employs. To believe that a sufficiently rigorous analysis will lead the analyst to an unarguable 'one best answer' which the consumer will immediately recognize and adopt, is simply to be naïve about the status of policy advice and the activity of policy advising. Where the underlying perceptions, assumptions, and values of analyst and consumer are at odds or, worse, simply do not relate to one another, then very little influence is likely to be exerted.

The approach in this book is, we hope, reasonably aware of most of the problems and traps indicated above. It emphasizes the political nature of the policy process, the subjectivity of much analysis, and the need for the analyst to concern himself with the consumption as well as the production of policy advice.

# Part II
# Analysis in the
# Policy Process

# 5

# Issue Search

## 5.1 The importance of issue search

The potential contribution which analysis can make at later stages of the policy process depends on when and how a potential public policy problem or opportunity is initially identified. The introduction of expensive policy analysis techniques for options appraisal may be wasted if the failure to identify a potential problem at an early enough stage means that many options are foreclosed because of time constraints, or that they can only be adopted at a much greater cost. All organizations in the public sector currently employ both formal and informal methods of identifying possible problems, opportunities, or threats to the organization. The questions to be explored are whether these existing channels, many of them 'political', are fully adequate for establishing the 'agenda' of public policy issues, or whether the use of more active issue search approaches might improve the overall issue-processing capacity of public organizations

## 5.2 Agenda setting in practice

How and why do some issues get on the policy agenda for discussion and perhaps action, while others do not or, if they do, receive only cursory or belated attention? There are, of course, different types and levels of agendas (see Cobb and Elder, 1972, on 'systemic' and 'institutional' agendas) and agenda items can also be categorized in various ways, such as annually recurring (for example, budget-related) items, less regular but cyclically recurring items such as demands for an incomes policy, and apparently 'new' items which, in turn, either become recurring items or quietly disappear.

To the extent that it is possible to generalize, however, an issue—especially a new issue—seems most likely to reach the agenda if one or more of the following circumstances apply. First, the issue has reached *crisis* proportions and can no longer be ignored (see Kimber *et al.*, 1974, on the origins of the Deposit of Poisonous Wastes Act, 1972), or is perceived as threatening a future crisis (for example, nuclear waste in the 1980s). Second, the issue has achieved *particularity* (Solesbury, 1976): for example, 'acid rain' has recently served to exemplify and dramatize the larger issue of atmospheric pollution from sulphur dioxide and other industrial emissions. Third, the issue has an *emotive* aspect or the 'human interest angle' which attracts media attention, such as the tragedy of the 'Thalidomide children' which aroused concern about the side-effects of modern drugs and the plight of the severely handicapped. Fourth, the issue seems likely to have *wide impact*: most 'pocketbook' issues (such as higher rate demands by local authorities) come into this category, as do health 'scares' such as the possible link between the contraceptive pill and certain types of cancer in women. Fifth, the issue raises questions about *power* and *legitimacy* in society, as in recent disputes about the 'closed shop' principle and the use of 'secondary picketing' by trade unions. Sixth, the issue is *fashionable* in some way which is difficult to explain but easy to recognize: for example, problems of the 'inner city' or concern about mugging and other forms of 'street crime'.

Such predisposing circumstances do not guarantee politicization and access to the public policy agenda. For a fuller understanding of why issues do or do not achieve political salience we need further study of the activities and influence of various *agenda setters*, such as organized interests, protest groups, party leaders and influentials, senior officials and advisers, 'informed opinion', and the gatekeepers of the mass media such as newspaper editors and television producers. Fortunately there has been growing interest among political scientists (for example, Anderson, 1975; Richardson and Jordan, 1979) in the politics of agenda setting. Certain policy areas, such as ecology and the environment, have been particularly well served (Brookes *et al.*, 1976; Downs, 1972; Kimber *et al.*, 1974; Sandbach, 1980; Solesbury, 1976; Stringer and Richardson, 1980) but agenda setting in other areas, especially the more 'closed' fields such as defence or science policy, requires further research and discussion.

## 5.3 The case for (and against) more active issue search

### 5.3.1 THE NEED TO ANTICIPATE PROBLEMS AND OPPORTUNITIES

Governments often become aware of problems or their ramifications too late to act upon them in the optimal way. The best time to start treating (or averting) a problem might well bo before a crisis forced the issue onto the political agenda. Relatedly, it often takes a considerable amount of 'lead' time to set up the organizational structure to deal with a problem. Thirdly, if a decision has to be made very quickly once crisis has arisen, it may be based on inadequate or misleading information. There may be inadequate time for definition of just what the problem is and for exploration of the implications of alternative options. Many of the techniques available to policy analysts can only he brought to bear if there is adequate time for analysis; hence anticipation of occasions when decisions may be required is a precondition for effective policy analysis at other stages.

There are, of course, formidable technical and intellectual problems in devising methods of ensuring advance warning. However, it is political factors which help to explain the relatively passive role of governments in problem search. There is a temptation for governments to concentrate on current problems requiring action now rather than hypothetical problems where any adverse political effects of not taking action now will not occur until the future, and perhaps affect a different political party. In Britain, because of the frequent reshuffling of ministerial posts, an individual minister also faces the temptation to concentrate on issues with an immediate impact, since 'He knows that he will probably not be in the same post long and therefore not be held responsible for the consequences of his policies' (Headey, 1974, 99). Similarly, civil servants are likely to have moved on before any hypothetical crisis actually materializes. On the other side of the coin, the rewards for foresight for both politicians and civil servants are negligible, and are just as likely to be reaped by others as by those actually responsible for the anticipatory action.

Thus, there may be a mismatch between what is 'rational' in terms of bringing analysis and programmes to bear on problems at the optimal time, and what is 'rational' from the perspective of the career rewards of policy-makers. Thus, more active issue search would entail not only the introduction of new techniques, but alterations to the political reward structure so that foresight is rewarded (and perhaps lack of it penalized).

### 5.3.2 THE NEED TO IDENTIFY PROBLEMS WHERE THERE ARE ONLY 'WEAK SIGNALS'

The type of information required for issue search may differ from that required for strategic planning or forecasting approaches, which tend to assume massive information input (see Ansoff, 1975, 22). If we are to be able to anticipate potential problems rather than merely identify problems which already exist we need to be able to respond to 'weak signals', particularly when there may be discontinuity from the present pattern. There is a paradox that a comprehensive planning approach is easiest (and arguably only possible) when it is least necessary, that is, when there is plenty of information and high continuity or certainty. On the other hand, incremental approaches are singularly ill-equipped to deal with large discontinuities, particularly those requiring long decision or lead times.

The purpose in seeking to identify potential threats or opportunities which are highly uncertain or may have only a low probability of occurring is to enable these to be taken into account when designing organizations and other policies so that a capacity to deal with potential problems is built in, or at least not precluded. In addition, it might be decided to establish a contingency or crisis team designed to carry out or co-ordinate contingency plans should the crisis actually occur. Such preparations may be politically sensitive, as indicated by the resistance of some local and health authorities to making appointments to posts concerned with civil defence preparations for nuclear war.

The identification of a potential problem on the basis of only limited information does not preclude fuller analysis later when more (or more certain) information becomes available, but at that stage it may be too late to start effective contingency preparations.

### 5.3.3 THE NEED TO RECTIFY UNEQUAL ACCESS TO THE POLICY AGENDA

We have already noted the political nature of any prescription for more active problem search, but the most explicitly political is the argument that access to the policy agenda is currently unequal, and therefore there is variation in the extent to which problems affecting particular groups get on the policy agenda. Policy analysts should therefore, it could be argued, take on the role of ensuring that the problems of all groups in society receive equal attention.

This issue is an academic minefield in terms of both descriptive and prescriptive models. In terms of descriptive models, there is a long-standing disagreement about the distribution of power in Western societies, both in terms of how issues get on the policy agenda in the first place and how this affects the final outcome (see Castles, Murray and Potter, 1971, part three; Jenkins, 1978, 105–16; Lukes, 1974; Polsby, 1980). 'Pluralist' writers tend to emphasize the widespread distribution of power among a variety of often competing groups and the existence of a multiplicity of channels for raising grievances, where-as 'class' or 'elite' writers emphasize the concentration of power in a particular elite group or economic class by virtue of office-holding, political power, or the way the State is structured to favour the interests of the dominant class. However, all but the most naïve pluralist theorists would accept that the ability of citizens to get issues on the agendas of decision-makers is not distributed evenly. A particularly relevant development in the literature is the concept of 'non-decisions', by which potential issues are kept off the agenda either by action or even by inaction on the part of those holding political power (see e.g. Lukes, 1974); pluralist writers, such as Polsby (1980) have attempted to cast doubts on the validity of the findings of those who claim to have empirical evidence of 'non-decisions'.

When we turn to the normative aspects of the models we can see the ideological problems which face a 'rational policy analyst' trying to 'improve' various stages of the policy process. If there is a tendency in the relatively closed British 'policy communities' of government departments and associated interest groups to raise issues which reflect only mutually shared values, how can a policy analyst, perhaps employed by the department, ensure that other issues are raised, and, indeed, is this a proper role for him rather than for elected politicians? Marxist models would indicate that the only way to remove the problem of unequal access—and indeed solve the substantive problems of society—is to overthrow the capitalist system. The pluralist writers would recognize the existence of inequalities in access to the political agenda, but would argue that this is inevitable in any political system and that pluralist societies represent the best, if unsatisfactory, form.

Thus to ask whether it should be the role of the policy analyst to seek to place on the policy agenda issues which are not currently receiving attention may also imply arguments for changing political institutions or for changing the distribution of political power, and the nature of the political system. For example, Stringer and Richardson (1980, 36–7) call for more open government in Britain on the grounds that more attention would be paid by government to the identification and definition of problems if these were subject to critical review from outside the government apparatus.

## 5.3.4 THE PROBLEM OF ANALYTICAL OVERLOAD

More active issue search would involve further problems receiving serious attention from government in addition to those it already considers. Even given a substantial increase in the analytical capacity of government, it would not be possible to bring costly analytical techniques to bear on all existing issues, let alone new ones thrown up by a deliberate search for more problems which might require analysis. However, this is an argument for explicit priorities in deciding which issues should be subject to analysis of the planning kind, and which should be decided by conventional routes. Such priorities should not be determined by default, through the failure to give consideration to some issues at all. We present procedures for drawing up priorities for the allocation of analytical resources in chapter 6 on issue filtration.

## 5.3.5 THE PROBLEM OF POLITICAL OVERLOAD

It could be argued that policy analysts should not actively engage in seeking out new problems for consideration by government, since this would entail increasing the demands made on the political system without necessarily increasing resources to meet those demands, 'supports' for the political system, or the capacity of the political system to resolve issues. Since many of the 'new' problems may be intractable (and this may be one of the reasons why these issues were not on the political agenda before), the effect of creating new demands without necessarily providing the resources for corresponding solutions may be to create additional strains on the political system.

Set against this are the counter-arguments that better recognition of the problems and opportunities that exist in a society would increase general support for the political system and would improve the capacity of the political system to cope with problems. If improved issue search was part of a wider improvement of decision-making, then fewer resources might be wasted on bad decisions (some of which arise from inadequate warning of problems).

However, it has to be recognized that the idea still has to be sold to the decision-makers who have to cope with more information and increased problems. Their reaction may be that they have enough problems already, thank you. Advocates of issue search have to convince decision-makers that there are political or other benefits to them as well as to 'society as a whole'.

## 5.4 Distinctive characteristics of public sector issue search

We should be cautious of simply transposing prescriptions from the management literature to policy analysis, since the nature of the problems, environment, and organizational structure all differ; arguably, these are normally much more complex and ambiguous in the public sector. However, some insights from the management literature are potentially relevant (see e.g. Aguilar, 1967). One of the themes of the management 'scanning' literature is the need to scan for problems and opportunities in a range of different contexts. For example, Hellriegel and Slocum (1974) draw attention to the different *modes* of scanning ranging from highly structured to quite unstructured:

(1) *Undirected viewing*. This is exposure to information without any specific purpose in mind. Thus firms 'keep their eyes open' for information about political, economic, and social developments, but without quite knowing what they hope to derive from this information.

(2) *Conditioned viewing*. This involves a degree of purposefulness in terms of the information sources to which the organization exposes itself and of the purposes to which that information may be applied. A manager travelling abroad may notice particular types of opportunity or methods of delivery which are potentially applicable to his own organization.

(3) *Informal search*. Here the organization is in a less passive or reactive stance. Branch managers or regional representatives might be requested to look out for certain types of information for specified purposes. For example, Inland Revenue tax inspectors might be asked to look out for signs of growth in the 'black economy'.

(4) *Formal search*. This involves quite deliberate scanning: the aim is to acquire specific information for specific purposes. This could include market analyses and forecasts; technological state-of-the-art surveys and forecasts; political analysis, etc. Sometimes a specific unit is set up within a firm for such purposes. More often it is a matter of policy information acquired by various departments within a firm: R. & D., marketing, finance, etc.

The last category, formal search, has an aura of being more sophisticated and more rational than other modes of scanning. However, it is these other modes which are likely to lead to the identification of problems and opportunities which had not previously been anticipated or which would not be thrown up by the appraisal of routine data. The problem is to ensure that all this information is passed on to the parts of the organization where it will be utilized.

Similarly, there is the problem of co-ordination of information from a variety of sources, both personal and impersonal, and of varying degrees of reliability. The problem arises from the fact that effective information flows do not necessarily correspond to either functions or formal hierarchies within and between organizations. The 'official' flows of information will tend to be impersonal: trade publications, trade shows, technical conferences, regular reports, scheduled meetings, etc. However, personal information is often potentially more important: business contacts, customers, bankers' advice, recruits transferring to the firm, even (or especially) gossip. Such personal, and often oral, information may not necessarily reach the relevant sections of the organization (especially if there is internal distrust) or may be discounted relative to supposedly harder, formal printed information.

Any organization will seek, or simply receive, different types of information. For a firm, these will include market information, technical information, information about broad issues such as general economic conditions, government policies, social trends, leads about potential mergers and acquisitions, and information about suppliers and resources. For most public sector organizations, information about the clientele served or target group regulated would be most important for the identification of future problems and opportunities.

Despite some similarities between scanning for industry and issue search for public policy, there are important differences, some of which reflect the less well-defined nature of public policy concerns, but others of which derive from the Government's special authority to collect data which it requires.

Arguably it is easier for industry to conduct scanning because there will be greater agreement about what to scan for, how to measure it, and how to interpret the findings in terms of their implications for the firm. Within government one can distinguish between economic and social data, with social data being more fragmented because of the lack of any central social theory (Moser, 1980, 9). However, even with macroeconomic data there is now less certainty about the policy implications, even within the known margins of uncertainty. The potential range of data that government has to scan is much wider than for firms, though some firms are now becoming sensitive to wider social and political implications of their activities.

Government has certain advantages in the different sources of information on which it can call. We can distinguish between *by-product statistics*, which are produced incidentally to the carrying on of the administrative process, and *survey statistics*, where the main purpose of collecting the statistics is to produce information (Thomas, 1980). Because of the scale of its activities, government generates a wide range of statistics on everything from crimes reported to the number of vehicles licensed to the volume of imports checked by customs and excise. In addition there are a number of statistics which could be said to be a main product rather than simply a by-product of a government activity: this is true of statistics of the numbers eligible to vote, which can be obtained from the electoral roll, and vital statistics collected as part of the process of registration of births, deaths, and marriages. While many by-product statistics are a valuable potential basis for scanning activity, care should be exercised that figures do not simply reflect administrative procedures rather than the phenomenon with which one is concerned. For example, figures for crimes reported or those registered as unemployed are not accurate measures of crime or unemployment, and changes in the statistics may not reflect corresponding changes in the phenomena (and vice versa) or may even be perverse in their measurement effects: a vigorous anti-crime campaign by the police may lead to a greater success in arrests, but because of that very success people may report crimes which previously they would have failed to report.

Government also has particular advantages when it seeks to collect information it needs. First of all, its sheer size means that it has the resources to carry out surveys of a type which might not be justifiable by smaller organizations. Secondly, government has the power to compel people to provide the information, such as business statistics from firms or personal details from individuals in the decennial census. However, much of the data that government does collect is through voluntary responses, as in the General Household Survey.

Government might, in principle, seem to have fewer difficulties in the transfer of information between public organizations than is the case in the transfer of information between firms which may be in competition with each other. However, this ease of transfer is not always apparent in practice. Central government is profoundly ignorant of the pattern of policy delivery at local level on many indicators. Even within central government there are problems of the transfer of data. As is so often the case in policy analysis, apparently technical questions turn out to have political ramifications.

Governments also have a wide variety of other sources of more informal information and demands, such as public inquiries, select committees (though much of the information they collect comes *from* government), consultative and advisory committees, interest-group representations, and information from MPs, as well as internal information-generating mechanisms such as reports from regional offices, embassy reports, intelligence and espionage activities, etc. The defects of these channels as mechanisms for agenda-setting have already been discussed in section 5.2.

## 5.5 Information needs and issue search

### 5.5.1 CHANGES IN CLIENTELE

For many public sector organizations, the largest potential source of change comes from their customers or clients. For some programmes, such as flat-rate old-age pensions, it is the number only which matters; for others, such as supplementary benefits or social work care, the intensity of condition also matters. At a routine level, information on such matters is necessary for budgeting, but changes may also have implications for how the organization goes about delivering its service and draws attention to 'needs' which would not be met simply by an expansion (or rundown) of the size of the organizations concerned.

In issue search it is particularly important to anticipate discontinuities such as an acceleration of the trend or a change in the direction of the trend. Analysis may have to be carried out at disaggregated level to spot key changes in trends. For example, for the health and personal social services it is not enough to consider only the total number of over-sixties/over-sixty-fives; estimates are needed of the changing proportion of those who are over 75, since they require substantially greater care than the 'young' elderly (see also 5.6.3).

### 5.5.2 NEW PROBLEMS

In addition to identifying problematic trends in existing clientele it is important to be able to spot as early as possible emerging new problems. These problems may be completely new or they may be existing phenomena which have passed or may pass a threshold which leads to them being important enough to require special government attention or of such a scale that it now becomes relevant to consider designing a separate apparatus to treat them.

Examples of such actual or potential new problems are new forms of pollution from new industrial processes, the increase in the number of household units of various kinds requiring social care, solvent abuse, 'diseases of affluence', and alleged problems of increasing 'leisure'. Many new problems are themselves caused by the 'solutions' to previous problems, such as high transport costs (both financial and time) for people relocated in peripheral council housing estates.

The identification of a new problem, opportunity, or 'need' does not automatically imply that instant or indeed any action by government is called for but rather the need for further definition and analysis of the policy implications. The existence of barely-used skateboard parks scattered through the country should serve as a warning against relatively costly instant solutions to suddenly arising problems which may (or may not) subsequently subside.

New problems are those that are least likely to be picked up by existing operational units within the organization, because they may not be collecting data on them and because their focus on the pre-defined problem which they are already tackling may mean that they do not realize the potential significance of information which happens to come their way.

### 5.5.3 NEW SOLUTIONS

Just as potential new problems arise, so too may new solutions, either better ways of delivering existing policies or (alas, a rare coincidence) a solution which emerges at the same time as a new problem. 'New' solutions may reflect changing perceptions as much as new technology. For example, the recent increased emphasis on 'community' rather than institutional care reflects changing political and intellectual fashion, whereas many new medical solutions are technologically derived (and may in turn cause problems both in terms of their own cost and increased need for post-treatment care).

Microtechnology is likely to provide a wealth of potential new solutions to policy problems, not all of them necessarily desirable or cost-effective. Computerization would enable the introduction of a local income tax and of new personalized benefit packages available from a single outlet rather than the present impenetrable maze of interacting organizations and rules. Microtechnology-related developments in communications might make it easier to maintain contact with the elderly or disabled, and thus enable new types of non-institutional care, while many new (and perhaps expensive) devices which will assist the disabled are already being developed.

In some cases a better or cheaper solution which emerges may not be a completely new one, but one which arises from a change in the cost-effectiveness mix. For example, in labour-intensive programmes the increased relative cost of labour may lead to more capital-intensive methods of delivery becoming relatively cheaper.

New solutions are not necessarily neutral in terms of bureaucratic politics. A new method of service delivery may pose threats to jobs or current professional values about appropriate forms of service delivery. There is a danger that only non-threatening new solutions will be placed on the agenda by existing service deliverers and that others which may be worth considering do not get raised unless they arrive by other routes.

## 5.6 Methods of more active issue search

### 5.6.1 INFORMAL SOURCES AND ATTITUDES TO ISSUE SEARCH

As writers on scanning in both business and the public sector have pointed out, the bulk of the potentially useful information coming into an organization comes from the more informal methods (see Hellriegel and Slocum, 1974; Bardach, 1978). Informal means of learning about threats and opportunities facing the organization will continue to be the most important source whatever techniques are introduced. Some of the methods outlined later in this section are not so much means of identifying new information as mechanisms for making explicit the implications of information already held.

The greater explicit use of informal sources of information requires (1) the recognition of issue search as a valuable activity for organizational maintenance (indeed survival); (2) incentives at the personal level to raise issues even (or especially) if they pose threats to the established order within the organization. The introduction of some of the more formal procedures outlined below may itself symbolize a change in attitude, but even formal techniques may 'evaporate' if top management is clearly uninterested in consuming the information they generate when making decisions.

### 5.6.2 ADMINISTRATIVE SOURCES

Administrative sources will also continue to be a major political source of issue search information, but there is a danger that as a result of inertia (or lack of any explicit thinking about policy relevance when the administrative data collection system was designed) inappropriate or inadequate sources of data may be generating misleading signals (see 5.4 above). Accordingly, it is advisable to carry out a review of administrative sources at least every five years designed to answer two questions: (1) Do the administrative sources currently being used present an appropriate and accurate picture of the state of the problem the organization is expected to tackle? (2) Are there sources of data currently being used purely for administrative purposes which might also be used for issue search? If the answer to the first question indicated deficiencies in the present statistics a number of alternatives might be considered. The type of information collected at the point of delivery or even the way the service is delivered might be altered to generate more meaningful information. If this was inappropriate or would fail to get round the problem, consideration could be given to carrying out regular sample surveys to collect the necessary information.

It is clear that more is required than drawing attention to the technical superiority of any proposed replacement to existing administratively derived data. In particular, change has to be introduced in a way that is as non-threatening as possible to those in the delivery organization.

### 5.6.3 DEMOGRAPHIC ANALYSIS

Analysis of future trends in the structure of the population can throw up a wide range of implications for public policy, particularly, but not exclusively, for the social services (see CPRS, 1977). Among these implications are fluctuations in the number of school children, the number seeking jobs in any given year (which also affects the number of potential recruits to the public sector), the size of the wage-earning (and therefore taxable) population, and the size of various categories of households such as single-parent families and the elderly, which may impose heavy demands on social security, social work, and health services. Detailed analysis may affect policy planning and budgeting at later stages, but here we are concerned with the alerting function which demographic analysis can perform.

Demographic analysis can provide no panacea in the form of firm forecasts of all aspects of the future age, household characteristics, and geographical distribution of the population. While it is possible to provide reliable forecasts of the future aggregate number of certain ages where they refer to age cohorts which are already born (and for which we can estimate death rates), it is much more difficult to make forecasts about variables which depend on human behaviour, such as birth rates (we can predict the number of women of fertile age, but not the number of children they will decide to have) or household formation. The fate of past forecasts of the birth rate points to the dangers of simply extrapolating current trends (see CPRS, 1977). Thus we can anticipate trends in the number of the elderly, but are much more uncertain about the number of primary school children there will be in five to ten years time. However, since uncertainty itself is a policy problem, it is helpful to carry out demographic analysis which will identify areas of uncertainty, the implications of which can be pursued at later stages of the policy process.

In performing an alerting function it is important that demographic analysis is conducted at appropriate levels of disaggregation. An initial breakdown into age categories which are related to demand or eligibility for certain services is desirable (e.g. school/working/pensionable age), but it may be important to carry out further disaggregation: it is not just the total school-age population that matters, but the balance between primary and secondary, and the identification of specific 'bulges' as they pass through the school system; a stable number of over-sixties/over-sixty-fives may conceal a growing proportion of over-seventy-fives requiring greater care. Disaggregation by area (which depends on assumptions about migration) is particularly important for local authorities trying to anticipate changes which might affect future service delivery.

Many organizations will be interested only in specific types of demographic analysis, such as the number of over-sixties/over-sixty-fives, or the rate of household formation. For multi-purpose local authorities virtually the whole range of demographic projections are potentially relevant.

### 5.6.4 SOCIAL INDICATORS AND SOCIAL DATA

A variety of other forms of social information are potentially relevant to policy, both those which are direct attributes of individuals such as state of health and those that refer to the conditions in which they live, such as age and facilities of housing and car ownership. In the late 1960s there were some hopes that policy-relevant social data might be developed to the state where they would not only identify problems needing to be tackled, but would also provide measures of the success of government programmes and might even be consolidated into a 'social report' or account corresponding to national economic accounts, which, it was argued, presented only a partial picture of the nation's well-being and, because they were measurable and social improvements were not, led to excessive concentration on economic targets (see Carley, 1980, ch. 11). The aspirations of this 'social indicators movement' have not been met, nor is it likely that they will be. This reflects problems over values (disagreements about the normative implications of changes in indicators), problems over our knowledge of social processes (which is necessary if we are to be able to assess the impact of government programmes on indicators) and also more technical problems of measurement (selecting indicators which are both *valid*, i.e. meaningful measurements of the problem with which we are concerned, and *reliable*, i.e. will consistently reflect changes in the problem). It should be noted that there is now much greater scepticism on all these matters about the economic indicators which the social indicators movement sought to emulate.

That said, there have been some advances in the collection and presentation of social data, especially in Britain, and considerable scope for further improvements both in collection and consumption by policy-makers. This is perhaps particularly true of their role in alerting policy-makers to problems which might require further investigation even if they cannot be used in an undigested form for policy planning and evaluation. For once we can say that this is an area of policy analysis where Britain has led the way, particularly in *presentation* of social data (see especially the annual *Social Trends*).

Much of the data compiled by central government organizations are at too high a level of geographical aggregation to be useful to individual local authorities and other public bodies operating in the localities. National or regional level indicators may, however, perform a useful role in alerting local authorities to issues whose possible local implications they should investigate. The decennial census provides a universal survey, broken down into small geographical areas, which includes some social data (e.g. about housing conditions) in addition to demographic data. However, the time gap between censuses is long, and the data are available only after a delay. Administratively derived data (see 5.6.2) may provide some indication of trends (e.g. on housing conditions from planning applications and its own council house records), but particularly for large authorities it may be worth conducting regular sample surveys of households in their area to provide timely data.

There is a certain amount of circularity in the argument that social data can be used for issue search: the availability of the data already implies that the policy relevance of collecting the data has been recognized. However, the implications of the data still have to be identified—the data themselves will not flash up a warning light, though this would be one of the aims of a fully developed set of social indicators. There is a danger even (or perhaps especially) with fully developed social indicators that they will fail to pick up precisely those new and unpredicted problems which it is a central aim of active issue search to identify. Social indicators must be supplemented by other methods, both formal and informal.

One-off snapshot surveys collecting social data may well draw attention to problems which had not previously been identified, but information suggesting the need to reconsider public policy is more likely to be generated if there is a change in trend (or expected direction) over time in data collected on a regular and consistent basis. Much of such data may never show an unexpected deviation and might therefore be considered 'useless' as a possible indicator for issue search and its collection and compilation as unnecessary extravagance. Other data collected by government might seem to have no present policy relevance. However, some indicators may be 'sleepers', that is show no unexpected deviations over a long period but then provide a direct or indirect warning of a potential policy problem. Abandoning or skimping on the collection of time-series data may destroy the value of having a long run of data to place current status in perspective.

## 5.6.5 JUDGEMENTAL TECHNIQUES

There are a number of judgemental forecasting techniques (i.e. those depending on intuitive judgements rather than quantitative analysis) which, it will be argued in chapter 8, are of dubious value as predictions of the future. However, as supplements to other methods of issue search some of these techniques may inject awareness of possible threats and opportunities, though they certainly cannot guarantee that problems will be foreseen. The use of such techniques may provide a formal avenue for the explicit articulation of insights gained through informal scanning.

The *Delphi* technique assumes that useful forecasts can be obtained from the intuitive judgements of people knowledgeable in the area of interest and that these are best obtained individually from members of a group, since it is argued that in a group meeting the views of some extrovert or higher status members will tend to be more influential than the others. The procedures for conducting a Delphi exercise are described in 8.5.1. Apart from its dubious predictive accuracy, Delphi has a number of features which limit its use as a potential technique for issue search. First of all, the possible range of problems or opportunities which might be identified is predefined by the selection of 'experts' of particular types and the issues raised in the initial questionnaire. Secondly, the consensus-generating aspects of the procedures mean that unlikely but important threats may be homogenized out before the final presentation.

'*Brainstorming*' is based on assumptions almost the opposite of Delphi: that there is some sort of 'synergy' involved in a group of people sitting collectively and rapidly listing possible future developments, however improbable. In other words, that ideas put forward by one participant may spark off other ideas in other participants which might otherwise have been overlooked. The exercise may then proceed with the participants attaching probabilities to the various hypothetical events listed and indicating which are the most important, with weightings or rankings being arrived at by consensus or averaging (see also section 8.5.2). Whether or not such exercises are likely to predict the future accurately, they may be of value to the participants in making them more future-oriented and more aware of the values and perspectives of colleagues. Brainstorming exercises might lead to the identification of possible threats or opportunities which might otherwise be overlooked.

## 5.6.6 LITERATURE SCANNING

The problem in active issue search is often not the creation of new information but the identification of existing sources of information and a means of extracting relevant information from them. Few influences on an organization have not previously been forecast or discussed in some journal or media item, perhaps one apparently unrelated to the concerns of the organization. Television tends to make a high impact, but according to Weiner (1976), 'Information disseminated by television reflects trends rather than presages them.' Accordingly, a systematic scanning of printed publications is likely to be most useful for the early identification of new ideas and technologies and changes in trends (see Weiner, 1976).

A large government organization may be able to run its own literature scanning operation, but where there are a number of similar organizations with their own association (as with local authorities) it may make sense for the association to conduct the operation provided that this is supplemented by scanning of local publications. In selecting the publications to be monitored it is important that a very wide range is included so that indirect influences will be picked up.

The individual monitors would be asked to prepare an abstract of any article which met two conditions: (1) the article deals with an idea or event that indicates a trend not previously identified or a discontinuity. (2) The implications to be drawn from the article have medium or long-run implications for the policy area(s) with which the organization is concerned or otherwise have implications for its operation as a public body (see Weiner, 1976).

Periodically, an abstract analysis committee would meet to discuss the implications of each abstract submitted during the previous period. The committee would summarize the meeting in a report which would give particular emphasis to information which added to or completed understanding of a phenomenon rather than making points which had been made before; a particularly important function of the committee would be to draw together implications from seemingly unrelated facts or ideas from a diversity of sources.

This committee (or another committee) could then decide on a perhaps less frequent basis which of the themes it wished to see developed into fuller reports analysing trends. Such reports, in addition to developing the theme, would discuss the implications for personnel, ways of delivering public policy, new policy problems requiring attention, and possible resource implications.

For a relatively modest outlay this form of literature scanning can make a useful contribution to issue search. As with all types of policy analysis, one of the key factors is to ensure that the analysis is actually consumed by those who influence decisions, for example, by having the committee which commissions the trend analysis reports composed of high officials from the organization or member authorities.

## 5.6.7 EVALUATION OF EXISITING POLICIES

In chapter 12 we will discuss the contribution which evaluation of policies can make to determining whether they have been successful in achieving their objectives. Here our concern is to draw attention to the important contribution that evaluation can make by feeding back into a new round of decision-making. Useful evaluations are those which do not mark the end of analysis in the policy process but provide information about badly designed programmes and changing circumstances. From the perspective of the issue search stage it is important that such information should be appraised not just in terms of the specific programme which has been evaluated but in terms of broader implications for policy design or for the emergence of or changes in problems which are the concern of more than one organization or the focus of more than one programme.

## 5.7 The institutional setting of active issue search

Apart from a few people who might develop their attention full-time to issue search, it would be undesirable to separate the issue search function out as one to be performed only by designated staff, since the aim is to make *everyone*, especially top management, more future-orientated and willing to recognize that greater explicit thinking about threats or opportunities may make their future tasks easier (or at least give them bad news early). Accordingly, the bulk of issue search activity will continue to be carried out in operating divisions and departments. It may be considered desirable to require departmental heads to ensure that adequate issue search is carried out within their departments, emphasizing that this is a management role ranking in importance with the supervision of the implementation of present programmes. It would probably be undesirable to compel departments to set up separate issue search units, leaving it to their own discretion whether or not this was considered appropriate for their departments.

There are, however, a number of snags with giving departments sole responsibility: (1) there is no means of ensuring that departments actually carry out systematic scanning, which they may allow to lapse because of its apparent lack of urgency; (2) there is a danger that, through inertia, statistics inappropriate for measuring the scale of a problem may continue to be used, especially where these are favourable to the views of the department; (3) issues with broad implications for more than one department or for the organization as a whole might be neglected or those broader implications may not be realized.

All these factors point to the desirability of having (in multi-departmental organizations) some formal issue search mechanism to carry out three main functions: (1) an 'auditing' function, carrying out periodic reviews of the procedures for issue search used within departments and advising on possible changes; (2) a 'clearing house' function, passing on ideas about issue search procedures which have worked in other departments and also dealing with issues originally identified within departments which those departments have passed on as having broader implications; (3) an issue search capacity of its own to enable the identification of organization-wide issues. Such central functions need not necessarily be given to any existing central planning or statistics unit. Indeed, given that many problems may be identified in ways that are not the product of standard planning or statistics-collection procedures, there is a case for establishing a separate mechanism for issue search overview. Such a mechanism need not necessarily be a full-time unit, and may be best handled by a regularly meeting committee consisting of representatives from departments as well as from any central planning or statistics unit, perhaps with a small back-up staff. The British government's now defunct 'think tank', the Central Policy Review Staff (CPRS), was the major example of a central policy unit with an issue search role; it would claim to have alerted ministers to the implications of demographic analysis for social policy and to the implications of microprocessors.

The appropriate institutional arrangements will vary according to the public body concerned; for a local authority with a strong commitment to a corporate approach and a policy analysis capability at the centre it may well be more appropriate to ask such a unit to take responsibility for the central aspects of issue search. The establishment of a planning unit will not of itself, however, ensure such a policy analysis capability nor a strong corporate approach.

A number of writers, including two with experience working inside central government, have independently arrived at the conclusion that it might be desirable to have some forum outside government which could examine the Government's collection and use of statistics. Moser (1980, 25–6) noted that Britain was one of the few advanced countries without a national statistical council and proposed the establishment of such a council, to which existing advisory committees would be linked. The council would have the roles of giving advice about issues of public statistics policy as well as priorities for statistical work, especially with outside users in mind; act as a forum for debate about issues of statistical importance; and serve as a liaison committee between statisticians, users, and academics. Moser noted that 'this idea never aroused much enthusiasm in Whitehall'. Similarly Rees (1981, 13–14) argues for 'some kind of autonomous institute or commission, on which government might be represented, which would be responsible for keeping the statistical data base for social policy under review'. Stringer and Richardson (1980, 38) draw on the Swedish example in suggesting an independent agency, supported by study commissions, to raise the standard of policy-making particularly at the issue search and issue definition stages. An additional role for such a council might be to consider the ethical implications of the collection and use of some kinds of data. As with all proposed institutional solutions, this one would be ineffective unless it were accompanied by a change of attitudes within Whitehall.

Consideration of the establishment of a review body outside government proper leads on to the more general question of the openness of government at the issue search stage. The general consensus in Britain among both academic commentators and past practitioners is in favour of maximum publication of government statistics and maximum openness in both directions (see Moser, 1980; Stringer and Richardson, 1980; Rees, 1981).

In seeking to remedy deficiencies of current methods of becoming aware of problems, government organizations should avoid assuming that they should treat issue search as a matter of techniques for internal consumption. Information passed on from outside the organization will continue to be a major source, and the quality of such information and comment may well be improved if the government is prepared to develop the dialogue by making generally available the information it has itself collected. Such a strategy may well make the organization more vulnerable to criticism based on its own data, but the scale of the problems public policy is designed to tackle will not be reduced simply because information about them is inappropriate, concealed, or too late to be useful.

# 6

# Issue Filtration

## 6.1 The key role of issue filtration

We saw in chapter 4 that sharply differing views exist about the best style of policy-making. At one extreme there are attempts to approximate to the ideal type of 'rational' or 'synoptic' policy-making which emphasizes the need for issues to be subjected to comprehensive analysis of values, objectives, options, and consequences. At the other extreme there is 'muddling through' with its emphasis upon the desirability as well as inevitability of pluralism, mutual adjustment, consensus-seeking, and incrementalism.

The confrontation of these extremes involves, as we pointed out in chapter 4, too simple a dichotomy. There is no 'one best way' of deciding all issues. For some situations and problems, the rationalist approach may be necessary and desirable; conversely the muddling through approach may be appropriate (or just inevitable) for other circumstances and issues. There will also be a large middle zone of cases where it is far from clear which policy-making style (or mixture of styles) is the more appropriate. We then have to *decide how to decide*.

This process of deciding how to decide is what Dror (1968) describes as 'metapolicymaking'. Simon, too, wants to divide decisions into 'programmable' and 'non-programmable' categories, with different styles of decision-making appropriate to each (Simon, 1960). Lindblom (1965) refers to the problem of 'choice among policy-making methods' in his book *The Intelligence of Democracy* and, in his later writing on muddling through (Lindblom, 1979), he indicates that some issues may be suited to 'strategic analysis' while others can be left to 'simple' or 'disjointed' incremental analysis. Etzioni (1967) calls for a third approach to decision-making through 'mixed scanning', with special problem areas being subject to more detailed scanning. None of these writers, however, provides specific or policy-relevant criteria by which one might determine the suitability of different issues for different degrees of analysis. The writer who has done most in this direction is Colin Wiseman (1978) in his work on 'the selection of major planning issues'.

Our concern in this chapter is with the selection of an appropriate mode of analysis as a practical problem facing decision-makers and not just as an abstract problem for academic theorists. The classification of issues (or issue filtration) does take place on a day-to-day basis in government, at all levels from the Prime Minister deciding (before 1983) to refer a problem to the Central Policy Review Staff to the individual civil servant sorting the contents of his in-tray into mental categories such as 'hold for further consideration' and 'pass on as quickly as possible'. However, just as theorists have failed to define criteria for metapolicymaking, so too have politicians and administrators 'decided to decide' in a highly intuitive and *ad hoc* way. The findings reported by Wiseman (1978) for the Scottish Health Service can be generalized to much British decision-making: 'for the most part past decisions about which issues should receive detailed planning study have been based on essentially political criteria often without the benefit of any systematic consideration of the underlying situation.' We are recommending a more 'systematic' or, at least, more self-aware approach to this important but rarely acknowledged aspect of the policy and administrative process.

From our own experience of teaching issue filtration, we consider that the most effective way for students to become aware of the importance of issue filtration and the significance of different criteria is for them to derive an initial list of criteria themselves through an exercise in which they play the roles of members of a public body trying to set up a planning system. Section 6.2 describes alternative organizational contexts for such exercises. When such simulations are run, it is best to do so before students have read the remainder of this chapter. The list of criteria they have compiled can then be compared with the one we offer in section 6.3 (we give no guarantee that our list is better!). The exercise may then be concluded by applying one or more of the procedures outlined in section 6.4 to the issues used in the exercise to see how they might be classified.

## 6.2 Issue filtration at different organizational levels

Issue filtration is not an activity relevant to only one level of an organization and it is certainly not something which should be the concern only of a central planning unit. Even at the level of the individual administrator there are some problems arriving in the in-tray which will be picked out for more careful review and deliberation, while others will be passed on with a mild ameliorative suggestion, and still others will be filed (at least mentally) under 'ignore it and hope that it goes away'. At the other extreme, in February 1982, the cabinet committee on innovation in policy and administration (MISC 14), chaired by the Chancellor of the Exchequer, decided to ask the Central Policy Review Staff, the government's 'think tank', to look into the relationship of real wages to unemployment, union monopoly activities, training, and foreign experience (*The Economist*, 6 February, 1982).

In each of these cases we are seeing issue filtration in action. In this chapter our purpose is to explore whether the implicit and perhaps inconsistent criteria presently involved in most decisions about how to process issues can be made explicit and systematized.

At the level of the individual with his in-tray, there is the danger—as the authors are well aware from their personal sins of omission—that 'the urgent will drive out the important'. Issues which have to be decided first will be dealt with first, and other, perhaps more complicated, issues which could in the meantime have undergone some analysis simply wait in a queue until they, in their turn, become urgent decisions requiring action before they can be carefully analysed. Where members of a policy analysis course are also administrative practitioners, a useful discussion can be based upon one member bringing in the actual contents of his in-tray for the previous day or week. He or she can then indicate how and why each item was classified for further handling, under such headings as: (a) for action by me this day/week, (b) requires further consideration by me, (c) refer to superior because of larger implications, (d) suggest reference to planning unit or outside consultants because of complexity of issues involved. The group can then discuss whether the in-tray 'heaps' into which the contents were implicitly or actually divided were the appropriate ones or whether better routing might be devised. This should lead naturally into a discussion of the criteria and procedures being employed. Would an explicit checklist of criteria, as outlined in section 6.3, be a useful way of standardizing filtration or would it add nothing to what is already done?

At a different level, some issues which are important because of their political significance, their scale, their complexity or intractability may have been referred to top management or to politicians, perhaps as a result of issue filtration lower down the organization. A decision then has to be taken as to how the organization should handle such issues. Where a unit for planning or analysis is available, which issues should be referred to it? What are the issues requiring highly specialized expertise which should therefore be referred to a particular professional group within the organization? Which issues should be left firmly in the hands of line management or those most closely involved with consumer and client groups? When is there a case for convening an inter-departmental committee, for setting up a special project team, or for bringing in outside consultants? Such decisions do have to be taken and they are not easy ones, not least because they have a political as well as an intellectual dimension. For example, there may be competition between professional groups or between line and staff officers (including planners); or staff associations may resist the use of external consultants. Arguably, questions about 'who should deal with what issue, and how?' are inseparable from top-level management and senior administrators should therefore make the necessary decisions or recommendations, although they should employ improved criteria and procedures in doing so.

## 6.3 Criteria for issue filtration

In this section we outline our own list of criteria to be taken into account when determining whether a particular issue is appropriate for formal analysis or should be handled by more conventional methods. We recognize that many of the criteria overlap and that others might come up with different checklists (see, e.g. Wiseman, 1978). There may also be disagreement about which way certain factors should point: for example, does the fact that an issue is politically highly salient mean that it should or should not be subjected to formal analysis (see 6.3.1.2)? While some of the criteria can be assessed on the basis of more or less objective considerations (for example, the number of people affected) others will involve much more subjective assessments. Further, the relative significance of different criteria is also subjective and may vary over time or between organizations. For these and other reasons, a checklist of the sort we suggest can only be a starting point and various procedures for using the criteria will be examined in section 6.4.

## 6.3.1 ISSUE'S CONTEXT

### 6.3.1.1 Is there time for analysis?

An obvious first question to ask (though one ignored by those who assume that systematic analysis is always desirable) is whether or not there is sufficient time available to carry out an analysis. Political or other constraints may require that a decision has to be taken in the near future (for example, because the minister has committed himself to make a statement by a specified date). If the need is for a 'decision' rather than a fully documented 'conclusion' there is likely to be little enthusiasm for formal analysis.

Shortage of time need not mean, however, that there is no role for analysis at all. The analytical input may take the form of a 'quick and dirty' exercise. If so, it should try to limit decisions to those which have to be taken in the short term and retain flexibility to allow subsequent alteration (Wiseman, 1978, 78). Clearly this will be easiest in cases where the minimum outlay of resources is low (cf. 6.3.4.2). In any case, time is rarely an absolute constraint (for example, ministers can sometimes be persuaded to make a holding statement) and if an issue scores high on other criteria indicating the need for further analysis, any time constraint may have to be reassessed. Also the time by which an issue has to be decided is only one aspect of whether or not there will be time for analysis; the other aspect is the length of time the proposed analysis will take, which will in turn reflect the complexity and significance of the issue (see 6.3.2.3 and 6.3.3.1). Where appropriate, the starting time of an analysis can be advanced (i.e. it can be given preference in the queue of problems awaiting analysis) and the minimum time involved can be reduced by concentrating analytical resources upon it.

### 6.3.1.2 To what extent does the issue have political overtones?

'Political' here is not confined to party political issues, though these are obviously important. There are many other types of politics: interdepartmental and intradepartmental politics, interprofessional and interregional politics, and many others. What often happens is that a disagreement about a particular issue falls along the same fissure-lines as those which already tend to divide parties, or departments, or professions on many other issues. This means that the particular issue in question will more readily become 'politicized'. It will thereby also become potentially more significant in the eyes of the organization, which might suggest the need for analysis. But the very fact that it is a 'sensitive' issue may serve to exclude analysis, especially where the organisation's leaders fear that an open, frank, and allegedly 'objective' analysis may expose them to criticism or exacerbate relations between contending groups. This sort of political sensitivity was one reason for the rejection by Whitehall departments of some subjects as potential candidates for PARs (programme analysis and review) in the early 1970s (Gray and Jenkins, 1983).

Thus the 'political' criterion is double-edged. A political issue may seem to require analysis, especially when it relates to fundamental questions of purposes and priorities within the organization; but a high degree of political sensitivity may mean that the issue does not lend itself to analysis.

### 6.3.1.3 Have fixed positions been adopted on the issue?

When an issue is 'political' in one of the senses indicated above, there is a tendency for party politicians or powerful figures within the bureaucracy to have preconceived ideas and to adopt fixed positions from which analysis is unlikely to move them. Indeed even the suggestion that an analysis should be carried out may receive very short shrift indeed. Thus, in Mrs Thatcher's Whitehall, it would be a brave analyst who proposed a study of alternatives to monetarism. Nor have recent Labour governments seemed likely to welcome a possibly critical review of comprehensive education.

### 6.3.1.4 How central to the concerns of the organization is the issue?

A final criterion related to the 'context' in which an issue presents itself (also to 'repercussions', see 6.3.3 below) is the extent to which it is perceived as having 'centrality'. This test is difficult to define but easy to recognize in practice. That is, some issues are seen as relating to the key values or purposes of an organization, or as bringing together many strands of policy, or as having long-term implications or widespread ramifications, or as creating precedents or guidelines for future decisions. For these or other reasons, such issues are seen as central rather than peripheral. Provided they are not too sensitive politically, they appear eminently suited to analysis.

### 6.3.2 ISSUE'S INTERNAL CHARACTERISTICS

### 6.3.2.1 Is there scope for choice?

It is important to establish what range of options is open in tackling the issue. The really difficult policy issues are those which require choices to be made, particularly where the choices involve large numbers of diverse factors. Where there are no real choices, or all options seem likely to produce much the same outcomes, or a policy line is heavily indicated by political or circumstantial factors (e.g. financial constraints), then there might seem little point in conducting in-depth analysis. Conversely where there appear to be genuine policy choices the case for reference to analysis would seem stronger.

### 6.3.2.2 How much consensus is there about the issue and the solution?

Related to the criterion of choice is the question of how much consensus there is about both the nature of the issue and the best policy for tackling it. If there is virtual consensus then analysts may have little to contribute, unless they can see value in acting as devil's advocate on occasion (e.g. when it seems that other options are being neglected or that the consensus is based upon an unquestioning 'conventional wisdom'). Where there is not only a range of choice but also disagreement, there might seem to be a particularly useful role for analysis.

### 6.3.2.3 How complex is the issue?

Systematic analysis would seem to have a major contribution to make where there is disagreement about the definition and scope of an issue or where there are many considerations and criteria to be weighed against each other in selecting a solution. Issues which involve a number of different factors have particular appeal for the analyst.

### 6.3.2.4 How much uncertainty is there about the issue and possible outcomes?

The complexity of an issue—and its appeal for analysts—will be increased if there is a high degree of uncertainty about the nature of an issue, the causal factors at work, the likely outcomes, and the feasibility of various solutions. Deciding between alternative solutions often involves choices between small, but fairly certain, gains and much larger, but also quite uncertain, gains. Analysis should have a good deal to contribute to issues involving the identification and consideration of probabilities. An issue might be expected to be of particular interest to an analyst if its outcome was both potentially significant (see 6.3.1.4 and 6.3.3) and highly uncertain.

### 6.3.2.5 How value-laden is the issue?

This may overlap with the question of political overtones (6.3.1.2) but the more general point is that the contribution of analysis is likely to be more obvious and acceptable when dealing with issues which lend themselves to fact-finding, quantification, the comparison of commensurables, and relatively 'objective' analysis. There are other issues which can only be considered in 'subjective' or value-laden terms. Abortion is perhaps an extreme example of an issue where the grounds of dispute are located in strongly held and widely differing value-judgements, related to ethical and even religious beliefs. Capital punishment is another example of a value-laden issue. This is not to say that analysis has no contribution to make to such issues, but the contribution will be limited to, say, appraising the validity of the 'facts' advanced by contending groups or clarifying the value differences underlying the debate. Given the limited resources available for analysis, it might seem wise to attach only low priority to value-laden issues.

### 6.3.3 ISSUE'S REPERCUSSIONS

#### 6.3.3.1 What scale of consequences is involved?

The resolution of a particular issue may involve bringing the organization (perhaps even the State) into a completely new area of activity, or terminating existing activities, or replacing an entire programme rather than altering it incrementally. An example might be deciding whether or not to omit the next generation of development of fission technology in civil nuclear policy and go directly in pursuit of fusion technology (the 'controlled hydrogen bomb'). As Americans say, the latter would be 'a whole new ball-game' with not only technological and industrial but also social, political, and military implications. Such a policy issue would clearly demand a larger input of analysis than other issues with less far-reaching consequences.

#### 6.3.3.2 Will many people be affected?

Different issues impact upon different sizes of 'constituencies' or affected groups. Some issues involve very large numbers of people. For example, legislation to make wearing of seat-belts in cars compulsory affects all drivers and front-seat passengers. Simple political reasoning suggests that issues which affect large groups of people appear more likely to justify the expense of large analytical inputs.

#### 6.3.3.3 How significant are the affected groups?

More advanced political reasoning will remind us that the size of an affected group is not the only determinant of its significance. In the health services, for example, a small 'client group' can be politically significant if its members are well-organized and vocal (such as the drivers of invalid cars) or evocative of popular and media concern (such as the thalidomide children). Such groups may be able to secure the attention of both analysts and politicians. Conversely, much larger but less organized client groups, such as sufferers from bronchial diseases, may receive little consideration.

### 6.3.3.4 How significantly is the group affected?

As Wiseman (1978, 78) suggests, 'A small client group which could be provided with life-saving conditions might therefore be as important as a much larger group where disease condition(s) can only be reduced in severity and not cured'. More generally, an issue which involves significant consequences for a significant group is likely to be given high priority on the agenda of both politicians and analysts.

### 6.3.3.5 Is the issue likely to ramify and affect other issues?

Many issues are relatively insulated, so that decisions on them will have little or no impact upon other issues, policies, or agencies. The need for analysis would seem to be limited accordingly. However, some issues tend to ramify, to have 'knock-on' or side effects, and to have far-reaching consequences for the parent organization and for other agencies. These may qualify for analysis on the grounds of centrality (6.3.1.4) and complexity (6.3.2.3); but analysts have a more direct contribution to make to such issues in terms of tracing and assessing their ramifications and repercussions throughout the larger system. This type of analytical activity may be particularly suitable for a central unit such as a corporate planning group in a local authority or the former Central Policy Review Staff in the Cabinet Office. The influential work of CPRS on population trends and their implications for public services is a good example of this sort of analysis (CPRS, 1977).

### 6.3.3.6 Will acting upon the issue restrict the agency's future flexibility of action?

Former US Defense Secretary McNamara used to warn his colleagues against adopting policy options which would 'foreclose' other options. British civil servants are taught to recognize decisions which may be quoted as precedents or 'decision rules' (Keeling, 1972) and thus commit their department. Any economist knows that the true cost of 'project A' is not simply the cash outlay ('accountant's cost') but rather the denial of the same funds to project B and C with the loss of opportunities for possibly higher returns ('opportunity cost'). These are all examples of the same insight, namely that certain issues (or certain ways of handling those issues) are important because they have the effect of seriously restricting the alternatives open to the agency and/ or limiting the agency's future freedom of action. Such issues and their resolution both require and lend themselves to analysis. As Wiseman (1978, 77) puts it:

Because there is usually considerable uncertainty about the future situation, decisions about the future should wherever possible be made in the future. When commitments have to be made, the level of flexibility of action they allow to be retained into the future is important in adapting to the inevitably changing circumstances. If any options are such that they will commit significant resources far into the future in a virtually irreversible way then very detailed and careful study of them will be required before any implementation should be contemplated.

### 6.3.4 COSTS OF ACTION AND ANALYSIS

#### 6.3.4.1 How large are the costs of acting on the issue?

Almost every policy issue will have a cost dimension. Issues which involve major costs (not simply in terms of money but also real resources of manpower, materials, land, etc.) might seem to be self-evidently those deserving high priority in terms of analytical inputs. However, there are other aspects of the cost question. For example, an agency head might insist that any 'spending option' involving an outlay of more than £100,000 should be referred for analysis. However, £100,000 is a significant sum for a small agency and almost insignificant for a much larger agency. Thus, if any rule of thumb about costs were to be applied, it would be more realistic to refer a spending option for analysis if it committed, say 2% or more of the budgeted revenue expenditure. In other words, relative cost is more relevant than absolute cost in determining any threshold for analysis.

#### 6.3.4.2 Cost increment or quantum jump?

The argument for incrementalism (see chapter 4) is that an agency can move from a known present into an unknown future by a series of small steps based upon trial and error and experiential learning, with little or no need for costly analysis. For example, it would be possible to introduce a small-scale traffic-management scheme in Bradford and, if it worked, to expand it gradually in other towns, even nation-wide eventually, without any prior or formal analysis being involved. Contrast this with the case, quoted earlier, of pursuing the 'fusion' option in nuclear civil policy. A fusion reactor cannot be developed incrementally (or, for that matter, terminated decrementally): both literally and metaphorically, it has a 'critical size' below which nothing will happen and the minimum commitment of resources involved in embarking upon such a policy initiative is enormous and irreducible (Schulman, 1980). Many programmes based upon advanced technology (Concorde, space travel, etc.) have extremely high 'entry fees' and the funding agency's budget will rapidly move on to a new plateau rather than increase gradually over the years. This used to be called 'lumpy expenditure' but has now attracted the more impressive label of a 'quantum jump' in expenditure.

Where tackling a policy issue will commit an agency to a very large minimum outlay, especially one which is virtually irreversible (e.g. Concorde), there is the clearest of cases for prior and extensive data-gathering, forecasting, research and analysis.

### 6.3.4.3 For how long a period will resources be committed?

J. K. Galbraith (1969) argues that one of the 'planning imperatives' in modern industry arises from the fact that the average 'lead time' of investment is increasing (i.e. the period elapsing between the decision to invest and any return on that investment). When large volumes of resources (see 6.3.4.2) are likely to be tied up for long periods of time, there would seem to be a strong case for planning to precede commitments, in the public sector as in industry. Among other considerations, the opportunity costs (6.3.3.6) of such decisions will be high.

Time considerations also add to the complexity (6.3.2.3) of a decision, since a pound spent (or received) today has a different value from a pound to be spent (or received) several years ahead. Modern methods of investment appraisal include provision for 'discounting for time' ('discounted cash flow' methods): although the calculations are fairly simple, some of the assumptions involved are controversial and such project appraisal is best put in the hands of professional analysts.

### 6.3.4.4 What will be the cost of analysis?

Perhaps surprisingly, given its emphasis on the rational use of resources, much of the policy analysis literature ignores the cost of the analysis itself. The resources of money and manpower available for analysis are usually severely limited. The resources committed to one analysis may be denied to another, potentially fruitful, analysis so that there are considerations of opportunity cost involved here as well. Other things being equal, analyses which would tie up many resources should be approached with great caution.

### 6.3.4.5 Will the analysis have pay-off?

Other things are rarely equal, however, and the cost of any analysis must be set against the anticipated benefit in terms of better policy, especially when the issue involved is central, complex, likely to ramify, and significant in terms of the various dimensions identified above.

## 6.4 Procedures for issue filtration

We have identified some criteria which can be used in deciding which policy issues both require and lend themselves to analysis. It may be that, in a real-life administrative setting, the above criteria will be employed only occasionally and ad hoc, as a mental checklist to assist in deciding how a particular issue should be handled, or more often, to whom it might be referred. (In working through issue filtration exercises with senior administrators, we have noted their tendency to ask 'Do we have to take this one on board at all? Could it be passed to someone else?'). However, issue filtration calls for a more systematic approach, especially in agencies where there are many policy issues competing for attention and, therefore, for selection and ranking in terms of suitability for analysis. This more systematic approach demands not only criteria but also *procedures* for applying such criteria consistently and comprehensively to a range of issues.

There is, of course, no single correct way to carry out issue filtration and an important consideration will be the *level* at which issues are considered. The civil servant looking for a way to improve upon his impressionistic assessment of the contents of his in-tray will want a procedure which can be carried out on a single sheet of paper in a few minutes. At the other extreme, a panel deciding how to allocate an analysis budget of tens of thousands of pounds can take time to develop and apply a more detailed, systematic and formalized set of procedures for the selection and ranking of issues for analysis. We shall now look at some different procedural approaches.

### 6.4.1 PRIORITY MATRICES

At a very simple level one can construct a matrix, as in Table 6.1, in which the criteria (or clusters of criteria) are listed down the side and

TABLE 6.1 *A simple priority matrix for issue filtration*

| CRITERIA | ISSUES | | |
|---|---|---|---|
| | A | B | C |
| **1. ISSUE'S CONTEXT** | | | |
| 1.1 Time for analysis? | √ | X | √ |
| 1.2 Not too politicized? | √ | √ | X |
| 1.3 Not fixed positions? | √ | √ | X |
| 1.4 Centrality? | X | √ | √ |
| **2. ISSUE'S CHARACTERISTICS** | | | |
| 2.1 Scope for choice? | √ | X | √ |
| 2.2 Absence of consensus? | √ | X | √ |
| 2.3 Complexity? | √ | √ | X |
| 2.4 Uncertainty? | √ | √ | X |
| 2.5 Not too value-laden? | √ | √ | X |
| **3. ISSUE'S REPERCUSSIONS** | | | |
| 3.1 Significant consequences? | √ | √ | √ |
| 3.2 Many people affected? | X | √ | X |
| 3.3 Significant group? | √ | X | √ |
| 3.4 Significantly affected? | √ | √ | X |
| 3.5 Tendency to ramify? | √ | √ | X |
| 3.6 Limiting future options? | X | X | √ |
| **4. COSTS OF ACTION AND ANALYSIS** | | | |
| 4.1 Costly to act? | √ | √ | X |
| 4.2 Quantum jump in cost? | √ | X | X |
| 4.3 Ties up resources? | √ | √ | √ |
| 4.4 Cheap analysis? | X | X | √ |
| 4.5 Pay-off from analysis? | √ | √ | X |
| NET TOTAL | 16−4=+12 | 13−7=+6 | 9−11=−2 |

the issues being considered are listed along the top. In each cell is placed a tick or a cross, depending on whether the criterion is considered to indicate for or against analysis for that issue. The ticks and crosses are then summed and issues with a net surplus of ticks can be considered worthy of detailed analysis. If time and resources do not permit the same degree of analysis for all the issues qualifying, then priority or emphasis can be given to those with the largest positive surplus.

Clearly, the procedure outlined in Table 6.1 is relatively crude. For each criterion the issue is assessed in a simple yes/no manner, whereas issues will vary considerably in their degree of complexity, size of minimum outlay, political sensitivity, etc. Accordingly, each issue could be scored for each criterion on a scale of 1 to 10, as in Table 6.2. the column totals would then produce a numerical 'suitability for analysis' score and those issues which achieved the highest totals would be routed for more detailed analysis.

A more significant weakness of both methods 1 and 2 is that they

TABLE 6.2 *A priority matrix with issue scores for each criterion*

| CRITERIA | | ISSUES | | |
|---|---|---|---|---|
| | | A | B | C |
| 1. | ISSUE'S CONTEXT | | | |
| 1.1 | Time for analysis? | 7 | 3 | 6 |
| 1.2 | Not too politicized? | 6 | 8 | 4 |
| 1.3 | Not fixed positions? | 7 | 8 | 3 |
| 1.4 | Centrality? | 4 | 9 | 6 |
| 2. | ISSUE'S CHARACTERISTICS | | | |
| 2.1 | Scope for choice? | 8 | 2 | 7 |
| 2.2 | Absence of consensus? | 7 | 3 | 7 |
| 2.3 | Complexity? | 9 | 6 | 3 |
| 2.4 | Uncertainty? | 8 | 7 | 3 |
| 2.5 | Not too value-laden? | 6 | 6 | 2 |
| 3. | ISSUE'S REPERCUSSIONS | | | |
| 3.1 | Significant consequences? | 7 | 8 | 6 |
| 3.2 | Many people affected? | 5 | 6 | 4 |
| 3.3 | Significant group? | 7 | 4 | 6 |
| 3.4 | Significantly affected? | 8 | 7 | 3 |
| 3.5 | Tendency to ramify? | 6 | 6 | 4 |
| 3.6 | Limiting future options? | 3 | 2 | 6 |
| 4. | COSTS OF ACTION AND ANALYSIS | | | |
| 4.1 | Costly to act? | 6 | 9 | 4 |
| 4.2 | Quantum jump in cost? | 6 | 9 | 3 |
| 4.3 | Ties up resources? | 7 | 8 | 6 |
| 4.4 | Cheap analysis? | 2 | 2 | 8 |
| 4.5 | Pay-off from analysis? | 8 | 7 | 4 |
| TOTAL SCORE | | 127 | 120 | 94 |

treat all criteria as if they were of equal significance. In fact, this is unlikely to be the case and those responsible for issue filtration will want to attach particular significance to certain criteria and less to others. Thus we can incorporate a system of weighting the criteria themselves to reflect perceived differences in their relative importance. In Table 6.3, each criterion is scored from 1 to 10 which, when multiplied by the issue score on that criterion, gives a cell total. Of course,

TABLE 6.3 *A priority matrix with issue scores and weighted criteria*

| CRITERIA (with weights in brackets) | ISSUES (scored as in Table 6.2) | | |
|---|---|---|---|
| | A | B | C |
| **1.  ISSUE CONTEXT** | | | |
| 1.1  Time for analysis? (9) | 9 × 7 = 63 | 9 × 3 = 27 | 9 × 6 = 54 |
| 1.2  Not too politicized? (8) | 8 × 6 = 48 | 8 × 8 = 64 | 8 × 4 = 32 |
| 1.3  Not fixed positions? (6) | 6 × 7 = 42 | 6 × 8 = 48 | 6 × 3 = 18 |
| 1.4  Centrality? (7) | 7 × 4 = 28 | 7 × 9 = 63 | 7 × 6 = 42 |
| **2.  ISSUE'S CHARACTERISTICS** | | | |
| 2.1  Scope for choice? (5) | 5 × 8 = 40 | 5 × 2 = 10 | 5 × 7 = 35 |
| 2.2  Absence of consensus? (5) | 5 × 7 = 35 | 5 × 3 = 15 | 5 × 6 = 30 |
| 2.3  Complexity? (6) | 6 × 9 = 54 | 6 × 6 = 36 | 6 × 3 = 18 |
| 2.4  Uncertainty? (7) | 7 × 8 = 56 | 7 × 7 = 49 | 7 × 3 = 21 |
| 2.5  Not too value-laden? (9) | 9 × 6 = 54 | 9 × 6 = 54 | 9 × 2 = 18 |
| **3.  ISSUE'S REPERCUSSIONS** | | | |
| 3.1  Significant consequences? (8) | 8 × 7 = 56 | 8 × 8 = 64 | 8 × 6 = 48 |
| 3.2  Many people affected? (6) | 6 × 5 = 30 | 6 × 6 = 36 | 6 × 4 = 24 |
| 3.3  Significant group? (6) | 6 × 7 = 42 | 6 × 4 = 24 | 6 × 6 = 36 |
| 3.4  Significantly affected? (7) | 7 × 8 = 56 | 7 × 7 = 49 | 7 × 3 = 21 |
| 3.5  Tendency to ramify? (4) | 4 × 6 = 24 | 4 × 6 = 24 | 4 × 4 = 16 |
| 3.6  Limiting future options? (7) | 7 × 3 = 21 | 7 × 2 = 14 | 7 × 6 = 42 |
| **4.  COSTS OF ACTION AND ANALYSIS** | | | |
| 4.1  Costly to act? (4) | 4 × 6 = 24 | 4 × 9 = 36 | 4 × 4 = 16 |
| 4.2  Quantum jump in cost? (9) | 9 × 6 = 54 | 9 × 9 = 81 | 9 × 3 = 27 |
| 4.3  Ties up resources? (6) | 6 × 7 = 42 | 6 × 8 = 48 | 6 × 6 = 36 |
| 4.4  Cheap analysis? (6) | 6 × 2 = 12 | 6 × 2 = 12 | 6 × 8 = 48 |
| 4.5  Pay-off from analysis? (9) | 9 × 8 = 72 | 9 × 7 = 63 | 9 × 4 = 36 |
| **TOTAL SCORE** | 853 | 817 | 618 |

all such rankings are subjective and must be determined by members of the agency concerned.

The matrix approach has both strengths and weaknesses. One advantage is that it gives not only an overall assessment of whether analysis seems worthwhile in relation to a particular issue but also allows various issues to be ranked in terms of their suitability for analysis, thus allowing more effective use of scarce analytical resources. Among the weaknesses is the spurious appearance of objectivity and precision which quantification of essentially subjective indicators can suggest. Also it may be felt that certain of the twenty criteria listed in section 6.3 are so much more important than the others that it makes little sense to rank them on the same ten-point scale.

### 6.4.2 USING DECISION TREES AS FILTERS

A different approach to issue filtration is suggested by the concluding comment above. If certain criteria are of a different order of significance from the others, then perhaps we can save a great deal of time by using these as preliminary tests which any issue must pass before subjecting it to more detailed 'filtration'. Such crucial criteria become 'gateways' which the issue must successfully pass through if it is to be of any further interest to analysts. The procedural format which this suggests is less that of the matrix than of the familiar 'decision tree'.

An illustrative fragment of a decision tree is shown at Figure 6.1. We have assumed that the policy issue has to be decided before a deadline which is absolute (although we have indicated our unease about such assumptions at 6.3.1.1): thus we ask first 'Is there sufficient time for analysis?'. If the answer had been 'No', no further attempt would have been made to filter out the issue for analysis. Next we ask 'Is the issue so value-laden as to exclude useful analysis?'. Here the 'correct' answer —i.e. the answer which allows the issue to survive—is 'No'. There may be half a dozen such crucial gateways to negotiate successfully. They will not always be the same questions in the same order: for example, when resources for both analysis of issues and action upon them are in very scarce supply the crucial gateways might be questions about the cost of analysis, whether acting upon the issue would involve a quantum jump in spending, the significance of the consequences and, say, centrality to the agency.

The decision tree approach, too, has its strengths and weaknesses. One obvious weakness is that a decision tree with simple Yes/No branches is similar in crudity to the ticks and crosses of the matrix in

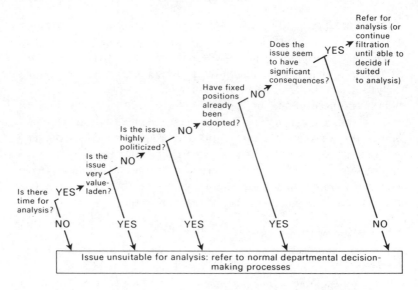

FIG. 6.1. Fragment of a decision tree for issue filtration

Table 6.1. In principle, decision trees with three or more possible answers at each decision point could be constructed but they would very quickly become too unwieldy to use. A related weakness is the oversimplification of possible outcomes when the choice is limited to 'proceed to further filtration' (when an issue has successfully passed through a crucial gateway) or 'unsuitable for detailed analysis'. In practice, as indicated in section 6.1, the choice is rarely as stark as it should be possible to consider a wider range of outcomes and destinations (e.g. full-fledged analysis by a central planning unit, referral to a project team for further consideration, return to line agency with recommendation that further consideration be given to certain aspects, and so on).

The main advantage of the decision tree approach, as already noted, is that it does not regard all twenty criteria as being of the same order of significance and saves much time by posing five or six crucial questions.

### 6.4.3 A COMBINED AND FLEXIBLE PROCEDURE

By now it should be obvious that the matrix and decision tree approaches are not so much alternatives as they are complementary to one another. We therefore recommend a procedure combining both approaches, as indicated at Figure 6.2. This approach also incorporates various feedback and other devices to make the procedure more flexible and dynamic.

The main features of the procedure outlined at Figure 6.2 are as follows:

(1) There is an initial coarse filter in the form of a decision tree, thus reducing the number of issues to be fed into the more comprehensive, detailed, and discriminating filtration procedure of the matrix with its many criteria and more elaborate weighting, scoring, and ranking provisions.

(2) In this initial stage, several clusters of the twenty criteria are conflated into broad tests or 'gateways'. More detailed testing, by criterion, can be left to the matrix stage if the issue survives the decision tree.

(3) The organization must decide for itself what are 'crucial' criteria for incorporation in the decision tree. We have used for illustration criteria related to time, political sensitivity, and cost of analysis in relation to expected pay-off.

(4) Neither time constraints nor political sensitivity should be regarded as invariably excluding analysis and provision is built-in for 'second thoughts' or further testing of assumptions.

(5) In considering, albeit impressionistically, whether expected pay-off from analysis is likely to justify the cost of analysis, relevant criteria will probably include centrality (1.4), scope for choice and absence of consensus (2.1, 2.2), complexity and uncertainty (2.3, 2.4), and all the criteria relating to 'repercussions' (3.1–3.6).

(6) If an issue survives the initial decision tree 'gateways', it is then subjected to the full matrix treatment, to confirm whether it seems both to require and lend itself to analysis and, if so, to decide its priority for analysis—as reflected, for example, in its place in the queue for analysis and the analytical resources committed to it.

(7) Another important procedural decision concerns the choice of an appropriate body to carry out the analysis (e.g. outside consultants, agency's own planning or policy analysis unit, *ad hoc* project team, referral back to line department concerned with recommendation for further consideration of certain aspects, etc.).

(8) Finally, we must emphasize the importance of periodic monitoring

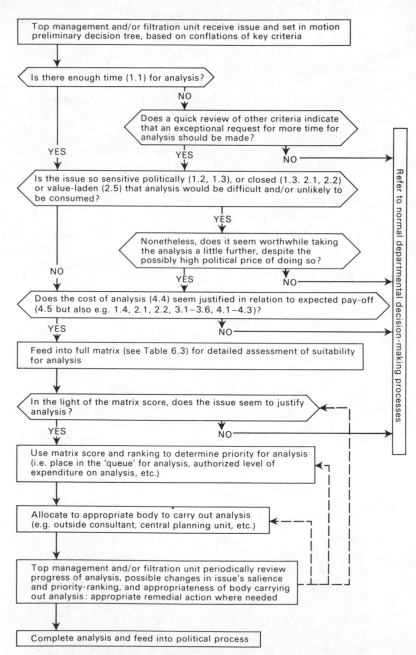

FIG. 6.2. Procedure combining decision tree and matrix approaches

and review in this as in all other aspects of decision-making. Decisions about the suitability of an issue for analysis, the priority and resources given to it, and the choice of an appropriate body to carry out the analysis all should be reconsidered from time to time with relevant considerations including the progress of the analysis itself and any changes in the wider context which may have made the issue more significant or more urgently in need of resolution.

# 7

# Issue Definition

## 7.1 Defining issue definition

The policy-making process, we have argued in previous chapters, begins with awareness of a 'problem', especially one which existing policies are failing to cope with at even a 'satisficing' level. Or the problem may be a novel one for which no policy stance has yet been adopted but which has begun to press for attention. To speak in terms of a 'problem' is a useful form of shorthand but it might be less restrictive if the term 'issue' were to be adopted, since the latter subsumes not only problems (or threats) but also 'opportunities' for positive action and, indeed, 'trends' which, while being perceived as having potential significance for the organization, could turn out on closer study to be either problem or opportunity. By issue definition, then, we mean the processes by which an issue (problem, opportunity, or trend), having been recognized as such and placed on the public policy agenda, is perceived by various interested parties; further explored, articulated and possibly quantified; and in some but not all cases, given an authoritative or at least provisionally acceptable definition in terms of its likely causes, components, and consequences.

Certain phrases in the above definition merit some further attention. First, we are concerned with 'processes' in the plural. Thus, within 'issue definition' are such activities as (a) becoming aware of a stimulus to thought or action, (b) interpreting that stimulus, and (c) relating it to what one already knows or believes—i.e. to a 'cognitive map'. Also the issue definition process or processes overlap with others which we discuss below (7.2).

Secondly, the above definition refers to issues being 'perceived' as such. Perception can best be understood as the process by which individuals or groups attach particular meanings and significance to events or other forms of external stimuli. It is a highly subjective process and it follows that different individuals, groups, or 'interested parties' may perceive the same stimulus differently—through different 'conceptual lenses' as Allison (1971) would say. We discuss this aspect more fully below under the heading of 'frame analysis' (7.5.5). The essential point is that few, if any, problems are capable of a completely verifiable or unarguable definition; they are not 'out there' somewhere waiting to be discovered and delineated, indeed they may not be objectively knowable at all. We each create our own 'reality' and this is nowhere more true than in the way we identify problems or issues, and interpret and relate them to our mental map of some larger situation.

Thirdly, while some persons or agencies may possess the legal or other right to offer their version of a problem as the official version, it does not necessarily follow that this version will be accepted by other persons or agencies. At best, only a 'provisionally acceptable definition' may be achieved for the purposes of initiating legislative or administrative action, while the larger argument continues unabated. Should the political party in power change, or one dominant group be succeeded by another, then the problem may be open to redefinition. As an extreme example, a change of government may lead to 'social security scroungers' being relegated almost to non-problem status while the 'real' problem of social security is restated as being 'the hidden iceberg of benefits unclaimed by those in need'. In other words, we are dealing with a process unfolding over time in which, as the above definition suggests, the issue will be iteratively subjected to further exploration and articulation.

Fourthly, our definition mentions the possibility of, but does not insist upon, 'quantification' of issues. We regard it as being less important that a problem, opportunity, or trend can be measured than that an attempt should be made to understand and explain it, in terms of what we have called its 'likely causes, components, and consequences'. Later in this chapter, we shall develop the reference to the 'components' of an issue under the heading of 'disaggregation' (7.5.7).

Finally, it is implicit in our definition that both agenda-setting and issue defining are highly political processes, in the sense that they are influenced by the distribution of power within or between organizations, or in society at large. Thus some groups or agencies are unable to obtain access to either process, others have access but do not have much impact, while a few are able to exercise considerable influence both over which issues get on the agenda and how they are subsequently defined. The position of such influential groups or agencies will be greatly strengthened if they are seen as having legitimacy as well as power with regard to a particular issue so that, for some time at least, their version of the issue will be seen as 'authoritative'.

## 7.2 Why issue definition is important—and difficult

We shall argue that issue definition is important in its own right, but it must also be seen in relation to other activities within policy-making and it is to these relationships and interactions that we turn first.

'Issue search' (or 'agenda-setting') will inevitably have involved some element of preliminary definition (see chapter 5)—otherwise how would members of the organization know they had a problem (or opportunity, or trend) meriting their attention? However, there is often an element of intuition, even political instinct, at work in the processes by which an issue is recognized and it is essential to move on to more explicit and deliberate processes by which the nature of the issue can be systematically explored and defined. If 'issue filtration' has been attempted, of course, the problem or issue will already have been characterized in certain ways, such as being value-laden or complex or likely to affect an influential group of people, etc (see chapter 6). However, the 'filters' we use in real life tend to be fairly crude and merely to say that an issue seems susceptible to an analytical or planning approach does not constitute an adequate definition of the issue itself.

Since we are interested in how the problem, opportunity, or trend will develop in the future, issue definition will overlap with forecasting and an inadequate definition of the problem can have serious consequences for both the 'modelling' and 'judgemental' aspects of forecasting (see chapter 8). How the problem is defined will also influence later policy processes such as objective setting, identifying 'relevant' options and appraising them, and suggesting standards of 'success' which will underlie policy monitoring and evaluation. An example for classroom discussion might be the way in which central and local authorities have defined the 'decline of the inner city' and how that definition has affected, and in turn has been affected by, other aspects of the policy-making process with regard to this 'problem' (see, e.g. McKay and Cox, 1978).

Turning to issue definition itself, there is some agreement among analysts that, first, this is a crucially important aspect of policy-making, and secondly, it is often the stage in the policy process at which decisions will be made which turn out to be unwise (with the wisdom of hindsight). Steiss and Daneke (1980, 124) set out some of the dangers succinctly;

A plausible but incomplete definition of the problem can be more dangerous than a wrong definition. If the problem cannot be stated specifically, then the analysis has not been of sufficient depth. Even an excellent solution to an apparent problem will not work in practice if it is the solution to a problem that does not exist in fact.

Wolman (1981, 436) develops the critique of much 'real life' problem definition as follows:

Too frequently rhetoric is substituted for adequate conceptualization, resulting in vagueness and lack of direction throughout the entire formulation and carrying out process. The end result is perceived to be a program which has failed to solve a problem even though no one is quite certain what the problem is . . . Policy agendas reflect the mobilization of political demands rather than a rational process of evaluating needs, values, and objectives. Thus 'problems' frequently appear on the decision-making agenda without having been adequately conceptualized or thought through.

Wolman argues that inadequate problem and hence programme conceptualization is particularly liable to occur with regard to issues which arise from crises or from intense political pressures requiring an immediate response. Even when time is available, however, issue definition is often an example of political and administrative 'satisficing', in the sense that a plausible or, perhaps, a convenient formulation of the issue is adopted too quickly, without sufficient gathering and analysis of data or testing of evidence and assumptions.

One reason why issue definition is both important and difficult is that it is an aspect of the policy process which is at least as much influenced by value-judgements as by the careful sifting of facts. The salience of values to policy-making has already been mentioned and will recur throughout this book, but there will be no more relevant point than 'issue definition' at which to give some specific attention to this question.

## 7.3 Values in policy-making and issue definition

One of the most admired British contributions to policy analysis has been Sir Geoffrey Vickers's discussion of the 'appreciation' function in policy-making, which he describes as follows:

An appreciation involves making judgments of fact about the 'state of the system', both internally and in its external relations. I will call these reality judgments . . . It also involves making judgments about the significance of these facts to the appreciator or to the body for whom the appreciation is made. These judgments I will call value judgments. Reality judgments and value judgments are inseparable constituents of appreciation . . . for facts are relevant only in relation to some judgment of value and judgments of value are operative only in relation to some configuration of fact. Judgments of value give meaning to judgments of reality, as a course gives meaning to a compass card. Information is an incomplete concept; for it tells us nothing about the organization of the recipient which alone makes a communication informative. [Vickers, 1965, 40].

In these elegantly cryptic comments, Vickers is describing what we have called issue search and definition, as well as some aspects of objective-setting. His emphasis upon the importance of perception, and upon the part played by values within the process of perceiving, is also one which we would endorse. Vickers gives many illustrations of values but does not define the concept at any length. For our purposes, we would define *values* as being:

—the beliefs, ethics, standards, and more specific norms
—which affect policy making processes at all levels (individual, group, organizational, and societal),
—through guiding and constraining the behaviour and actions of participants in policy making,
—by influencing their perceptions of both desirable end-states (terminal values) and of acceptable means (instrumental values) for achieving those end-states.

A *value-system* involves:

—an interconnected pattern or structure of values,
—occuring at any level (individual, group, organizational or societal),
—with values ideally being ranked in hierarchical order of significance or, more realistically, with rough weighting of some values as being more important than others;
—such a system normally being relatively stable or slow to change,
—and having the capacity to influence both general policy-making behaviour and specific choices or decisions.

Finally, a *value-judgement* occurs:

—when a value or value-system is applied
—in a particular policy-making situation or to some aspect of the policy
  'process,
—usually with the connotation that more objective, analytical, or
  factually based inputs to the policy-making process have been subordinated to essentially subjective and normative inputs.

The relationship between 'values' and 'facts' is, of course a difficult
and controversial one which has been discussed at length by writers in
many disciplines. In common usage, facts are commonly regarded as
having their basis in knowledge, especially knowledge which is capable
of verification, while values are based upon beliefs or standards which
are not capable of being proved right or wrong. In Vickers's (1965, 71)
version: 'The value judgments of men and societies cannot be *proved*
correct or incorrect; they can only be *approved* as right or condemned
as wrong by the exercise of another value judgment.' However, Vickers
also argues that facts and values are closely interwoven, since policy-
makers use only a *selection* of facts and both the process of selection
and the *validity* attached to alleged facts are influenced by value
judgements as to what is 'relevant' and, perhaps, by what the policy-
maker has already decided to do. This view of the relationship between
facts and values is one which we share in general terms.

Thus, what policy-makers define as problems and how they define
them will be deeply influenced by the values they bring to the policy-
making process. If a society is highly stratified, for example, even the
most fully-documented evidence that particular groups are suffering
from discrimination will not be seen as a problem or, at least, as a
problem which need concern government. Only if a different value-
system begins to emerge will factual evidence of inequality or discrimination begin to acquire significance and be viewed as a matter for
concern. Since societies do not usually undergo major value shifts
spontaneously, it is more probable that a politically dominant group
will initiate the change, as may be happening at the present time in the
attitude of the South African Government towards 'Coloureds' (though
such a change would appear to be a matter of expediency rather than
conviction). As Carol Weiss (1972) suggests, 'Politics is the system we
have for attaching values to facts.'

Values both facilitate and complicate policy-making. They facilitate
the process by providing a ready-made 'model of the world' within

which many decisions can be made more or less automatically, and to which even new types of problems can be referred for a 'quick steer'. Value-judgements, combined with only a very limited and selective search for 'facts', do offer a short cut for the 'satisficing' decision-maker, as Simon and other writers have argued (see chapter 4). Carley (1980) also suggests that value systems:

are considerably less complicated than the world and this is a great virtue: a few standards apply in a multiplicity of situations . . . (and provide) a basis for orientation in, and interpretation of, a complex world and for formulation of the appropriate responses to that world.

However, values are also a complicating factor. The individual decision-maker will be influenced by several value considerations and may find it difficult to reconcile them (when they conflict) or to rank them (when they are compatible but competing). Values may be largely implicit, diffuse and confused. Above all, decision-making usually involves more than one person, so that questions about 'whose values?' must arise. At the higher levels of public policy-making, many agencies may be involved and the question of conflicting or competing values will often be acute, as will the issue (discussed in chapter 9) of the appropriate *level* for resolving such disagreements.

### 7.4 Can issue definition be 'improved'?

Given the importance we have attached to values and perception in the definition of problems, it might seem that the analyst has relatively little, if anything, to offer at this stage of the policy process. If the activity of defining issues is wholly subjective, how can anyone claim that their perception is 'better' than anyone else's? Should the analyst not accept that the statement of a problem is 'given' and that his or her contribution will begin at the point when forecasts are being made of how the problem will develop?

Despite undoubted difficulties, we would argue that it is worth seeking to extend the analytical approach to issue definition: first, because 'who defines, decides', that is, the outcome of the issue definition stage will deeply influence the later stages of the policy-making process; and secondly, because some analysis is possible in most, though not all, cases of issue definition. We have already set out at some length (chapter 6) our view that analysis is not applicable to all issues and that some 'filtration' is essential if analytical resources are to be used to best effect.

We do not wish to give the impression that we regard 'improvement' in this context as being derivable solely from a larger input of analysis. Issue definition is a stage in the policy process at which there is a particularly strong case for wider participation by those in a position to say whether there is a problem and, if so, what they see the problem as being. In practice, opportunities for participation tend to be provided, if at all, only at the later stages of the policy process, such as commenting on 'options' provided by officials. By then most real choices will have been foreclosed, whereas an opportunity to participate in how the problem was defined would have opened up a much wider range of possibilities. It is, of course, disconcerting for a local authority or central department to discover that those citizens most directly affected do not agree with the 'experts' about the nature of the problem. They may even deny that there is a problem or argue that there are much more important or pressing problems. Worst of all, they may suggest that the 'real problem' is the local council or government department itself! These strike us, however, as excellent reasons for rather than against participation in issue definition. At a minimum, it would require officials to articulate and explain their view of the issue more fully and persuasively.

## 7.5 Approaches to issue definition

While we believe that policy analysis can contribute to issue definition, we have also made it clear that this is not an aspect of the policy-making process to which the analyst can bring a neat package of techniques, far less guaranteed solutions. In this situation, we revert to an approach which will become increasingly familiar to readers of this book, namely the use of a checklist of questions. These are offered in the hope that they will help to sharpen up the discussion of a given problem—not least by asking, on occasion, whether the problem can be accepted 'as given'.

### 7.5.1 WHO SAYS THERE IS A PROBLEM? WHY?

We do not want to cover ground already transversed in terms of 'issue search' (see chapter 5), but it cannot be denied that whether a problem is recognized as such, and *how* it is then perceived, will depend in part upon *who* has sought to place it on the agenda, from what level and for what reasons. For example, various groups (representing working wives, single-parent families, divorced persons, children in poverty, the unemployed, etc.) have tried over many years to draw the attention of politicians and officials to specific legal, financial, tax, housing, and other problems of families, without attracting a great deal of attention or serious consideration of how these various problems might be related to one another. When, however, two party leaders and successive prime ministers—Mr Callaghan and Mrs Thatcher—publicly expressed their concern about 'the family' in the late 1970s it both became a policy issue to which higher priority was attached and one which was recast in much more global terms, including the interaction of many aspects of public policy and their cumulative impact upon the family unit.

In opposition, then, Mrs Thatcher wanted a very broad view taken of the problem, and her social services spokesman told the 1977 Conservative Party conference that a future Conservative Government would require 'family impact statements' to be attached to each new policy proposal from departments. Adverse comments were made upon the Labour Government's failure to deal with 'the poverty trap' and much else. In office, however, the Thatcher Government has not dealt particularly effectively (to date) with these or other, related problems and various commentators (e.g. Jones, 1982) have suggested that the definition of the problem has subtly altered, with the Government being increasingly concerned to reduce the dependence of families upon 'the State', incidentally reducing some major items of public expenditure and thus contributing to a policy objective which has very high priority in Conservative Government circles.

The independent analyst can take a broader view of 'the family' and, indeed, a more global perspective has been sustained in a series of reports published by the privately funded 'Study Commission on the Family', culminating in a final report (1983) on *Families in the Future*, sub-titled *A Policy Agenda for the 1980s*. However, the administrator-as-analyst, while he need not agree with how politicians define the problem nor sympathize with their motives for doing so, must be aware of the currently prevailing formulation at political level, if only on the grounds that 'what you would change, you must first know'.

### 7.5.2 IS IT A 'REAL' PROBLEM? IS IT TREATABLE BY GOVERNMENT?

Certain problems may appear to some observers to be less real or substantive problems than the result of a process of 'labelling'. That is, they are defined as 'social problems' because a sufficient number of people—or a sufficiently influential group—think that they are problems and are able to have them so defined in terms of prevailing social conventions and, in some cases, of the law. An obvious British example would be the way in which (male) homosexuals were treated as criminals because they departed from a generally held view of what constituted 'normal' or acceptable sexual behaviour. More recently, homosexual activities (provided they take place in private and between 'consenting adults') have been decriminalized. Conversely, recent attempts to suggest that the law relating to paedophilia should in some respects be relaxed led to a wave of revulsion in Parliament and the media.

'Deviance' is not, of course, limited to sexual behaviour or, to put the same thought differently, 'labelling' is sometimes alleged to extend to pursuits as diverse as social security scrounging, selling or watching video nasties, living off the 'black economy', certain types of what was once called 'madness', or sniffing cocaine. As examples of resulting 'arbitrariness', we may be told that using or trafficking in 'soft drugs' (itself a splendid example of labelling, albeit of a more fashionably liberal variety) is seen as a problem, whereas heavy reliance upon and medical prescribing of tranquillizers is not. The 'power of labels' might also be illustrated by the way in which 'glue sniffing' has in Britain come to be described as 'solvent abuse' whereas in some American circles it is now called 'recreational inhalation'.

Attitudes to what are regarded as 'social problems' (Etzioni, 1976) may change over time as more 'facts' emerge (e.g. more about different types and degrees of 'madness') or as 'values' alter (e.g. about sexual behaviour) or as the distribution of power in society shifts from those who perceive a problem (e.g. 'undemocratic trade union practices') to those who do not.

Are such observations of interest only to academic social scientists or should politicians and those who advise them also be aware of the possibility of 'labelling'? Their perspective might be different since, if sufficient voters think there is a problem, then for politicians it becomes a 'real' problem. Even so, they might be encouraged to question the priority given to the problem or helped to gather data in an attempt to generate more light and less heat. Above all, at a time when it is often said that governments attempt to do too much, questions might be asked about whether -or in what specific respects-- it is likely that government intervention would be both justifiable and feasible. We shall return to this theme at various points below. Conversely, of course, there will be occasions when the role of the analyst or adviser is to suggest that there are some 'real' problems which merit attention although they have not yet been recognized or defined as such.

### 7.5.3 IS THERE LIKELY TO BE AGREEMENT ON THE PROBLEM?

Politicians and their advisers will often want to know if an emerging issue is one which is likely to produce consensus or dissensus. Some of the factors likely to condition the degree of agreement are, first, the numbers of different agencies or interests involved at this stage of the policy process; secondly, the availability and reliability of relevant information; thirdly, the extent to which the issue is value-laden; and fourthly, the range of perspectives or 'frames' bearing upon the issue.

Even problems which seem quite technical can lead to a surprising amount of disagreement. An example from one large Scottish city was the problem of subsidence in built-up areas. The delays and difficulties in arriving at a 'corporate' view of the problem were caused by several types of subsidence which existed almost side by side; the different professional concerns and perspectives of the various local authority departments concerned (Planning, Architectural Services, Environmental Health, Building Control, Housing, etc.); the often divergent interests of the local authority, the National Coal Board, landlords, tenants associations and building contractors; and the surprising amount of room for disagreement even among the experts about such factors as the probability of a suspected subsidence actually occurring, its timing and likely consequences, and the action which should be taken to prevent, minimize, or remedy those consequences.

### 7.5.4 IS IT TOO SOON TO ATTEMPT A DEFINITION?

The timing of the decision to 'firm up' on the definition of an issue can be difficult. On the one hand, it is obvious that issue definition is an extremely important activity which will deeply influence the entire policy process. Moreover it is an activity logically prior to most others, so it should come early rather than late in that process. On the other hand, it is essential that the definition should not be arrived at too early. That is, policy-makers should try to avoid the premature adoption of a single, too restrictive definition of the issue. More information may have to be collected and analysed, more views and opinions canvassed, before any operational version of the problem is agreed.

## 7.5.5 DO THOSE DEFINING THE PROBLEM HAVE A PARTICULAR POLICY 'FRAME'?

Etzioni (1976) has described the different 'approaches' which several participants may bring to the definition of an issue. Young (1977) writes of their 'assumptive worlds' and Allison (1971), in his 'organizational process model', emphasizes the way in which large organizations function according to regular patterns of behaviour, with members tending to define problems in a stereotyped way. An interesting treatment of such closed perspectives is provided by Jeremy Baker in an unpublished paper, 'CPRS, the Car Industry and Chrysler: A Case of "Misframing"?' Baker uses the concept of 'policy frames', which he defines as self-contained models for seeing a policy problem. He argued (in 1977) that the Central Policy Review Staff's report on *The Future of the Car Industry* had framed the question of governmental support for the British car industry in conventional economic terms of productivity and efficiency and ignored other, more political, perspectives on the problem, so that the utility of their recommendations to the Cabinet was severely constrained. In his terminology, this was an example of 'misframing' or 'the deliberate or unconscious framing of a problem in a way that is irrelevant; i.e. the incorrect choice of frame'. Baker recommends that '"Framing" should be a conscious moment in any large-scale policy project' and that, although 'the process of choosing the policy framework cannot be a totally rational one' it can be improved by being undertaken 'consciously'. In training analysts we similarly recommend that they should be critically aware of the 'assumptive worlds' or 'policy frames' of policy-makers—and of the biasing effect of their own assumptions or background (e.g. previous training as lawyers or economists).

### 7.5.6 ARE THERE ALTERNATIVE POLICY FRAMES?

One way of exposing and, perhaps, limiting the bias in one's own perception of a problem is deliberately to identify, even generate, alternative ways of 'framing' it. Thus Baker argues that, at least in the case of policy issues which are both important and complex, an attempt should be made, first, to list as many policy frames as possible, secondly, to describe each briefly but sympathetically, and thirdly, to compare these with the policy frame prevailing within one's own agency.

This might seem a counsel of perfection, inapplicable to most issues, but there are some cases to which it could well be appropriate. For example, in defining issues within foreign policy or defence strategy, part of the professional skill of the diplomat or strategist lies in being able to understand the perspectives of the other 'players'. Even in domestic policy, those involved in the handling of an industrial relations dispute may need to be able to empathize (even though they do not sympathize) with the 'frame' adopted by, say, a trade union leader who is seeking to fight off his own militants as well as his opponents across the bargaining table. More than that, however, they may occasionally have to face the much more difficult challenge of re-examining their own framing of the issue and decide if it is unduly restricted, logically inconsistent, or unable to accommodate some empirically verifiable features of the situation.

Even if the analyst is sufficiently open-minded to consider and possibly accept other policy frames, however, there will be problems in persuading senior officials and politicians to do the same. If policy frame analysis is to be sold to them it may have to be in terms of the political advantages to be derived from doing so, such as anticipating the moves of other participants or of withdrawing gracefully from a policy position which would prove dangerously unpopular or simply untenable.

### 7.5.7 WHAT IS THE APPROPRIATE LEVEL OF AGGREGATION?

The terms in which a policy issue is placed upon the agenda are sometimes closer to a slogan or a call to arms than a useful or specific definition of the problem, opportunity, or trend. For example, one of the authors was involved in a politically inspired study of certain aspects of 'homelessness'. This proved to be a singularly imprecise and over-generalized remit and it was only when a commissioned piece of research broke it down into several sub-categories that any focused discussion could get under way. Thus the 'homeless' were *disaggregated* into such subcategories as: (1) evictees (but people could be evicted for rent arrears or for anti-social behaviour, so the need for some subcategorization was indicated); (2) victims of marital or other domestic disputes; (3) incomers to an area (e.g. in search of employment) and other transient homeless; (4) victims of civil emergencies (floods, etc.); (5) families without a satisfactory home (i.e. not 'roofless' but, for example, a young married couple living with in-laws in crowded conditions because they could not obtain or afford a home of their own); (6) the single homeless (a subcategory which has had more attention in recent years and been further disaggregated in a variety of ways); and (7) 'travelling people' (Romanies, etc.).

Such disaggregation is not only useful in itself but can lead, on occasion, to helpful *reaggregation*. For example, the young married couple living with in-laws might more relevantly be viewed as an aspect of the problem of securing access to loan capital than as part of the homelessness-as-rooflessness problem. A better example might be those problems of the physically disabled, such as social isolation, which have less to do with disablement than with the relative poverty which too many disabled persons must endure but which they also share with other groups in society, such as the unemployed or the elderly.

Finally, there will on occasions be scope for moving up the scale of *aggregation*: that is, for seeing the general in the particular or, in medical terminology, the syndrome among the individual symptoms. Obvious examples include recognition in the 1960s of 'multiple urban deprivation' and in the 1970s of 'the decline of the inner city'. This is not to say that these problems have been adequately defined, but at least attempts have been made to understand the linkages between such individual indicators as poor housing, inadequate health standards, low levels of educational attainment, high rates of unemployment, and so on.

### 7.5.8 IS THE CAUSAL STRUCTURE OF THE PROBLEM UNDERSTOOD?

While greater sophistication in recognizing the *symptoms* of problems and of aggregating them appropriately (above) is to be welcomed, it might seem more important that issue definition should be able to go on to the more difficult task of suggesting *causes* and providing explanations. A useful example is the Home Office research study on *Tackling Vandalism* (Clarke, 1978). Figure 7.1 is a diagrammatic representation of some of the groups of factors that are seen to contribute, or predispose, to vandalism. The variables in groups 1 to 5 are those seen as 'conducive to a general predisposition to offend' while groups 6 to 8 'deal with variables which directly influence the decision to commit a particular offence'. The Home Office study accepts that the entire causal structure of vandalism would be almost impossible to investigate. 'Policy relevant' research has to be selective but the problems involved in selection are succinctly described:

First, we do not know the relative explanatory power of the groups of variables . . . It is conceivable, for example, that 'situational' features play a much greater part in an act of vandalism than the fact that the individual responsible comes from a broken home—but this is not

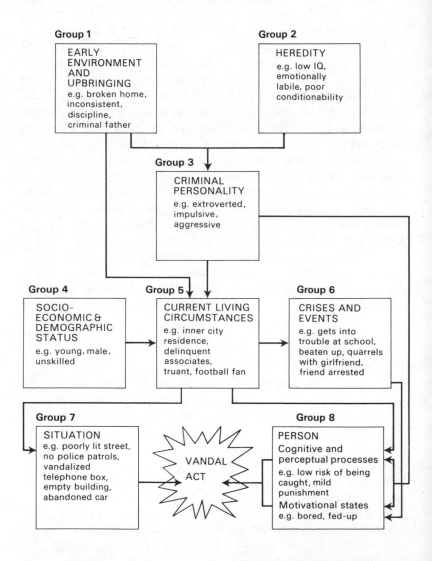

FIG. 7.1 Groups of variables contributing to an explanation of vandalism

Source: Clarke (1978, 4).

©Crown Copyright 1978. Reproduced with the permission of the Controller of Her Majesty's Stationery Office.

certain. Second, there are some variables, such as the individual's emotional state at the time of the offence, which may be relatively important in explanation, but about which it would be very difficult to obtain reliable information. Third, the explanatory power of particular variables does not necessarily match their importance for prevention . How can one make parents, who are not so disposed, love their children. What can be done about the demographic position of crime-prone individuals, or indeed about their particular personality characteristics?

The Home Office study chose to concentrate on 'those variables more immediately impinging on the offence itself as these might be expected to yield more direct and immediate implications for prevention'. The variables chosen were those in group 7 ('situation'), though there was some study of group 5 ('current living circumstances'). In other words, the strategy implied was one of concentrating upon particular high-risk groups of persons and limiting their opportunities for committing acts of vandalism in poorly lit streets or empty buildings. This selection of more readily treatable causes is open to criticism, but at least the analysis was conducted in awareness of how such factors fitted into a model of the overall causal structure.

This discussion of the factors leading to vandalism indicates that division of a problem into symptoms and causes may often be oversimplified: there can be a range of factors at various stages of remove from the specific events or acts which are the initial focus of attention. In this case the Home Office study chose not to go too deeply into root causes but to stay fairly close the the site of the offences themselves, on the grounds that preventive action was more likely to be effective if it concentrated upon immediately predisposing circumstances and situations. Of course, the longer-term consequences of such an approach might be worrying. For example, does the removal of opportunities to commit acts of vandalism in one area lead to the elimination of the problem or simply to more such acts being committed elsewhere (i.e. problem displacement) or, perhaps, to other forms of anti-social behaviour (i.e. problem substitution)? Problem structures are rarely self-contained but tend to overlap and interact with others. To treat one may lead to spillover effects elsewhere. Indeed the cure for one problem may be the cause of another (see chapter 13 on policy succession and termination).

Social policy is particularly liable to complexity, interdependence, and knock-on effects. It has produced such interesting theories as those of 'problem attraction' or Dexter's more general 'Law' which suggests that 'Whenever a piece of legislation creates a demand for a particular service or activity or even attitude, that demand is likely to be fulfilled' (Dexter, 1981, 424). There is also Steiss and Daneke's concept of a 'problem hierarchy', suggesting that problems 'are seldom mutually exclusive' because they 'often exist in a hierarchical relationship to one another, and the solution of one problem may depend on the solution of another, either higher or lower in the hierarchy' (Steiss and Daneke, 1980, 133).

Fortunately, however, there are other situations which are less complex and where it does seem possible to suggest that too much attention is given to the suppression of symptoms and too little to dealing with underlying causes. A simple example is that of litter in city centres, especially at weekends. Resources are often concentrated upon coping with the all too visible symptoms of the problem, but some time and thought should be given to asking why the problem appears to have got noticeably worse in recent years. A recent study in one city suggested that some contributory factors were: (1) deteriorating standards of behaviour; (2) underprovision of litter bins plus new bins which blended so skilfully with the environment that the public did not identify or use them as such! (3) proliferation of hot food takeaways; (4) refuse from restaurants having to be put into lanes where various scavengers overturned bins or ripped open bags; (5) inadequate enforcement by police of litter laws, etc. While the first of these factors did not seem open to short-term ameliorative action, steps were taken to deal with most of the others, including a survey which indicated that the 'dropping zones' for take-away food containers were unrelated to the availability of rubbish bins. A partly successful attempt was made to persuade take-away purveyors to 'sponsor' (with suitable advertisements) the provision of additional bins in the dropping zones.

### 7.5.9 CAN THE IMPLICATIONS OF THE PROBLEM BE SPECIFIED, EVEN QUANTIFIED?

Politicians and senior officials are interested not only in the symptoms and causes of problems but also, and perhaps especially, in the consequences of the problem and the demands it will make upon them as policy-makers and implementers. It is important that these consequences and implications should be specified as far as possible and, where appropriate, specification should extend to quantification. For certain issues, the method of issue search employed (see chapter 5) may already have provided much of this information, as with some forms of demographic analysis or social indicators. For other issues, special investigations may be necessary, ranging from secondary analyses of existing data to specially conducted surveys. We set out below some of the main features of an issue which seem to require specification and quantification (see also Rossi, Freeman, and Wright, 1979, ch. 3).

First, it is useful to specify both the *scale* and *intensity* of the problem. How widespread is the problem? For example, how many houses are affected by dampness, how many miles of river are polluted by industrial effluent? How serious is the problem for those affected: for example, is the river pollution a threat to amenity or a more serious threat to health? Next, what is the *incidence* of the problem? This is not the same as asking how widespread are its effects, since the problem may not impinge equally on all those affected. If incidence is not uniform then the appropriate policy responses will have to be more complex and discriminating and a simple 'package' will not suffice. The *characteristics* of those affected are relevant: for example, while dampness in housing is a problem for all residents, it is a particularly serious problem for the very young and the very old, since the health risks will be greater for these less resilient subcategories of residents. Variations in the incidence or intensity of suffering will have implications for the *targetability* of programmmes: obviously we should try to direct resources where they will do most good but often we need more specific (and disaggregated) data before we are in a position to do so. Any scope for problem *attraction* should be identified. For example, it may be recognized that single-parent families headed by a mother are in acute poverty and a programme of relief payments established. However, if there is no corresponding programme for two-parent families in poverty, there will be an incentive for the father or other male adult to desert the family (in appearance if not in reality) so that it can qualify for relief.

Other relevant features which need to be specified and quantified include the *rate of change* of the problem. For example, incremental policy responses may be adequate to deal with inflation which is increasing only slowly and uniformly but if inflation appears to be accelerating sharply or fluctuating wildly then different corrective measures may have to be adopted. Where past trends are unclear or underlying causal factors are not understood, the future development of the problem may be difficult to predict, but some attempt must be made to quantify the degree of *uncertainty*. Where there is considerable uncertainty, the emphasis may have to be on 'wedge forecasting' (a range of possibilities between the 'most optimistic' and 'most pessimistic' extremes) and associated 'contingency planning'. To determine policy responses on the basis of a single most likely (or wished-for) development is a common fault in policy-making.

At this stage in issue definition the focus is obviously beginning to shift from the issue as such to the range of appropriate policy responses open to the public agencies concerned. Attempts must be made to specify the availability and relevance of *existing programmes* and to establish whether a new programme will be necessary to cope with the emerging issue or whether the latter can be accommodated by an extension of existing programmes, agencies, and personnel. If only an extension is required, it will be necessary to quantify *current shortfalls* in terms of funding and real resources—including, for example, the need to train existing staff in new skills. Where a new programme is required, there will obviously be a need to specify in some detail what will be involved in terms of new resources, organization, and personnel. This may involve consideration of the necessary *threshold level* of resources. That is; there may be a certain minimum level—or 'critical size'—of policy response below which there will be little or no impact upon the problem, or the ratio of resource input to achieved output will be unacceptably high (Schulman, 1980). If there are such threshold effects, they must be identified and specified as accurately as possible if resources are not to be wasted or used ineffectively.

### 7.5.10 WHEN AND HOW WILL THE ISSUE BE REVIEWED?

While every effort should be made to specify, disaggregate, and explain issues, there will obviously be limits to our understanding and to our ability to predict how an issue will develop in the future. Where the issue is important, uncertainty is acute, and the scale of any attempted solution is likely to be large, consideration should be given to running an experimental or pilot programme. Often that will not be practicable (see references to the 'threshold' effect at 7.5.9 above) and it then becomes essential to monitor the actual development of the issue, probably as part of a larger monitoring exercise directed at the relevant policy or programme. As fuller information emerges about the issue, including feedback from the programme developed to deal with it, it may then seem appropriate to undertake a full-scale review of the problem, opportunity, or trend, to determine whether it is possible to refine or, indeed, necessary to alter the earlier definition of the issue.

In other words, it is important to remember that few issues will ever be fully, finally, or authoritatively defined; that even a long-standing formulation of a problem should be regarded as only a provisionally acceptable definition; and that either the issue itself or our perception of it may change over time as a result of new facts, changing values, or a combination of both.

# 8

# Forecasting

## 8.1 The policy analysis approach to forecasting

The approach in this chapter is not that of a technical expert in forecasting who is 'selling' forecasting techniques. Rather, the appropriate frame of mind in which to approach the subject of forecasting in policy analysis is one of humility. When we consider the problems involved in understanding the past and the present (e.g. in issue search and issue definition) it may seem the utmost temerity to try to understand the future.

What then is the justification for carrying out forecasting? Quite simply, because it is necessary. The choices we make now affect the future, and the outcome of those choices is affected by events in the future. In making choices we are implicitly or explicitly making assumptions about the future. Forecasting involves making those assumptions explicitly and rigorously, the assumption being that the resulting choices will in some sense be 'better'.

The policy analysis approach to forecasting requires knowledge of what techniques are available and of their limitations in theory and practice, but is not obsessed with methodology or numbers as such. Forecasts cannot predict the future but they can assist decision-makers to cope with uncertainty and change and to explore the implications of policy options. The policy analysis approach to forecasting also recognizes the crucial importance of how forecasts are consumed by *decision-makers* rather than simply with how forecasts are carried out by 'experts'. Forecasting can be costly and a balance has to be struck between possible benefits from forecasting and the costs of carrying out forecasts and consuming them.

## 8.2 Problems of forecasting

### 8.2.1 THE DIFFERENCE BETWEEN PREDICTING IN SCIENCES AND FORECASTING FOR POLICY-MAKERS

In the natural sciences, probabilistic thinking is replacing simple determinism because of the need to allow for the operation of random factors. But in forecasting social events the natural science solution is not readily applicable, because whether a phenomenon, such as pollution, will continue to increase depends on whether a decision to introduce countermeasures is taken. In other words, the probability of any predicted future is subject to major modifications by deliberate action within the time-span for which the prediction is supposed to hold. These actions may, indeed, be the consequence or purpose of the 'prediction' having been made.

Forecasting in policy analysis is therefore not concerned with predicting the future—since in most cases this is impossible—but with attempting to assess the implications of different assumptions. There is, however, a danger in some cases of self-fulfilling prophecies—of actions taken by government as a result of forecasts itself leading to the fulfilment of the assumptions made in the forecast. Arguably, this has been true of some transport forecasts made in Britain in the past (see Gershuny, 1978). Forecasts of the future numbers of cars by the Transport and Road Research Laboratory assumed a continuation of existing government policy towards road provision, traffic restraint, public transport, etc. Thus the forecasts predicted *policy* as part of their forecast. This seems to defeat much of the value of forecasting in policy analysis, which is to help the examination of policy options.

Given the differences between prediction in science and forecasting for public policy-making, we would argue that forecasting in policy analysis should always indicate the sensitivity of forecasts to assumptions, and in particular should always indicate the extent to which the outcome of forecasts is capable of policy manipulation.

### 8.2.2 FORECASTING THE PRESENT AND THE RECENT PAST

In forecasting the future our first task is to forecast the present and the recent past. The information we have may be three months, a year, or even longer out-of-date, and may be subject to revisions greater than the original changes shown by the figures or greater than the size of the change we are seeking to achieve, and perhaps in an opposite direction, for a period of several years. For example, figures for national income may still be subject to revision *seven years* after the year concerned, though the bulk of the revision occurs in the first three years. The data for UK employment in *1961* were revised between February *1976* and December 1976. A classic case of massive revisions and changing directions of revisions over a long period (ten years) occurred with the figure for savings in 1958, which was revised from £1,341m to £616m between 1959 and 1968, and the savings ratio (savings as a percentage of personal income) was revised from 7.1 per cent to 3.3 per cent between 1959 and 1968.

### 8.2.3 LACK OF DATA

We have already noted that available data may be out of date and subject to revision. However, we may not have the data we need ready to hand at all, and it may be costly and time-consuming to obtain it.

### 8.2.4 APPROPRIATE LEVELS OF AGGREGATION

In making our forecasts we are likely to be concerned not simply with the overall picture in year $x$, but with the *spatial* distribution of the outcome (e.g. we are concerned to know *where* to build schools), with various subcategories (e.g. secondary schools relative to technical colleges), and with the distribution *over time* (e.g. *when* and *whether* to build new schools). The issues thrown up by profiles over time can cause more problems than the figure in a single year some time in the future.

### 8.2.5 LACK OF UNDERSTANDING OF PROCESSES

Even if we have the necessary raw data, we will not be able to make forecasts if we do not understand the social or economic processes involved. Economists would be obliged to admit that their understanding of some of the basic economic processes is less than perfect; our knowledge of social processes is even more inadequate. Yet without theoretical underpinning, forecasting exercises are mere number-crunching or speculation.

### 8.2.6 THE COSTS OF FORECASTING

Many forecasting techniques, particularly those which involve the analysis of large amounts of data, are very expensive and in many cases are more expensive than the potential benefit to decision-making which might arise from having the forecast available. Also, it is important to include not just the direct costs of forecasting. The costs of forecasting can be listed as:

the costs of data collection
the costs of processing and analysis
the costs of presentation
the costs of consumption

The costs of not forecasting are:

the extra costs of making provisions for unforeseen but foreseeable
contingencies at non-optimal times and non-optimal forms
or the costs arising from failure to make provision

The implications of these costs of forecasting will be discussed further
in the final section of the chapter.

### 8.2.7 THE TIME AVAILABLE FOR FORECASTING

Forecasting takes time, and the time taken may lead to the foreclosing
of options which would have been taken if the forecast had been made
available earlier. This is particularly the case where a long lead time in
implementing a policy is involved (e.g. nuclear power stations).

### 8.2.8 THE CONSUMPTION OF FORECASTS

A point which can hardly be made often enough is that the purpose of
forecasting in policy analysis not to produce large numbers of neat
tables or to prove methodological prowess but to assist decision-makers
to take decisions. Yet most books on forecasting concentrate entirely
on methodology and appear to take it for granted that the outcome of
the analysis will be consumed. This cannot be assumed, and particular
care is needed in presenting forecasts to ensure that they are consumed.

## 8.3 Types of forecast

### 8.3.1 ONE-OFF AND ITERATIVE FORECASTS

Forecasting can be regarded as a one-off activity carried out before the
programme design stage or as a continuous input to the policy process.

In general, one-off forecasts will be adequate only where we are
concerned with a single lumpy good or where there is total knowledge
and understanding of the present state of affairs, total predictability or
of control over all the influences on the processes concerned, and total
agreement among political actors about the objectives to be pursued.
Even if a one-off forecast turns out to be accurate, this may not mean
that the assumptions behind the forecast are correct or that the policy

was successful. Fortuitous changes in the opposite direction may have concealed other errors.

Iterative forecasting stresses the importance of continuous updating and feedback of information if policy is to cope with a changing world; some of these changes will be predictable but there will always be an element of unpredictability. Iterative forecasting will be more expensive than a single one-off forecast, but may well be cheaper than a series of *ad hoc* one-off forecasts.

### 8.3.2 WHAT SHOULD BE FORECAST?

How wide-ranging should we be in the subjects we include in our forecasts? The differences between the Simon and Lindblom models are relevant here (see chapter 4). For example, in industry policy should we be concerned only with forecasting demand for a product or with political and social factors as well? What we want to forecast will depend on the objectives we want to pursue (see chapter 9).

Considerable care should be exercised in deciding what are the appropriate things to forecast in relation to a problem; the obvious ones may not in fact be the most important ones. For example, forecasting the use of microprocessors over the next ten years depends more on economic and social forecasting than on technological forecasting, since the technology likely to be applied already exists and it is the commercial application of it that has to be determined (see Barron and Curnow, 1979).

### 8.3.3 RELEVANT PERIODS FOR FORECASTING

Clearly, the relevant period for forecasting will vary because of the varying lead times and consequences of decisions. The construction of nuclear power stations is an example of a decision involving both long lead time and long-term consequences, both in terms of energy provision and their implications for society. Forecasting the unemployment implications of economic decisions involves short-to-medium-term lead time and impact. Relevant considerations here are the *flexibility* of decisions, including their degree of *lumpiness* and their *reversibility*.

The terms 'short-term', 'medium-term', and 'long-term' are often used, particularly of economic predictions. They are not used rigorously, but are often used to mean the following: up to one year, one to five years, and over five years. However, the relevant period for forecasting will vary from policy to policy, so the following classification seems more useful:

(a) forecasts about the effects of decisions already made or where major influences are already revealed. It is possible to predict with a very high degree of accuracy the number of old age pensioners in Britain in twenty years time because they are already born (though some uncertainty is generated by life expectancy and migration, and there is always that chance of nuclear holocost—though presumably we would then be more worried about things other than our forecasts about pension costs being out). However, it is much more difficult for the Government to predict the size of the public sector borrowing requirement over the next year, because this depends on a number of influences which are difficult to forecast.

(b) forecasts where some but not all major influences are already apparent. We know to a high degree of accuracy one of the major influences on the number of children of primary school age in ten years time—the number of women of fertile age—but not one of the others—the birth rate.

(c) forecasts where we have little or no control over events or where straightforward projection of exisiting figures is an inadequate guide (e.g. number of nought-to-five-year-olds in twenty-five years time). Our area of concern in twenty-five years time may be profoundly affected by changes in society and technology not yet apparent.

## 8.4 Extrapolation

Extrapolation involves projecting into the future existing trends and making forecasts on the basis of these. In a sense, modelling techniques (see 8.6 below) also involve extrapolation in that the models are based on our understanding of relationships in the past and present, but not all extrapolation techniques are so sophisticated or require the same theoretical underpinning.

The main problems arising with extrapolative techniques are the measurement and interpretation of past trends (which may have to be disentangled from a variety of cyclical or special effects) and the possibility that unpredicted factors will upset predictions based on the continuation of present trends. However, many predictions made, particularly by politicians, are based on relatively crude extrapolative techniques.

Distinctions can be made between linear, exponential, S-curve, cyclical, and discontinuous change (we are not always necessarily always dealing with *growth* in forecasting). These are illustrated in Figure 8.1. In linear change, there is a constant rate of change. In exponential change there is a constantly accelerating rate of change. With an S-curve the accelerating rate of change will level off and decelerate.

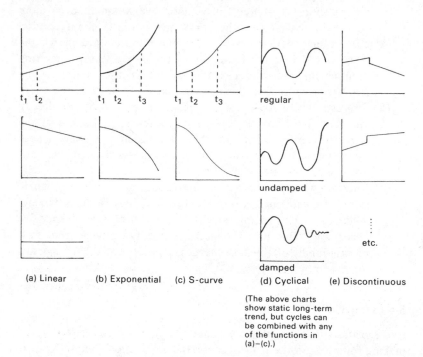

(a) Linear    (b) Exponential    (c) S-curve    (d) Cyclical    (e) Discontinuous

(The above charts show static long-term trend, but cycles can be combined with any of the functions in (a)–(c).)

FIG. 8.1 Different types of trends

However, it may be difficult to work out what the long-term trend is in the variable we are concerned with, particularly on the basis of a trend over a relatively short period. For example, in (a) to (c) in Figure 8.1 the change in the period $t_1-t_2$ is much the same. How can we establish whether the long-term trend is linear, exponential or S-curve? It may matter little if the decisions we have to make are relevant to only a relatively short time period ahead, and we are able to cope with a sizeable margin or error. If we are concerned with making decisions about time $t_3$., however, the linear and exponential paths have diverged sharply, though the exponential and S-curve paths are similar; after $t_3$ the exponential and S-curve functions also diverge sharply.

To make matters worse, there are other paths which change can take (cf. Rose, 1976a, ch. 1). Figure 8.1 (d) and (e) illustrate only a few of the many paths which cyclical or discontinuous functions can follow. A projection of live births in Britain made in 1965 extrapolated on the basis of a sharp increase of a linear nature, whereas 1965 actually marked the peak of a cycle in live births, which proceeded to decline sharply; by 1974 the divergence between the 1965 based projection of 1.1m for 1974 and the actual figure of 0.7m was about 0.4m (see CPRS, 1977, 8).

Again it may not matter too much which of a range of possible paths we assume providing we are prepared to accept a wide margin of error and/or are dealing with a relatively short time period; e.g. it may not matter too much if the path is static linear or regular cyclical if we are prepared to accept a margin of error equal to the gap between top and bottom of the cycle. In general, however, we will be unable to extrapolate a trend where the nature of the trend is ambiguous or to assume that the trend will continue in the future unless we have some understanding of the processes at work and what affects them.

There is a form of extrapolation called the 'envelope curve', which seeks to project into the future the trend of a series of products, projects, etc., by drawing a curve tangential to all the individual product curves. Such an envelope curve might, for example, help a manufacturer predict the point at which he will no longer be able to charge a premium price for his product. However, as with all extrapolation, envelope curves depend on the assumption that existing trends will continue.

We may be obliged to use extrapolative techniques because of our lack of understanding about social and economic processes or because of a lack of data for modelling, and the results may often turn out to be adequate for our purposes. However, in the absence of a theory or a model of the processes at work we have no indication in advance of the reliability of our predictions, and if they turn out to be incorrect we may be unable to work out why and use this information to improve our forecasting techniques.

## 8.5 Judgemental techniques

This group of techniques is largely concerned with forecasting possible futures on the basis of intuitive judgements rather than more 'objective' methods such as modelling or extrapolation. A number of these techniques are neatly 'packaged' and have specific names, but this does not necessarily confer any theoretical legitimacy on them. A number of techniques involve sometimes quite complex computation using nunbers derived from weighting or ranking by participants, but the fact that such calculations are numbers in no way confers additional theoretical value on the technique or makes the results any 'harder' than 'soft' qualitative statements arising from intuitive judgements.

Given the potentially infinite range of judgemental approaches and combinations thereof, mention will be made here of only a limited number of these. Some of these techniques can be used in combination with each other or with modelling or extrapolative techniques.

## 8.5.1 DELPHI

The Delphi technique assumes that useful forecasts can be obtained from the intuitive judgements of people knowledgeable in the area of interest and that these are best obtained individually from members of a group, since it is argued that in a group meeting collectively the views of some extrovert or higher status members will tend to be more influential than the others.

In a typical Delphi exercise a panel of several experts is selected and each member receives a questionnaire listing possibilities in, say, technological development in the area of the study. A typical questionnaire will ask when each of the specified techniques will materialize, and perhaps also ask for reasons. The organizers of the exercise then summarize this information to indicate the spread of responses about timing. This summary is circulated and panel members may revise their estimate in the light of the summary and any arguments (e.g. most optimistic and most pessimistic) shown in the summary. There may be a number of such rounds of summary and circulation.

There are few a priori grounds for assuming that this technique will make accurate predictions, and some technical grounds for doubting it (see Sackman, 1975). There are problems of assessing Delphi in terms of its results, since many of the Delphi exercises so far conducted cannot be fully assessed since the dates referred to are not yet fully passed (Delphi exercises only started to be produced in numbers after 1963). However, it is clear that while some forecasts have been reasonably accurate, many have not, and perhaps more significantly, many events which have already occurred were not forecast. More worryingly, some of the items in the forecasts were so vaguely worded as to be inherently difficult to evaluate.

The Delphi technique is, then a highly controversial one. Both pro and anti Delphi viewpoints are contained in a symposium of articles which appeared in *Technological Forecasting and Social Change*, volume 7, no. 2, 1975. For an exposition of the Delphi method see Linestone and Turoff (1975).

## 8.5.2 BRAINSTORMING

We have already noted (in 5.4.5) that brainstorming may play a role as one method of seeking to identify possible future problems and opportunities. Similarly brainstorming might identify possible future events or trends which it is important to consider in policy planning.

The first stage of brainstorming (after any 'warming up' exercise) is the generation of a large number of ideas in a short time period within a small group (of between five and twelve). It is important that at this stage no attempt is made to evaluate or comment on the feasibility of ideas since this might lead to the premature rejection of ideas which turn out to be worth consideration and would interrupt the spontaneous and interactive generation of a large number of ideas. Rawlinson (1981, 38–40) argues that success in this stage of brainstorming depends on the application and enforcement of four guidelines: suspend judgement; free-wheel; quantity of ideas; cross-fertilize.

It is only after this creative stage is completed that the ideas generated are evaluated, including attaching probabilities to the various hypothetical events listed and indicating which are the most important.

There is little reason to assume that brainstorming will necessarily produce good predictions, but it may well lead to the identification of possible future 'rogue events' (perhaps with a low probability of occurring but with important implications if they do) which ought to be taken into account in policy planning but would not be spotted by extrapolative techniques. Brainstorming can also be used as a means of generating options for tackling problems and this seems to be the main use to which it is put in management applications (see 10.2 and Rawlinson, 1981, chs. 1–5).

## 8.5.3 CROSS-IMPACT MATRICES

Cross-impact matrices can be used with Delphi or brainstorming approaches. The technique concentrates on the actual and potential relationships between the forecast events. 'Using Delphi, it is quite possible that forecast events may be mutually reinforcing or exclusive and thus that a totally unrealistic "consensus" may be reached' (Encel, Marstrand and Page, 1975, 83).

The procedure for compiling the matrix is that panel members are asked to classify the interaction between events, specifying both the type of interaction and an estimate of its 'strength'. This should throw up which events are 'dominant' (i.e. have a strong impact on other events) and which are 'sensitive' (i.e. are strongly affected by other events). Computations may then be carried out to produce revised probability estimates for the occurrence of individual events; this phase is likely to rely heavily on simulation.

Cross-impact techniques will at least help to ensure that studies based on intuitive judgements do not produce forecasts which are internally inconsistent. However, as Encel et al., (1975, 85) point out, 'No amount of simulation and manipulation can turn a poor Delphi forecast into an excellent one.'

One of the originators of cross-impact analysis (Helmer, 1981) has pointed out that existing cross-impact models suffer from a number of defects, both logical inaccuracies (e.g. there may be no guarantee in some models that probabilities will fall in the interval 0 to 1) and factual inadequacies (e.g. only pairs of occurrences are considered in cross-impact analysis, whereas in reality the effect of A on B often depends on other conditions, C). However, Helmer argues that despite these shortcomings futures researchers should not feel discouraged from attempting to place cross-impact analysis on as sound a basis as possible, because of its use as a potential aid to long-range planning in conditions of 'nonexistent theory of how events affect one another in a multi-disciplinary context' (Helmer, 1981; see also Helmer, 1977). Interactive forms of cross-impact modelling can be used as a means of exploring the implications of policy options (see Lonsdale, 1978; McLean, 1976).

### 8.5.4 SCENARIO WRITING

Scenarios are 'hypothetical sequences of events constructed for the purpose of focusing attention on causal processes and decision points. They answer two kinds of question: (1) Precisely how might some hypothetical situation come about, step by step? and (2) What alternatives exist, for each actor, at each step, for preventing, averting or facilitating the processes' (Kahn and Weiner, quoted in Encel et al., 1975, 86).

It would obviously be a vast task to attempt to set out all possible steps to all possible outcomes, even in a fairly narrow context. Scenarios may, in principle, broaden the horizons of decision-makers and indicate the scope for action on their part. They may also be more compre-

hensible (i.e. easier to 'consume') than more computationally sophisticated techniques. It would however, be difficult to judge what impact
such scenarios have on decision-makers. However, the writing of scenarios
does assume an agreement about causal relationships that may not
exist, and there is no way a priori of ensuring that all major possibilities are identified (e.g. failure of many scenario writers to predict
the 1973—4 oil crisis).

'Scenarios' can also be generated by computer models. All that is
required is the list of outcomes predicted on the basis of different
assumptions about the conditioning variables. Finally, science fiction
can be considered to be a form of scenario writing.

## 8.5.5 THE USE OF JUDGEMENTAL TECHNIQUES IN POLICY PLANNING

One of the chief weaknesses of judgemental approaches is that there is
no way of assessing the likely accuracy of the forecast in advance. Not
only that, but if the conditioning variables, etc., are not clearly defined
it will be impossible to tell whether the forecast is working out as time
progresses and it may even be impossible after the 'event' to tell
whether the forecast was 'accurate' or not. Thus if our concern is with
planning for policies which require us to work on the assumption of
outcomes lying in a certain range to a specified degree of probability
we should be looking to modelling techniques; judgemental techniques
are of uncertain value for this purpose.

Can such techniques ever be of value? Although the view here is that
judgemental techniques are oversold—particularly the more sophisticated
ones ('sophisticated' here used in its older sense of 'adulterated')— there
are circumstances when such techniques can be of value in public
policy, particularly if combined with 'harder' techniques such as modelling or extrapolation. If, for example, we are concerned to spot
opportunities or to be prepared for problems with a low probability
of occurence but with important consequences if they do occur, then
these are more likely to be thrown up by judgemental techniques (see
5.6.5). Such techniques will not enable us to assess probabilities, but
if the issues are sufficiently important, contingency plans can be drawn
up (e.g. biological warfare attack), regulations tightened (e.g. nuclear
reactors in power stations) or flexibility introduced to take advantage
of possible future developments (e.g. leaving clear routes for possible
new communications systems).

Judgemental techniques may also draw attention to possible

relationships not revealed by modelling or extrapolative techniques. This is likely to be particularly the case where a new relationship is developing or an old one undergoing a qualitative change. Wherever possible, such impressionistic judgements should be verified by empirical evidence and fitted into a forecasting model, since only then can the importance of the relationship and its impact on forecasts be assessed in quantitative terms.

## 8.6 Modelling techniques

Strictly, modelling is the only intellectually reputable technique of forecasting, since unless we have some kind of understanding of the processes involved in the issues we are concerned with based on a 'model' of those processes, any prediction we make will be a shot in the dark, and we will be unable to learn from failures in our forecasts as part of an integrated information system. Modelling need not necessarily involve numbers (some important variables may be yes/no or nominal variables) but, generally, mathematical models are likely to be more rigorous.

### 8.6.1 THE ECONOMETRIC APPROACH

As noted in 8.2.1, scientific disciplines have been moving in recent years from deterministic to probabilistic (stochasic) formulations of their theories. This has also been reflected in econometrics (see Ramsey, 1977). It is valuable to think of economic and social relationships as stochastic rather than deterministic, since we live in an uncertain world. In calculating probabilities and using them to predict events and make decisions, we use conditioning variables—the circumstances under which the trial or experiment is performed—which determine the conditional probabilities of an event occurring.

Thus, in making an economic prediction an economist should say that if government policy and international trade conditions remain constant (the conditioning variables) there is only one chance in $x$ (the conditional probability) that the unemployment rate will fall below $y$ per cent. Frequently, we see figures quoted in the media which simply state that unemployment will be $y$ per cent, but their apparent precision is spurious; the reason why economic predictions quoting precise figures are usually wrong is that there is always a very low probability that any specific figure will turn out to be correct.

If we relax the assumptions about the conditioning variables, then we will have a set of predicted outcomes, each of which will be expressed in the form that there is a certain *probability* that the outcome will lie within a particular range. This point is important, since the assumption about government policy remaining constant is rarely valid. If we are concerned with predicting the future rather than making conditional statements we either have to relax the assumption within the range we think likely, or include politics in our model in some other way.

The testing of stochastic formulations is obviously more complicated than the testing of deterministic relationships. If the formulation of a hypothetical statement is put in terms of the conditional probabilities of the occurrence of events, testing the theory involves checking probabilities. We have to calculate from a large number of observations the probability of the event and compare it with the prediction. The testing of stochastic relationships thus requires much more data.

A necessary part of this approach is that the model has a theoretical underpinning; whether the theory was arrived at inductively or deductively matters not, providing that it has been tested. In the absence of a theory there will be no justification for making assumptions about the relationships and how they will operate in the future; mere correlation between sets of numbers is insufficient.

We have to *specify* the variables, i.e. define them in an unambiguous, theoretically meaningful, and measurable form (this is difficult enough even in economics; e.g. we have no theoretically meaningful measurement of unemployment readily available). Another important requirement of modelling is *identification*—the procedure by which relationships between two variables can be isolated from complex interactions among large numbers of variables. Because it is rarely possible in the social sciences to isolate such variables and carry out an experiment on them, we need a theory about their relationships and, in particular, the direction of causality. Our model would consist of a number of these relationships, normally a large number. There then remains the technical problem of assigning numbers to the unknown values of the coefficients in the mathematical model.

Such a model would not enable us to predict what the future will be, but the chances of an event occurring in certain circumstances. This is, in fact, an advantage, since it enables us to test the effects of different policy decisions. But, 'Forecasts are merely statements about the probability of an event occurring, and their usefulness depends on the correctness of the theory used and upon the "accuracy" of the assumptions about the underlying circumstances' (Ramsey, 1977, 34).

We will rarely be able to meet the rigorous requirements of such an approach: much economic forecasting fails to live up to them. We will often be unable to specify variables clearly or to obtain data on them to enable us to test hypotheses; we will often be unable to identify the relationships between sets of variables; our theories about society are often poorly developed and sometimes inherently untestable. Thus we perforce have to adopt less rigorous techniques of forecasting, but we should recognize that not only does this not entitle us to make firm statements about specific outcomes, it means that we are not even entitled to make statements about the probabilities of outcomes lying within a certain range. We will be uncertain about the degree of uncertainty of the future.

## 8.6.2 THE SYSTEM DYNAMICS APPROACH

Econometric approaches rely largely on the statistical estimation of relationships between indicators and they attempt to make conditional forecasts based on these statistical relationships as altered by judgement. The econometric model as a whole consists of sets of relationships between individual indicators. As Encel *et al.* (1975, 5) note, 'The individual relationships in these models are often sound with apparently little error, although the total model is usually far less satisfactory.' An alternative modelling approach, the system dynamics approach, relies on the prior identification of relationships in the model as a whole and draws on non-statistical as well as statistical data to define these relationships and feed in assumptions. The system dynamics approach treats all variables as endogenous (i.e. internal to the system being analysed), unlike the econometric approach which treats some variables as exogenous (i.e. external to the system) and therefore not affected by changes to variables within the system.

The system dynamics approach has been developed mainly by Forrester. The following quotation is taken from Forrester's *World Dynamics* (1971), which together with the development of the approach in Meadows *et al.* (1972), *The Limits to Growth*, has produced one of the most controversial applications of the system dynamics approach:

The most important concept in establishing the structure of a system is the idea that all actions take place within 'feedback loops'. The feedback loop is the closed path that connects an action to its effect on the surrounding conditions, and these resulting conditions in turn come back as 'information' to influence further action. We often erroneously think of cause and effect as flowing in only one direction. . . . Within the feedback loops of a system, the principles of system structure tell us that two kinds of variables will be found — levels and rates. The levels are the accumulations (integrations) within the system. The rates are the flows that cause the levels to change.

Advocates of the system dynamics approach argue that it can be applied to issues of concern where econometric approaches are entirely inadequate, such as pollution and urban change, and that it has a number of advantages:

it lends itself to communicating with the public, dealing with long time horizons, choosing the appropriate level of aggregation, emphasizing policy choices, making all the variables endogenous, joining the arena of political controversy, and drawing on the rich and diversified mental database. System dynamics can accept nonlinearities. It can incorporate structures known to exist and whose behavior will be important in the future, but whose influence has not yet become strong enough to be manifested in available quantitative data. [Forrester, 1982, 104.]

It can also be argued that the approach can reveal counter-intuitive consequences of certain policies; e.g. policies to control pollution might accelerate ecological collapse. Forrester has applied his approach to industrial organizations and urban change as well as the world as a whole.

Economists and others have criticized applications of the system dynamics approach on the grounds that the predictions are a pure arte- fact of the initial assumptions, that the variables are inadequately specified and that the models are not properly tested (see Greenberger, Crenson and Crissey, 1976; Encel et al., 1975). While it is true, as Forrester argues, that the construction of a model may reveal 'the consequences and internal inconsistencies of our assumptions and fragments of knowledge', it does not necessarily ensure the construction of an adequate model where our understanding of basic processes and interaction is weak. The modeller may rely unduly on supposedly 'expert' knowledge. To some extent, the criticism can be overcome by 'counter-modelling'—alternative formulations of the model or dif- ferent assumptions, but this would very quickly become a very expensive business.

## 8.7 Morphological analysis

Morphological analysis simply means analysis in terms of components and their configuration, both actual and hypothetical. It could be considered a form of judgemental technique, but it is worth consider- ing separately because of its particular application to technological forecasting. It involves: (1) taking a particular object or technical system; (2) analysing its components in terms of their function; (3) looking at alternative forms these components could take, both existing and hypothetical; (4) analysing the different possible configurations of these components.

In morphological analysis, the initial definition of the system is very important, and there is a danger that this definition may be unduly influenced by existing technical configurations. For example, a 1954 morphological analysis of a clock failed to spot the developments which have actually taken place in terms of quartz crystal and LCD displays and did not cover the various clock/radio, etc., combinations which have come on to the market.

Morphological analysis should perhaps be seen not so much as a forecasting technique as a learning or opportunity-spotting device. This is not to denigrate its possible usefulness: morphological analysis may be self-fulfilling if it leads to the adoption of a successful new product or policy not previously considered.

## 8.8 The political roles of forecasting

Although we have argued that an understanding of available techniques, their advantages, and their limitations is important in the policy analysis approach to forecasting, it is also important to have some understanding of how far forecasts may be used, abused, or ignored by decision-makers and others involved in the policy process. It is important to recognize that this process is often highly politicized and that this has consequences for the ways in which forecasts will be used. Forecasts may be used not as a form of information to help shape a decision but as a justification for a decision already taken on other grounds, and forecasts which are not useful in this way (e.g. produce ambiguous predictions or contradict the arguments in support of the decision) may be ignored or supressed. Opposition to a proposal on policy grounds may masquerade as a critique of the methodology used to generate the forecast. Given that all forecasting methodologies are vulnerable to challenge, this is a tactic which can be used by any opponent with some knowledge of forecasting methodology (indeed this chapter provides plenty of potential ammunition for that purpose).

Forecasts which make the most political impact may not be those based on any kind of rigorous methodology. One of the 'forecasts' which has had the biggest political impact in Britain in recent years was Enoch Powell's 'Rivers of Blood' speech in 1968: Powell's purpose in making the speech was to paint a vivid scenario of what would happen if government failed to adopt Powell's views on immigration and repatriation. Whatever forecasting methodology is used, ability to paint vivid word pictures of its policy implications will assist its injection into political debate. This use of 'off-the-cuff' forecasts to support a political case for policy change is a common one, including much less dramatic ones than Mr Powell's.

A common political use of forecasts is the production of forecasts which paint a favourable (or unfavourable) picture of a party's performance (e.g. figures given at elections about inflation or unemployment the following year). Politicians would be wise to be cautious in this sort of predictive exercise, since their predictions may backfire when the future arrives and disproves them, and their predictions are quoted back at them.

We have stressed in this chapter that if forecasts are to be of full value in policy planning, the assumptions underlying them must be set out and policy-malleable variables identified. However, this is far from being the case in practice in terms of the way in which forecasts enter into policy debate. Forecasts may embody important assumptions about the desirability or inevitability of certain economic, social or political patterns (e.g. that economic growth is desirable or that roads must be provided for all cars which would want to use them). Such forecasts may then be used to legitimate the values or assumptions which are built into the forecast in the first place. Such forecasts may be difficult to challenge in public (especially if the forecasts are stated to embody government policy in the first place). A particular problem may arise if the institution producing a forecast in support of its policies has a monopoly of the expertise necessary to produce the forecasts (e.g. aspects of electricity generation). Given that forecasts are often very expensive to produce, it may be difficult for anyone else to produce an alternative but equally 'respectable' forecast. Thus forecasting (and other expensive forms of analysis) may be used to reinforce existing distributions of political resources.

Much of the literature on forecasting implicitly assumes that the client is the 'decision-maker', but we have noted that forecasts may be of use and be used by other actors in the policy process. Some forecasts may be produced without the intention or expectation that they will be used directly be present decision-makers. For example, Forrester (1982, 105–6) in talking about the forecasts produced by world modellers argues, 'the audience must be the public in general . . . World modellers should be talking not to present governments but to that whole spectrum of people beginning with school children who will elect and who will be future governments.' Rather arrogantly, Forrester (1982, 106) argues that 'The modeller must see himself as a leader'.

Turning back to the forecasts for which the client is a decision-maker in government, we find that while the forecasting literature assumes that the client is the decision-maker it tends to neglect how the product of forecasts should be packaged to ensure that they are readily consumed in a useful way. Flooding the decision-maker with masses of detailed figures will not assist him to discover the salient points. On the other hand, simply to present him with a central forecast or even alternative forecasts may be highly misleading, given the assumptions and corner cutting which are inevitable even in the best forecasts. Our own view is that the best approach is to indicate to the decision-maker the sensitivity of the forecast to changes in key assumptions (probably but not necessarily in numerical form) and in the context of the specific decision to be taken to indicate the relative importance of:

the *size* of the 'central prediction'
the width of the possible *range*
the *direction* of change
the degree of *uncertainty* (if this can be measured)

In other words, which of these features matter most to the decision to be taken?

Is there a danger that these caveats will be lost as forecasts pass up from the original forecasts through various policy-level officials each of whom for the best of reasons simplifies and annotates the material? Could this be avoided by ensuring that the official closest to the 'sharpest' end of forecasting sees the brief that goes to the final decision-maker? Experience in British central government suggests that departments vary considerably in the extent to which this currently takes place.

Part of the consumption of forecasts is salesmanship, i.e. convincing a superior or sponsoring department that your figures are valid or worthwhile. Given that forecasts are always open to challenge, one tactic is for the forecaster to try to get his client to agree to method ology and assumptions before the figures are produced. 'Co-opt your client' is always a useful motto.

## 8.9 Forecasting and policy planning

The emphasis in this chapter on the difficulties and uncertainties involved in forecasting might seem to point towards an incremental approach, both in preparing forecasts and in using the information thrown up by them. In other words, that you should not attempt to plan ahead but only take relatively small-scale decisions for a short period ahead, thus providing the opportunity for adjusting policy if forecast events fail to materialize in the way expected. However, this is not necessarily the correct conclusion to draw. If by postponing a decision you are not unduly foreclosing options for a relevant future time period then it makes sense to postpone the decision, since the uncertainty involved will, other things being equal, decrease as the time period approaches. However, if by postponing the decision you are foreclosing options to an extent which might impose unacceptably high costs or an unacceptable risk of outcomes falling outside a desired range, then decisions should be taken now as far as is necessary to ensure that the risk becomes acceptable. In considering the foreclosing of options we are rarely talking about absolutes, rather about the relative costs of taking action at various times. A list of the various possible strategies for coping with uncertainties thrown up by forecasts—or the certainty that there will be large fluctuations—is shown in Table 8.1.

A clear message of this chapter is that, depending on the policy problem and the forecasting techniques used, the range of possible outcomes, the degree of probability attached to the forecasts, and the sensitivity of outcomes to variations in the assumptions fed in to the forecasts are often more important than the central prediction. Building in flexibility or adopting one of the other non-incremental strategies shown in Table 8.1 in order to meet outcomes within an acceptable margin of error and to an acceptable degree of risk is therefore often more important than attempting to achieve a 'spot on' hit on a single target, which is rarely the outcome which actually emerges.

There are obviously severe practical and political problems in attempting to follow through non-incremental strategies in response to forecasts. For example, there are problems in the management of government if an attempt is made to combine flexibility with accountability and the avoidance of waste. Building in flexibility to a programme itself produces costs, which have to be set against the (possible) costs of duplication, postponement, etc. For example, in shipbuilding the best productivity comes from purpose-built facilities for a single type of

TABLE 8.1 *Strategies for coping with uncertainty or fluctuating trends thrown up by forecasts*

| | |
|---|---|
| Incrementalism | Appropriate where start-up, expansion, or cutback can be achieved quickly once uncertainty has been reduced. |
| Plump for single targetted solution | The 'hope for the best strategy'. Only worth considering where consequences of getting it wrong are low. |
| Build in margin to cope with most of probable range of outcomes | Worthwhile when it is extremely important to be able to respond to all likely outcomes but is likely to be very expensive. |
| Flexibility (e.g. multiple-use facilties) | Worthwhile when demand has to be met if it arises but there is a risk of under-utilization if and when demand falls. One way of attempting to cope with cycles. |
| Multi-stage decision-making | Design early stages so that they are compatible with a range of outcomes, with later stages being selected once uncertainty is reduced. May be appropriate for some large projects with long lead times. Some versions may be very expensive (e.g. running two versions of project at an early stage and abandoning inappropriate one at second decision stage). |

ship. However, these are more vulnerable to demand fluctuations. On the other hand, building in facilities for flexibility may be more expensive. The point is for policy-makers to think explicitly about these trade-offs, and for forecasting to provide the information necessary for making an assessment. Finally, it should always be remembered that forecasting and the consumption of forecasts take place in particular organizational and political contexts. This has implications for willingness to build in flexibility, particularly if the flexibility is to take the form of potential multiple use which crosses organizational boundaries. For example, if it were proposed that all new schools should be built with scope for conversion to alternative use when school numbers fall, then educational departments would be likely to resist the cost of flexibility being charged to them.

Does the inevitable uncertainty which results from even the most meticulous forecasts imply a need for greater frankness by governments about the uncertainty of the environments in which they operate and their ability to delivery policies to precise targets, and a greater tolerance on the part of scrutinizers of policy of the need for an acceptable margin of error where those responsible for delivering a policy have little control over the demand placed on the service? For example, the Prison Service is attacked for waste if it embarks on a prison building programme which turns out to be unnecessary (in the short term) because the number of prisoners falls, and is attacked for over-crowding if it fails to anticipate a sharp rise in the number of prisoners. (The prison problem also raises the point that the requirement of prisons to accept all those so sentenced is itself a policy-malleable variable.) Perhaps the Government should even sponsor rival forecasts or critiques of its own forecasts to help avoid the dangers of the spurious accuracy of single predictions? The study of forecasting therefore raises questions of how decisions are and should be made and not just an understanding of the techniques available.

# 9

# Objectives and Priorities

## 9.1 The centrality of objectives

### 9.1.1 OBJECTIVE SETTING IN THE POLICY PROCESS

This chapter examines the place of objectives in theories of policy-making, in the rationale of recent administrative reforms, and in policy planning. We contrast the treatment of objectives (or goals) in the literature on management, administrative reform, and policy planning with its treatment in the literature on organizational analysis, especially in view of the latter's emphasis on the problematic nature of organizational goals. We suggest a more realistic treatment of goals and objectives in analysis of, and analysis for, public policy-making. Finally, problems associated with the 'prioritization' of objectives are considered: that is, how organizations cope with the need to select between, or place in some sort of rank order, several objectives which are competing for limited resources.

Objective-setting is linked to the stages of issue search, issue filtration, issue definition, and forecasting, which we have already examined in chapters 5 to 8, as well as to options analysis, implementation, evaluation, and policy succession and termination, which we will examine in chapters 10 to 13. For example, it is difficult to identify, classify, and define an issue without relating it to the larger purposes and concerns of the organization. If no such relationship can be established, it is unlikely that the issue will get on the organization's agenda in the first place. In looking at issue definition, we emphasized that this involved a preliminary appraisal of whether the organization was capable of a policy response and, if so, with what broad aims in mind.

The link to forecasting is also obvious. Forecasting is concerned with statements of an *expected* future or, in more sophisticated approaches, of various *alternative* futures, given different assumptions about the behaviour of key variables. Objective-setting, by a natural progression from forecasting, is concerned with statements of a *desired* future.

The linkage between objectives and 'options' is less clear-cut, and depends in part on whether one is speaking prescriptively or descriptively. In managerialist prescriptions, the 'logical' progression is from definition of ends (objectives) to identification of various means (options) of achieving those ends. This is typical, for example, of the sort of thinking involved in Cost-Effectiveness Analysis or PAR (Programme Analysis and Review). Descriptively, however, it is difficult to quarrel with Lindblom and others' views that ends–means analysis is more spoken about than practised. In the real world, politicians and administrators often do little more than attempt to improve existing policies incrementally, without asking more fundamental questions about underlying objectives.

Thus objectives and objective-setting are central to much of administrative and political rhetoric, but there is room for doubt about the part they play in the daily reality of government. An awareness of this discrepancy appears to have underlain many proposals for reform in the public sector in the 1960s and early 1970s.

In this section we examine the key role of objectives in managerialist writings and in administrative reform and planning, while in section 9.2 we contrast these treatments of objectives with the emphasis in organizational analysis on the problematic nature of organizational goals.

### 9.1.2 OBJECTIVES AS A KEY ELEMENT IN MANAGERIALIST MODELS

The managerialist approach, associated with such writers as Harrison (1975) and Albanese (1975), tends to assume that the policy-maker has a high degree of control over his environment. He retains considerable freedom of choice and is able to choose a course to follow rather than being compelled to follow a course set by forces beyond his control. The policy-maker not only can, but also should, adopt a pro-active and manipulative approach. In particular, he should adopt a positive and specific approach to objective-setting. While individuals, groups, and departments will have particular interests and objectives, they can, and should, recognize and give priority to larger collective goals in terms of the overall organization or programme. Organizational or programme objectives, once set, should be pursued actively and with minimal acceptance of deviation, in the short run at least. Administrators should be able and willing to evaluate on-going programmes in terms of the programmes' original stated objectives. Finally, the effectiveness of administrators should be judged by their ability to achieve their part of programme objectives, unless external circumstances prove to be exceptionally unpredictable and non-malleable.

This approach can be contrasted with that of writers such as Lindblom and his followers within the pluralist/incrementalist tradition. Writers in the latter tradition would tend to assume that policy-makers have relatively little control over their environment and their freedom of choice or ability to control the direction of events is extremely limited. Policy-making will inevitably be more reactive than pro-active and programmes will be re-examined only when they are clearly failing to cope with problems. Any fundamental re-examination of 'ends' is exceptional and administrators tend to focus upon 'means' (i.e. existing policies and programmes). Moreover the changes made in such existing means will be incremental rather than radical. Such instinctive incrementalism is based upon an understanding of the falsity of the assumption of sufficient foreknowledge or control of events to draw up realistic and attainable long-term objectives. Moreover, there is positive value in many small 'ends–means and means–ends adjustments' since policy-making should be an experience-based, experimental, learning process keyed to limited human capabilities.

The incrementalist approach considers that organizations and programmes do not have 'objectives': only individuals and groups have (largely self-interested) objectives and what we may retrospectively dignify with the title of, say, 'corporate objectives' will actually have been the result of the interplay of many interests exercizing such influence as they can (Lindblom's 'partisan mutual adjustment'). Even when objectives have been stated for an organization or programme, they are unlikely to prove accurate predictors of what action is subsequently taken. Actual policies are liable to be adjusted in the light of experience, or a change of direction may be the result of shifts in the power-balance within the organization. To evaluate actual policy outcomes in terms of earlier stated objectives is therefore largely irrelevant and is unlikely to be attempted. Administrators will also resist attempts to judge their performance in relation to organizational or programme goals. Instead of admitting 'bad execution' they will attribute non-achievement of earlier objectives to 'bad luck' or even to a 'bad policy' in the first place.

### 9.1.3 OBJECTIVES AS A KEY ELEMENT IN ADMINISTRATIVE REFORM

An emphasis upon specification of, and commitment to, goals or objectives was central to much 'business' thinking in the 1950s and 1960s. British government was subjected to several waves of administrative reform in the 1960s and early 1970s which owed something to these business influences. Thus 'management by objectives' was adopted as 'accountable management' by the Fulton Committee on the Civil Service (Fulton Report, 1968). The Plowden Report's (1961) proposals for changes in public expenditure control were added to by experiments in 'output budgeting', PPBS (Planning, Programming, Budgeting Systems) and PAR (Programme Analysis and Review), all emphasizing the need to define and cost objectives. The corporate planning movement, as we shall see in section 9.1.4, highlighted objectives. Even organizational design adopted objectives as an aid to both organizational differentiation and integration.

This concern with objectives reached its zenith in the White Paper on *Reorganization of Central Government* in 1970 (HMSO, 1970). The Heath Government announced that it would seek to decide its 'strategic objectives', against which lesser policy proposals and programmes would be measured. The adoption of output budgeting and PAR would require 'explicit statements of the objectives of expenditure' and allow much more systematic identification and appraisal of the Government's options and their relation to these larger strategic aims. To assist the Cabinet in defining and implementing its objectives, changes would be made in the machinery of government at Cabinet, departmental, and intra-departmental levels. Thus the need for improved 'central capability' would be met by setting up the Central Policy Review Staff (CPRS) within the Cabinet Office, which would help ministers to assess 'policies and projects in relation to strategic objectives'. Next, the allocation of responsibilities to departments would result in super-departments each defined by reference to 'objectives to be attained'. Finally, the internal organization of each department would reflect the Fultonian principle of accountable management—or management by objectives (MbO).

Similar tendencies have been observable in the USA in the 1960s, notably in the PPBS movement. As defined by its arch-exponent, C. L. Schultze (1968), PPBS 'calls for careful identification and examination of goals and objectives in each major area of government activity . . . (and for) the analysis of alternatives to find the more effective means of reaching basic program objectives . . .'. (PPBS and other budgetary techniques are discussed in 10.6.) As late as 1973, President Nixon initiated a review of the objectives of twenty-one federal agencies, requiring the head of each to prepare a statement of the most important objectives he intended to achieve during the next year (see Rose, 1976b; Newland, 1976). A total listing of about 200 objectives was ultimately given presidential approval, ranging from the broad (Housing and Urban Development's 'Foster the construction of good new housing') to the specific (Environment's 'Achieve health-related air quality standards for particulated matter and sulphur dioxide in areas where violations are most severe').

### 9.1.4 OBJECTIVES AS A KEY ELEMENT IN PLANNING

Corporate planning in industry lays great emphasis upon such questions as 'what lines of business are we in?' and 'what are our objectives within each line?' (see, e.g. Argenti, 1974). The same central place is given to objectives when one examines the standard documents on corporate planning in local government. The following are extracts from the Scottish Paterson Report (1973) on the process of corporate planning:

The main steps in the process can be summarised . . . identify, measure and analyse existing needs and new (and changing) problems within the community . . . specify the desired objectives for the provision of services to meet those needs and quantify them . . . consider the various alternative means of achieving those objectives . . . produce action programmes to achieve the stated objectives . . . measure real achievement in relation to the stated objectives . . .

Similar evidence could be drawn from the plans made by individual local authorities (e.g. Strathclyde Regional Council's over-arching objectives of fighting unemployment and tackling urban deprivation), the remits of planning units in Whitehall departments and CPRS within the Cabinet Office (see section 9.1.3 above), and the many planning documents produced by the National Health Service. If the rhetoric of corporate and policy planning could be summed up in a single word, that word would surely be 'objectives'—with 'priorities' (the weighting of objectives) as runner-up.

## 9.2 Objectives as a key—but problematic—element in organizational analysis

The naïvety of much of the rhetoric about objectives by administrative reformers, policy planners, and some policy analysts becomes very clear if one is also aware of the much more searching and sceptical treatment of objectives in the literature of organizational and behavioural analysis. That literature emphasizes the problems both of *identifying* existing organizational and programme goals and of *specifying* goals for the future development of organizations and programmes. Some of these 'problematic' aspects of goals are briefly discussed below.

### 9.2.1 PROBLEMS OF IDENTIFYING ORGANIZATIONAL GOALS

There is disagreement about the methods which should be used to identify existing goals. Silverman (1970) outlines several of the principal methods in use. Often goals are imputed to organizations, but this is hardly a reliable method. A researcher might ask organizational members about their perceptions of the organization's goals. Or he could study relevant documents, such as the wording of statutes or ministerial statements. The danger of such methods is that what one is hearing or reading may only be expressions of what are regarded as 'legitimate' goals and the 'real' goals may not be revealed. The most satisfactory, but also the most difficult, method would be by observation of actual behaviour. That is, goals should be guides to action and predictors of behaviour. When claimed goals do not appear to relate to observed action and behaviour, then the investigator may hypothesize the existence of other, 'real' goals and try to identify these by further observation. In practice, goals are often diffuse, unclear, unspecific, or internally inconsistent.

### 9.2.2 ORGANIZATIONS DO NOT HAVE GOALS, ONLY PEOPLE DO

The argument here is that to talk about an organization having goals is to fall into the trap of reification, i.e. the attribution of thought, will, desires, or preferences to an abstraction of social construct such as 'the State' or ICI. Only individuals or groups of like-minded individuals can, it is argued, have thoughts, preferences, or interests to advance although, for tactical reasons, they may advance these as the 'goals of ICI, or the 'objectives of the British armed forces' and, if they are powerful enough, they may have their claims accepted as 'official' statements of organizational purpose. J. D. Thompson (1967) suggests that the goals *of* the organization are in fact the goals *for* the organization held by those in the dominant group or coalition within it.

### 9.2.3 STATED AND REAL GOALS MAY BE DIFFERENT

For many reasons, including those touched on above, the stated (or official, or legitimate) goals of an organization may not be the real goals of the organization or, at least, of powerful groups within it. E. Gross (1969) suggests that 'Two kinds of evidence are necessary before one can confidently assert that a goal is present: intentions and activities'. By 'activities' he means 'what persons in the organization are in fact observed to be doing, how they are spending their time, how resources are being allotted'. A similar distinction is made by Perrow (1961) in his distinction between *official* and *operative* goals: the latter tell us 'what the organization actually is trying to do, regardless of what the official goals say are the aims'. The gap between the two may not be understood even by members of the organization.

### 9.2.4 EVEN STATED GOALS ARE MULTIPLE AND OFTEN INCOMPATIBLE

Where there is genuine consensus on goals or a widely shared intent to achieve some outcome on behalf of an organization then stated and real goals may be the same. But even such stated or official goals are likely to be multiple rather than unitary, and only a naïve rationalist will assume that these several goals are necessarily compatible with one another. Thus prisons, for example, have several goals including the protection of society and the rehabilitation of offenders; but the former goal may impose so many restrictions upon prisoners as to make unlikely the more positive goal of achieving their rehabilitation.

### 9.2.5 GOALS MAY CHANGE OVER TIME

Even where there has been an original consensus on goals this may break down over time. Simple goals may become complex and multiple. Real goals may depart from stated goals. For a discussion of 'goal displacement, succession, multiplication, and expansion' see Etzioni (1964). The tendency to 'goal displacement' is usually deplored ('when an organization substitutes for its initial or legitimate goal some other goal for which it was not created' or 'when means become ends in themselves that displace the original ends of the organization') but some 'movement' in goals is inevitable and even desirable as circumstances alter over time (see section 9.4.10 below).

### 9.2.6 THERE ARE MANY TYPES OF GOALS

One common distinction is between ('proximate') goals which are means to some higher end and the higher (or 'ultimate') goals themselves. An influential (but often unclear and arbitrary) classification is that of Perrow (1970) in terms of societal, output, system, product, and derived goals. Simpler and perhaps more useful is the distinction made by Mohr (1973) between a *'transitive*, externally oriented, or functional goal, and a *reflexive*, internally oriented, or institutional goal'. Organizations, that is, may claim the achievement of certain social or external (transitive) goals but they must also meet the internal (reflexive) goal of institutional survival if they are to do anything: to ignore the latter is to fail to understand many aspects of real-life organizational behaviour.

The questions raised above are not meant to deny either the theoretical or the practical importance of goals. But if we are to identify current goals with some precision and to specify future goals in a realistic and operationally useful way, we must first learn to handle the concept of goals or objectives with some care and discrimination. We shall deal with this topic in the next section.

## 9.3 A realistic approach to objective-setting

The emphasis of the organizational analysis approach upon the 'problematic' aspects of goals is a useful corrective to the more naïve assumptions and aspirations of the 'neo-rationalist' administrative reform movements of the 1960s and early 1970s but it can also lead to excessive cynicism and defeatism. The concept of an organization whose members lack any sense of collective purpose or of a wholly aimless policy seems unlikely as description and unappealing as prescription. Thus, while recognizing the many problems involved—intellectual, value-related, and practical problems—we believe there is a strong case for regarding objective-setting as an important activity within the larger policy process and one which can be improved by making it more overt, systematic, and realistic. Objectives have their uses and are worth rescuing from both over-optimistic planners and over-pessimistic sociologists.

Objectives which are reasonably specific and widely understood can give a sense of purpose and direction to an organization and to its various policies and related programmes. While groups within the organization will undoubtedly develop their own interests and goals, there will usually be quite widespread acceptance, no matter how grudging in some cases, that priority has to be given to superordinate objectives if the larger organization is to survive and flourish. To that extent, objectives will provide a measure of integration and unity. From the perspective of the organization's leaders, the existence of such super-ordinate goals will legitimate and support attempts to monitor and control subsequent performance. They may also act as a motivating device, since groups and individuals often derive satisfaction from being seen to contribute to larger organizational or programmatic purposes.

Anyone who is concerned with formulating, implementing, or evaluating a public policy is likely to benefit from asking two key questions. What are we trying to do? How will we know when we've done it? Moreover, these are questions which have to be asked not once but repeatedly as the policy develops, since objectives and associated standards of performance may alter over time because of changes within, or external to, the policy and the responsible organization. If stated objectives have ceased to be predictors of, or guides to, action then current activities or earlier statements of intent, or both, are in need of review. Such a review may help to revitalize a policy. It is also possible, of course, that asking such questions may lead to the un-pleasant recognition that an entire policy or particular programme is no longer justifiable and should be terminated.

Thus objectives are worth rescuing from their denigrators. But they also need to be defended on occasion from their supporters. At its most prescriptive and rationalistic, the managerial/planning approach emphasizes the need to define objectives at all levels and in great detail. Objectives, it is said, should be specific and quantified, compatible and mutually supportive, and linked in a 'hierarchy' or systematic progres-sion, so that personal objectives can be seen to contribute to larger group and unit objectives which in turn feed into departmental and corporate objectives.

Such a prescription is not particularly attractive, in that it would require a monolithic and highly centralized organization. It also seems unrealistic in the light of most findings about behaviour in actual organizations. Where attempts have been made, as in various PPBS and planning initiatives, to develop full-blown hierarchies of objectives they have often collapsed within a few months or years under the sheer weight of paperwork and time-consuming procedures involved.

Our approach is more selective and, we hope, more realistic. Con-stantly to fret about objectives is a formula for paralysis. However, there is value in occasional introspection, as when key members of an organization review their activities and try to agree some linked goals and priorities for the future. At various points in the life-cycle of a programme, too, it is useful to ask where it is going and why.

Thus in the next section we offer a simple and relatively non-jargonized 'checklist' of ten questions which might from time to time be asked (preferably by themselves) of the leaders of an organization or programme.

## 9.4 A checklist of questions about objectives

### 9.4.1 WHERE ARE YOU NOW?

Before deciding on a change of direction, it helps if a traveller has a map or other means of knowing accurately where he is now. The equivalent of a map in policy-making may be a 'position statement'. For many local authorities this is the first step in the corporate planning process, defined in one official report (Paterson, 1973) as 'the production of a document or series of documents summarising the authority's existing policies and activities'. A typical position statement by a Scottish District Council sets out broad 'programme areas' (such as Housing, Arts, and Recreation, Community Health), then identifies more specific 'programmes' within those 'areas' (such as House Letting or Improvement of Housing Stock), and finally 'activities' within those 'programmes' (such as Housing Waiting Lists or Caretaking in Multi-Storey Flats). These areas, programmes, and activities are then costed, using 'output budgeting' techniques, so that councillors can more readily see how they are actually deploying their resources among various competing ends. The findings of such statements are often received with disbelief, or at least surprise, since what an organization thinks it is doing is often very different from what it is actually doing as measured by the use of resources.

There is an obvious overlap here with the familiar distinction between stated and real goals (see 9.2.3 above). An alternative to position statements might be for an organization's leaders to hire an external consultant to compare actual resource-consuming activities with stated intentions and priorities. Uninvited critiques may, of course, be more outspoken and an excellent example is the study by Lodge and Blackstone (1982) of the extent to which post-war governments have fulfilled their stated commitment to greater educational equality. Their case-studies of nursery education ('one of the first items to suffer when cuts are imposed'), raising of the school leaving age ('promised in 1944 and achieved in 1973'), positive discrimination, abolition of selection at eleven, and developments in higher education all add up to an indictment of both the will and the capacity of politicians and officials to pursue, let alone achieve, their stated ends. For any reforming government, Lodge and Blackstone's chastening findings would provide a basis from which to consider future educational priorities and what would be needed to attain them.

### 9.4.2 WHERE DO YOU WANT TO BE?

A position statement may drive the leaders of an organization to look for programmes and policies closer to their original values and objectives. In business policy circles this process is often called 'gap analysis'. It is stimulated by awareness that there is 'a gap between the existing state of affairs and some desired state' (Steiner and Miner, 1982) which in turn leads to analysis of causes and to a search for new or improved policies to close the gap. In effect, the questions asked of the organization's managers at this stage are: 'Now that you know where you are, is it where you thought you were? Is it where you wanted to be? If not, where *do* you want to be and how will you get there?'

### 9.4.3 WHAT'S STOPPING YOU?

To continue this one-sided discussion, one might go on to ask of the managers: 'Now that you know where you want to be, what's stopping you getting there?' That is, the identification of constraints upon intended action or impediments to a desired line of advance is an integral part of the goal-setting process. Some constraints will be within the organization itself while others will be in the organization's external environment.

### 9.4.4 WHAT DO YOU NEED FROM OTHER AGENCIES?

'The most salient aspect of an organization's environment [is] . . . other organizations' (Perrow, 1970). This is obviously true of business organizations in a competitive market, but modern public sector studies also emphasize the importance of inter-organizational and, especially, intergovernmental relations in determining how far any single agency, such as a local authority, can pursue its own objectives. This explains why local authority corporate plans often refer at length to actions required of central government agencies or of other local authorities. At their most cynical, such references constitute a form of public pressure upon other organizations or may even set them up as potential scapegoats for any subsequent failure by the local authority to achieve its own objectives. But local councils are often genuinely dependent upon the co-operation or compliance of other agencies for the success of their plans. If the required actions are not forthcoming the council will either have to modify its goals or seek new ways of manipulating the inter-organizational network to its own ends. References to what is required of other agencies are, then, a valid and useful aspect of objective-setting—provided that the next question on our checklist is also posed.

### 9.4.5 WHAT IS REQUIRED OF WHOM IN YOUR OWN AGENCY?

It is convenient but also dangerous to talk in terms of 'the organization' and its objectives. Any sizeable organization is likely to be a very complex and imperfectly integrated collection of different specialisms, interests, and outlooks. It will often be difficult to agree or to impose a set of objectives for the organization as a whole and even more difficult to ensure that these objectives are actually and effectively pursued by the organization's component parts. Without seeking to introduce an elaborate goals hierarchy, it does seem essential to clarify who within the organization has to do what, when and how, if agreed goals are to be achieved. Moreover, such delegated tasks need frequent monitoring, clarification, and reinforcement over time. So the questions to top management at this point in the checklist are: 'Within your own agency, what actions are required if your objectives are to be achieved? Required of whom, at what levels? Do they know? How do you know they know?'

### 9.4.6 HOW WILL YOU HANDLE MULTIPLE OBJECTIVES?

Organizations and even programmes rarely have a single objective. The existence of multiple objectives is neither surprising nor necessarily a problem. However, managers should again be asked some pertinent questions.

One question is about different types of objectives. Some of the standard distinctions have been outlined at section 9.2.6 above. Thus it is worth identifying the 'ultimate' goals of the organization (or programme) as a whole as opposed to 'proximate' goals which are means to those larger ends. Another distinction is between 'transitive' (externally oriented) and 'reflexive' (internally oriented) objectives. The cruciality of some goals is emphasized by MbO theorists in the concept of 'Key Results Analysis' (KRA). KRA is usually applied to the individual manager but can be extended to the organization as a whole and the identification of those 'key' objectives which must be achieved if its overall mission is to be fulfilled.

Top management must be aware of actual or potential incompatibility between multiple objectives. This may arise from divergence between official goals of the organization as a whole and the unofficial goals of groups within it. But there may be incompatibility between official goals as well. Thus managers, in examining from time to time the multiple objectives of the organization (or programme), must be able to categorize goals as compatible or incompatible, complementary or competing, interacting or independent of one another, and so on.

Finally, there are usually more objectives than there are resources to pursue all of them adequately. Thus the most important decisions that the leaders of an organization have to make are choices among competing objectives. The 'prioritization' problem is so important, however, that it is dealt with at length in section 9.5 below.

### 9.4.7 WHAT WILL YOU REGARD AS 'SUCCESS'?

The questions to managers at this point are: 'Now you've decided what are the really important things you have to do, how will you know when you've *done* them? What will you regard as 'success'? Have you told the other people involved, such as your colleagues—or your clients? Have you thought who your 'clients' are? Might they have their own, possibly quite different, definition of your success or lack of it?' These questions need little elaboration at this stage (see chapter 12 on evaluation), but their importance should not be underestimated, since there are many recent examples of legislation where it is difficult to obtain any clear view of what success would look like—in race relations, perhaps, or in enterprise zones.

Success should be defined at a level above that of minimally acceptable performance. On the other hand, it is rarely useful to set some ideal standard which is likely to be self-defeating. The point is well illustrated by White (1979) in his discussion of 'How polluted are we— and how polluted do we want to be?' He suggests that over-ambitious campaigns for pristine pure rivers or zero pollution of food supplies create an 'economic credibility gap' and argues for a more modest and pragmatic approach, such as 'water quality objectives' which can be negotiated on a flexible case-by-case basis.

## 9.4.8 SHOULD SUCCESS BE QUANTIFIED?

The typical MbO manual emphasizes the need to have performance standards' or other indicators of success which are not only specific but also quantified. In some areas of governmental activity such quantification is feasible and appropriate but in other areas it is difficult and may even be dangerous—in the sense that an emphasis upon numbers may drive out non-quantifiable but important considerations. Ken (1976) gives the example of targets which were set for the processing of certain benefit claims, in terms of a reduced 'turn-round' period. While this target was achieved, subsequent investigation showed claims-clerks tending either to ride roughshod over considerations of fairness and equity or resorting to the popular but expensive slogan of 'when in doubt, pay out'. Also quantification is more relevant to administrative activities than to the assessment of policy outcomes. Thus we tend to be rather heretical in this area and, while emphasizing the need to define success, do not accept that success should always be quantified.

## 9.4.9 ON WHAT CONDITIONS IS SUCCESS CONTINGENT?

Any policy incorporates a theory of cause and effect: that is, a postulate that if $X$ is done now, $Y$ will follow (Pressman and Wildavsky, 1973). In practice, the expected sequence may not occur for one or more of the following reasons. First, $X$ may not be effectively performed, so that $Y$ does not follow: this is a failure of execution. Secondly, $X$ may be carried out in full but the expected effect, namely $Y$, does not occur: this is probably a failure of policy-making, in that the policy was based upon a fallacious theory of cause and effect. Thirdly, $Y$ may not follow $X$ because of unpredicted and adverse external circumstances: that is, neither bad execution nor bad policy but sheer bad luck has caused the failure. The last case obviously relates back to some of the points made at 9.4.3 (about external constraints) and 9.4.4 (concerning actions required of other agencies). The failure of the Labour Government's 'National Plan' of 1965, with its objective of achieving 5 per cent growth per annum over five years, was an interesting example of all three causes of failure—an inadequate theory of economic growth in an open economy, irresolute execution, and a hostile environment.

It is important that the assumptions and conditions upon which policy-making and goal-setting are based should be considered and, where possible, tested before large-scale resources are committed. Managers at any level should learn to ask the following questions:

'Have you thought through the assumptions on which your policy rests and, in particular, have you identified the crucial conditions which will have to be met if your objectives are to be achieved? How certain or uncertain is it that these conditions will apply in reality? What will you do if they don't?' This brings us to our final question on the checklist.

### 9.4.10 WHAT WILL YOU DO IF OBJECTIVES ARE NOT ACHIEVED?

As we shall argue in chapter 12, it is essential that policies should be monitored and performance compared against expectations. This should provide an early warning about the sort of failures described above and may allow of remedial adjustments to the policy or its implementation. But the possibility of failure should be accepted from the start and managers should be asked the following questions: 'What will you do if objectives are not being achieved (i.e. performance is ineffective) or are being achieved but at much greater cost than you expected (i.e. performance is effective but inefficient)?' Clues to possible action can be derived from the conditions identified at 9.4.9. Thus, if failure seems traceable to poor execution, attempts can be made to improve implementation and bring performance back on schedule. If, however, the problem appears to be an invalid policy or adverse external circumstances, then it will be necessary to adjust the policy and its objectives as being unrealistic.

The conditional nature of all objectives makes it essential to regard plans as provisional and it may be advisable to have alternative 'contingency plans' available. But, while this is easy to say, there are often considerable psychological and political difficulties involved. In particular, administrators and politicians appear to dislike any public adjustment—especially downward adjustment—of targets and objectives. Yet we must endorse Albanese's view that 'Goals are not static and inflexible guides to behaviour. Rather they are dynamic guides that respond to experience and to forces inside and outside the organization' (Albanese, 1975).

If objectives are to be operationally useful, then, they must be robust rather than rigid, and capable of being adjusted without losing their ability to influence action.

### 9.5 Prioritization of objectives

We have already noted the problem of 'multiple objectives' within policies or agencies, mainly in terms of the potential for confusion created by incompatible or contradictory objectives. Now we must examine the difficult problem of multiple objectives which may be compatible but are seen as competing. That is, how do the members of organizations cope with the need to select among, or place in some kind of rank order, several objectives which are all desirable but which cannot all be given sufficient resources from the same limited pool? Such difficult choices are endemic to the present situation of cutbacks in public spending when most agencies face 'hard choices for hard times' (Wright, 1980; Hood and Wright, 1981), but they are never absent from government.

Our governors often seem to find it difficult to make choices since almost any choice tends to disappoint some interests and voters. The *will* to choose is important, then, but may be lacking—especially among elected politicians. Equally important is the *power* not only to choose but also to have one's choice prevail. This in turn depends upon a combination of legitimacy (the perceived right to choose on behalf of others) and some control over the real levers (social, economic, or, in the last resort, coercive levers) by which influence can be exerted. Finally governors need the technical *capacity* to choose, which in turn may be subdivided into possession of adequate data, criteria (or values), procedures, and machinery, including staff with the appropriate qualities and skills. The study of policy analysis is mainly concerned with attempts to improve 'capacity' but it would be foolish to ignore the other aspects, since policy advice on priorities is useless unless it is consumed by politicians who have both the will and the power to make choices.

Indeed, *who* is given the task of determining priorities will to a large extent predetermine the other aspects of priority-setting, namely the selection of *criteria* for determining priorities, the *dimensions of choice* in which the priorities are expressed (e.g. by geographical area or type of service), the *type of resource* in which allocations are denominated (e.g. money, manpower quotas), and the *mechanisms* by which priorities are actually implemented and enforced (if indeed priorities are in practice implemented). For example, if professionals are given a big say in determining priorities they will tend to use professional or pseudo-professional criteria, and if they have an important role in the administration of policy they may be able to subvert or ignore statements of priorities determined from outside, as has happened in the National Health Service (see Haywood and Elcock, 1982). The decision (or failure to take a decision) about who will determine the criteria for priorities is very much a metapolicymaking activity (Dror, 1968).

We shall list a number of types of criteria for determining priorities and it will be seen that some of these criteria can be discussed in reasonably factual, objective, or technical terms; others will involve an element of subjectivity and several are almost entirely matters of political judgement. Information relevant to a number of aspects of these types of criteria should already have been generated at the issue definition stage (see chapter 7):

1. *Intrinsic criteria*. The extent to which each potential opportunity is ripe for development (e.g. fields of scientific research and development) or each problem is seen as susceptible to treatment (e.g. street crime versus house burglaries). In part this may be a question of 'professional judgement', but there is also a political dimension since one must ask 'developable or treatable at what cost?'

2. *Demand*. The extent to which a user or customer (whether private or public sector) is willing to pay for a service. A notable British example is the 'market' principle associated with the Rothschild Report (1971), with its espousal of the customer/contractor relationship, which said that a much more significant proportion of funding for government research and development should be derived from the willingness of a user or customer to pay for the research.

3. *Need.* the concept of 'need' is often quoted in the context of priority-setting in the social services, but Lind and Wiseman (1978) demonstrate the many meanings which can be given to this term. Are we talking about patients' 'felt need', articulated 'demand' for services, or need as defined by some group such as clinicians, or civil servants, or politicians? A more radical view would argue that, since the definition of 'need' cannot be reduced to statistical indicators and must involve ethical and social judgements, a larger role should be played in decision-making about medical priorities by public opinion, community groups, and, say, consumer surveys. Bearing these points in mind, there are several criteria which can be considered under the heading of need: (*a*) the *prevalence* of various conditions or problems (e.g. street crime versus house burglaries), which can to some extent be measured objectively;

(*b*) the *severity* of the impact of each of these problems (e.g. the disabling nature of different diseases): such assessments are often as much subjective as objective and may depend in part upon (c) and (d);

(*c*) *who* is affected: how many and how much sympathy do they attract?;

(*d*) the amount of *political* concern about each problem and support for those affected.

4. *Net social or economic benefit*. In its most rigorous form, as reflected in cost-benefit analysis (CBA), discussed at 10.6.3, this type of criterion seeks to compare the stream of costs (both financial and social) with the stream of benefits over time. In a looser sense, ministers of science and technology in Britain in the 1960s tried to move the criteria for funding R. & D. away from the 'intrinsic' criteria used until then (see 1 above) to external or 'extrinsic' criteria and to concentrate resources upon selected fields of R. & D. which, it was hoped, would have exceptionally high rates of social and economic return to the nation. In practice, great problems were encountered both in identifying fields for preference and in implementing such preferences (but see Gunn, 1966; Weinberg, 1963). In principle, analysts can contribute to the formulation of criteria and their application to questions of relative priority in resource allocation.

Again, it can be seen that the selection of which type of criterion to employ in setting priorities is itself a high-order analytical decision, which all too often is allowed to be taken by default.

The issue of criteria obviously overlaps with, but is not necessarily identical to, the issue of the number of *dimensions of choice* within which relative priorities can be expressed in operational terms. The problem for decision-makers is the multiplicity of dimensions which have to be considered. For example, priorities for the health service in Britain can be expressed along at least six dimensions (Lind and Wiseman, 1978):

(1) between geographical areas (see the useful but less than con-clusive reports of the English Resource Allocation Working Party (RAWP) and the Scottish Health Authorities Revenue Equalisa-tion (SHARE)) (DHSS, 1976; SHHD, 1977);

(2) between population groups (occupational groups, social class groups, various 'at risk' and 'multiply deprived' groups, etc.);

(3) between disease and dependency groups (the elderly, mentally ill, cancer sufferers, etc.: but should a group be given preference because it is sicker, or because it is facing long-term care and therefore requires the best conditions possible, or because it has better prospects of being effectively 'treatable'?);

(4) between different service or care activities (with particular regard being given to 'quantity, quality, effectiveness, and efficiency' in deciding priorities between, say, in-patient and out-patient hospital services);

(5) between different forms of intervention (for example, giving more attention to prevention rather than cure);

(6) between different agencies (within the NHS but also extending to external agencies such as social work departments and community or voluntary organizations).

These dimensions are obviously inter-dependent: for example, giving priority to a particular form of service provision such as long-stay facilities would tend to benefit particular disease and dependency groups. But most attention has been focused on dimensions (1) and (3), partly because they seem the most direct points of entry to questions about priorities, and partly because they appear to offer the best hope of developing commensurable indicators for comparison.

Even when choices are made along these dimensions the questions arise of the *type of resource* in which the allocation determined by the priorities is to be made and the *mechanisms* for carrying out and enforcing the priorities. Money is the most obvious type of resource in which to denominate priorities, but the link between budget categories and dimensions of choice may be weak. Where priorities are expressed between geographical areas or between different agencies (the first and sixth dimensions of choice above) then budget allocations are fully adequate mechanisms for specifying and enforcing priorities. However, for other dimensions of choice (e.g. between population groups), existing budget categories may be irrelevant, and even retrospective information about resource allocation among priority groups may be poor. *De facto* priorities may continue to be set by choices made at the point of delivery (e.g. by doctors, social workers). Consideration might be given to redesigning budget categories, and by implication management responsibility for resource allocation, to conform more closely to the dimensions along which priorities have been chosen (see also the discussion of output budgeting in 10.6.2). However, where individual work units or even individual members of staff are engaged in tasks which straddle priority groups, budget allocations to priorities are inevitably notional.

In cases where priorities require specialized staff, it may be appropriate to specify priorities in the form of manpower targets, perhaps in conjunction with money allocations. However, through such devices as contracting out and dilution of skills, priorities specified in manpower terms are easily subverted.

Even when priorities are denominated in money or manpower budgets, it is far from inevitable that these priorities will actually be followed through. The annual Public Expenditure White Paper sets out British central government's priorities between and within broad areas of public expenditure as a whole. However, detailed spending decisions on many of these are the responsibility of local authorities and other bodies (which may have their own sets of priorities), and the bulk of central government funds to local authorities is in the form of a block grant not allocated to particular programmes. Even where specific grants are made available to promote increased spending on a particular priority, it may be difficult to ensure that the money is actually used as additional rather than replacement funding.

Of course, local authority spending allocations are made within a framework of a large quantity of permitting and mandating legislation, but individually and collectively such laws are rarely expressed in such detail as to amount to statements of priorities. Exhortation in, for example, government circulars, may be a useful way of communicating priorities, particularly if these priorities are agreed between local authorities and central government, but such circulars are not in any sense self-enforcing.

Central government departments themselves frequently fail to spend according to the priorities expressed in the White Paper, indicating problems of maintaining priorities in the context of external change, lack of political will in sticking to priorities, and practical administrative problems in ensuring that priorities are actually reflected in the pattern of policy outputs.

It is clear that moving from statements of priorities along particular dimensions, through the allocation of resources, to ensuring that priorities are actually reflected in the policy outputs produced, is a process that requires careful thought. The appropriate mechanisms (e.g. redesigning budget categories, new legal requirements, negotiations) are likely to vary for different policies and different types of dimensions along which priorities can be expressed. Policies delivered in the form of a service rather than goods or cash can cause particular problems, as can expressions of priorities which cross-cut existing organizational and budget boundaries.

Also requiring consideration is the time-span of changing allocations where desired priorities differ from the current allocation. In the English health service, reallocation between regions has been done at the margins to try to avoid any region actually becoming worse off; however, at a time of low growth this means that resource allocation continues to reflect the historical legacy as much as it does stated priorities.

Following through on priorities should not be seen as a simple problem of enforcement, and it makes sense to involve implementers and possibly clients in priority-setting exercises. However, the question of enforcement cannot simply be ignored, otherwise there is a danger that the priorities themselves may be ignored. Existing methods of resource allocation and monitoring may need to be reconsidered in the light of their suitability for promoting the types of priorities chosen. However, the question of following through priorities in practice also raises broad questions about implementation, which is the subject of chapter 11.

Finally, it is important to stress again that priority-setting is not simply about analysis but about choices actually taken by decision-makers. Analysis should be designed to assist that task, not to replace it. Thus we share Lind and Wiseman's (1978) lack of enthusiasm about approaches to priority-setting which depend heavily upon statistical standards and norms, since these often disguise largely unargued assumptions and values and tend to concentrate on what is measurable (e.g. numbers of beds) rather than what is important (e.g. quality of medical care). They are also critical of the 'health status index' approach, which would 'reduce the different dimensions of ill health to a single scale measure', given problems about the reliability and weighting of data and even a lack of agreement about what constitutes 'health'.

Analysis for priority-setting is most likely to be useful when it does not rely on a purely mechanistic approach but is a process of dialogue between analysts and decision-makers, with the analyst assisting the decision-maker to make explicit choices about criteria, dimensions of choice, and mechanisms of allocation, and setting out information on the likely effects of choices.

# 10

# Options Analysis

## 10.1 What is involved in options analysis?

Selection from a number of options is at the heart of both politics and policy analysis. The applicability of more analytical or 'objective' methods of assessing options may be quite limited, since many issues are so dominated by political or value-laden considerations that there is little scope for analytical inputs (see chapter 6 on issue filtration).

Where scope does exist for a more analytical approach, what are the various subprocesses involved?: (1) identify readily available options and consider whether additional, less obvious options should be generated; (2) define options carefully; (3) appraise and compare them, using a wide range of criteria (political as well as technical) and analytical techniques; (4) present a prefered option or a small number of feasible options to the decision-maker. In the following sections we will look at the potentially applicable techniques as well as the constraints at each stage.

## 10.2 Identifying and generating options

By 'identifying' options we mean the relatively passive or reactive process by which readily available options or those which have 'backers' within the organization are collected for appraisal and comparison. By 'generating' options we mean the more active search for options which do not have existing backers and may not even by known to the organization.

The process by which options are identified and generated is one of the crucial missing links in policy analysis. As we shall see in 10.5–10.6, there are many techniques available to assist the decision-maker to appraise options. But where do these options come from? Are many options considered or only a few? Who decides which options are considered and by what means?

There seems to be a fairly widespread assumption that the range of alternative solutions considered by policy-makers is typically very narrow. The only options which reach the agenda may be those which have influential supporters within the organization. Also most organizations develop their own 'conventional wisdom' and many options are therefore almost literally 'unthinkable'. Certain options will be associated with particular personalities. Groups inside and outside the organization may seek to protect their position by suppressing certain options. Finally, key members of the organization will simply be ignorant of some options.

There is, however, little point in becoming so alarmed by such observations (or allegations) that one looks to ideal-typical formulae for assistance. The 'pure rationality' approach would involve generating all conceivable options and considering each in great detail, and this would clearly be impossible and self-defeating in most practical situations (see 4.2). On the other hand, token or desultory measures to improve options-identification are likely to be inadequate.

Options generation is regarded by Herbert Simon (1976, 263–5) as an activity which requires creative rather than mechanically rational thinking. Dror, too, argues that 'insofar as novel alternatives must be found, rationality can play only a limited though important role' (Dror, 1968, 179). The most promising ways of improving creativity would seem to be to recruit persons capable of original thinking and to provide an organizational climate which supports rather than suppresses such thinking.

Suitable procedures can also help and one of these has already been discussed in 5.6.5 and 8.5.2, namely 'brainstorming'. As with its use in issue search and forecasting, the initial stage of brainstorming would involve a group of people suggesting a large number of possible options in a short time, without any attempt at that stage being made to raise questions of feasibility, desirability, or side-effects. Only after the list of ideas is generated is any attempt made to winnow out those ideas which are worth further definition and appraisal (see Rawlinson, 1981; Argenti, 1969). Brainstorming is most likely to be effective when it is accepted that the problem is an important one, and there is scope for novel solutions, and that inputs are required from several sources and specialisms. It is, however, only a procedure and there is no guarantee that the ideas which participants bring to it will be useful or original.

Another source of options is that public bodies may borrow from industrial experience or from one another. The UK Government can learn from the experience of one of its component countries (e.g. from Scottish procedures for initiating prosecutions or for dealing with young offenders) or from foreign experience (e.g. Swedish methods of dealing with maladministration). Care must be taken with such borrowing, since the conditions which make the practice successful in one country may not exist in another.

Another source of social innovation is scientific and technological advance. For example, a breakthrough in nuclear fusion technology could transform a country's energy policy options. Advances in computer-based technology have already given us the potential not only to handle but also, perhaps, to generate more options. Dror (1968, 179) suggests that: 'In a few relatively simple cases, such as some military problems, pure rationality techniques can identify new alternatives, for example, by programming computers to randomly synthesize new alternatives and to learn from feedback.'

## 10.3 Defining options

Options vary greatly in their characteristics and contexts, the types of data and criteria seen as relevant, and the extent to which analytical techniques seem applicable to appraising and choosing between them. For example, decisions among options vary in terms of whether they require the selection of a particular point on a *continuous* range (e.g. the exact size of budgeting allocation) or one or more of a number of *discrete* options, some of which may be mutually exclusive. Where the choice is from a continuous range of options, the relationship between the decision variable (e.g. size of budget, number of staff) may not be a straight-line one. In certain parts of the range a choice in the decision variable may make little or no (or even a perverse) difference. For example, evidence suggests that differences in teacher–pupil ratios in a limited range on either side of the current average make little or no difference to educational outputs; however, we would expect important effects from ratios of 1:4 or 1:50. With a continuous range of options it is particularly important to identify any points of discontinuity in the relationship between decision variables and policy outputs. Any constraints that limit the feasible range of options should be identified.

Some of the decision-aiding techniques described in section 10.5 operate only on discrete options, but they can still be applied by grouping parts of a continuous range. Clearly, it makes sense for this to be done in such a way as to highlight the effects of any discontinuities.

Some sets of options will involve political choices, usually on relatively soft data, such as: (1) spending on defence vs. spending on welfare services; (2) ways of dealing with the problems of Northern Ireland; and (3) various possible modes of devolution to Wales and Scotland. More technical choices include those requiring the exercise of professional judgement, such as clinical decisions about various ways of treating kidney disease. They also include choices which can be reduced to routine, quantitative, formula-style solutions, such as deciding which type and size of computer would best meet the requirements of an organization.

From the policy analyst's point of view (see chapter 6 on 'Issue Filtration') the 'best' type of options exercise is one which does not fall wholly within either the political or the technical category but is multi-factoral, including some factors which are relatively 'soft' and others which are relatively 'hard'. However, he may be able to contribute even to very technical issues by opening the discussion out a little: e.g. decisions about treatment of kidney disease have cost (including 'opportunity cost') as well as clinical dimensions and, less obviously, various consequences for the patient's domestic circumstances and the welfare of his family. Equally, the policy analyst can bring a degree of rigour, precision, and objectivity to the discussion of even highly political options. See, for example, Rose (1976d) on Northern Ireland, and Gunn and Lindley (1977) on devolution.

One obvious question for the analyst is about the feasibility of an option. Feasibility includes purely technical considerations: for example, if a bridge over a Scottish estuary is contemplated as an alternative to a ferry service, has a sufficiently rigorous geological survey been done to establish whether the estuary floor will support the bridge's piers? Even such technical questions rarely allow of a simple yes/no response, since the next question must be 'feasible at what cost and to whom?' For example, how expensive would it be to provide the piers of the estuary bridge with secure foundations? If this and other costs were to be very high, might this suggest the need to charge tolls to users of the bridge? An analyst would also want to consider 'opportunity cost'; for example, would building the bridge mean that other civil engineering projects competing for the same funds would be postponed or even lost, and if so, how serious would these lost opportunities be—and again, serious for whom?

An option may be feasible in technical and economic terms but non-implementable on other, usually political grounds (see chapter 11). Implementability has to be considered at several levels. For example, will the option require legislation and, if so, will the Bill have sufficient support? Once enacted, can it be effectively executed, or will the problems of securing co-operation from powerful interests or from other public agencies obstruct implementation?

Most of the remaining questions are about benefits, or, more broadly, about consequences. Briefly, the analyst might ask: (a) what benefits or consequences would follow from adoption of this option? (b) who would be the beneficiaries? (c) would there be any losers and, if so, who? (d) how certain or uncertain are the assumptions which have been made about both costs and benefits? Thus, in the case of the estuary bridge, questions should be asked about, for example, benefits in terms of shorter journey times, consequences (both positive and negative) for the distribution of population and industry, and the reliability of forecasts about the volume of traffic likely to use the bridge as well as any transitional costs arising from disruption during the construction period.

Finally, it is important to consider the timing implications of each option. Do options vary in terms of the time at which they can be commenced? Are there variations in the total time taken to complete each option? Would the option allow for partial utilization before the project was completed (possibly in the case of a road-widening but not in the case of a bridge!).

## 10.4 Appraising and comparing options

There are many ways of appraising and choosing among options. They may be appraised in political terms and a choice made by vote—in committee, in the legislature, or by referendum (as in the case of the devolution option in·1979). Even a political decision can be informed and perhaps influenced by prior analysis. Or a decision may be made on more technical grounds by experts and administrators, either directly or indirectly by influencing their political 'masters'. If there is a separate role for the policy analyst, it is not that of making the final choice but rather that of helping politicians and their advisers by ensuring that (i) sufficient options are generated, (ii) the options are defined as precisely as possible, (iii) the pros and cons of each option are made clear, and (iv) such techniques as are available to assist the process of choice are used to best effect.

Thus we come to that aspect of options analysis with which many text books on 'decision theory' both begin and end, namely methods—especially 'quantitative methods'—and specialized techniques. It should be obvious by now that we regard the process of identifying and deciding among options as involving much more than mastery of a technique or even a battery of techniques such as cost-benefit analysis or linear programming. These techniques do not or certainly should not 'make' decisions. Many have severe deficiences in the range of relevant factors which they can process or take into account. They can, at best, assist decision-makers and perhaps persuade them to adopt a more systematic approach to identifying relevant criteria and data and to testing assumptions about the probabilities of events and outcomes.

The need to deal in probabilities and to assess the degree of risk and uncertainty associated with particular options brings us to an important aspect of the policy-making process. Strictly speaking, we should distinguish between *risk* and *uncertainty*:

Risk assessment involves the analysis of a large amount of data on past occurrences of a series of events, which enables probabilities of occurrences to be assigned to the same events in the future . . . Uncertainty, on the other hand, usually means an ignorance of the exact probability distribution for future events, or even of the nature of the future events themselves. (Carley, 1980, 115).

In most models of 'perfect rationality' the policy-maker is assumed to have perfect knowledge not only of his options but also of their outcomes. In the real world, however, no such perfect knowledge exists and we sometimes have to live with uncertain futures and subjective assessments of probability. Policy-makers vary in their willingness to accept risk. One who is *risk averse* will place a premium on avoiding the worst possible case or cases. Another who is *risk seeking* will choose the option with the highest possible pay-off, even if the events which would lead to that option occurring have a very low probability. However, it is not only differences in the personalities of decision-makers which influence the readiness to take risks; another important factor is, or should be, the nature of the decision itself—and the consequences of getting it wrong.

In briefly examining various techniques, we shall divide them into two very broad categories: (1) operation research and decision analysis (considered in 10.5) and (2) economic, financial, and budgetary analysis (considered in 10.6).

## 10.5 Operational research and decision analysis techniques

This section introduces a number of techniques which may assist decision-makers to select the option which best meets their objectives. Some of these are specifically designed to cope with priorities among multiple and even conflicting objectives in the context of considerable uncertainty about future events which might effect policy outcomes. The different decision contexts in which each technique is potentially applicable are shown in Table 10.1. A number of practical applications of operations research (OR) techniques to local authority problems in Britain are described in Pinkus and Dixon (1981), while a good introductory guide to the potential relevance of decision analysis is a British Civil Service College Handbook (Chapman, 1981).

### 10.5.1 LINEAR PROGRAMMING

Linear programming is an operational research technique for allocating resources between products (or objectives) when the products or objectives require the same resources and the supplies of these resources are strictly limited. The products or objectives are weighted, either to produce a minimum cost or maximum benefit or reflecting an explicit value judgement about relative priorities. These products or objectives are referred to as the control or decision variables, and the expression containing them is known as the objective function. This function has to be maximized (or minimized as appropriate) subject to constraints. The optimal solution can then be calculated mathematically using a method which can readily be carried out by computer. There may be no feasible solution given the objective function and the constraints specified, indicating a need to respecify objectives or priorities, or to find some means of relaxing one or more constraints. Linear programming assumes full knowledge of constraints and applies only where relationships are linear, i.e. can be represented by a straight line. For an introduction to linear programming and potential applications to public policy, see Stokey and Zeckhauser (1978, ch. 11).

### 10.5.2 DYNAMIC PROGRAMMING

Dynamic programming consists of a set of computational procedures to find the optimal policy in complex sequential decision problems. Such

TABLE 10.1 *The characteristics of decision-aiding techniques*

| Technique | Decision context | Copes with risk or uncertainty? | Allows different risk preferences? |
|---|---|---|---|
| Linear programming | Single strategic decision; continuous options | No (though interactive packages make adjustment of constraints and trade-offs possible) | N/a |
| Dynamic programming | Decision-rule for series of linked decisions; discrete (though quasi-continuous) options | Yes. Sensitivity analysis possible for some problems; also learning procedures where initial information is poor and procedures to handle random effects | Potentially |
| Pay-off matrix | Decision at single point in time amongst discrete options | Yes | Yes, highly explicitly |
| Decision tree | Series of interrelated decisions over time among discrete options | Yes | Yes, highly explicitly |
| Risk analysis | Large, innovatory project | Yes, central concern | Yes |
| Queuing theory | Single or varying allocation of service delivery patterns; continuous options | Yes | Yes |
| Inventory models | Guidelines for stock levels and reordering decisions; continuous options | Yes | Yes |

TABLE 10.1 *cont.*

| Multiple objectives or values allowed? | Commensurability required? | Potential policy relevance |
| --- | --- | --- |
| Yes, in form of product mix and constraints | Partial | Determination of optimum mix of policy outputs |
| Yes, in form of product mix and constraints | Partial | Policy problems which can be broken down into a chain of decisions with later decisions dependent on earlier choices |
| Yes | Trade-offs must be specified if no dominant strategy | Any policy decision taken at single point in time amongst discrete options |
| Yes | Trade-offs must be specified if no dominant strategy | Policy problems which can be broken down into a chain of decisions with later decisions dependent on earlier choices |
| Focus on risk; risk and cost both possible objectives; implicit original policy objective | Interactions have to be specified | e.g. Nuclear power stations |
| Yes | Partial | Hospital waiting lists; queues in social security offices; maintenance schedules, etc. |
| Yes | Partial | e.g. Defence supplies |

problems most obviously include a series of related decisions over time where the future available options will be shaped by earlier decisions, but also include apparently 'one-off' decisions which involve a series of interrelated choices, such as which office departments should be allocated to which buildings in order to maximize the use of space while keeping departments intact. Dynamic programming procedures apply to discrete options, though appropriate procedures can cover a wide, effectively continuous, range of options. Various procedures are suitable for *deterministic* problems (where all relevant factors are known in advance), *learning* problems (where factors are not known in advance but can be discovered as stages of the problem unfold) and *stochastic* problems (where random factors affect outcomes at all stages). In each case the procedures are designed to find the optimal policy; that is, a decision rule which defines an action for every possible state at every decision stage.

Dynamic programming is particularly appropriate for highly complex problems where the nature of the possible events and the options available at each stage of a problem show a repetitive pattern. Where there is a high degree of irregularity in the pattern of events or options at each stage of the problem, decision-tree analysis may be more appropriate (see 10.5.4 below). For an introduction to dynamic programming techniques, see Norman (1975), who also discusses the similarities and differences between dynamic programming and decision-tree analysis. Those who suspect that textbooks on techniques never cover problems relevant to a real-world policy setting might like to consider this example discussed by Norman (1975, 46), seven years before the Falklands War: 'suppose it is required to install generating equipment to supply electricity to a remote island on which a battalion of troops is to be stationed, probably for 5 years, possibly less, but certainly not more'.

## 10.5.3 PAY-OFF MATRIX

This decision analysis technique can be used to display the consequences of different options in the context of uncertainty about conditioning events. Pay-off matrices apply to a decision at a single point in time. The technique enables the implications of different attitudes to risk (risk-averse, risk-neutral, risk-seeking) to be reflected in the option selected. Pay-off matrices can be used for multiple objectives, but may only give a unique result if the objectives are explicitly weighted. Otherwise the 'best' option may differ for different objectives. Strictly, pay-off matrices do not apply when options or conditioning events are continuous variables, but these can be artificially divided into discrete categories. A pay-off matrix is constructed by (1) listing all the options available to the decision-maker; (2) listing all the conditioning events which can affect the result of adopting a particular option; (3) calculating the 'pay-off' (i.e. cost or benefit) which will result from each possible combination of options and conditioning events. Any option which when compared with one of the other available options never offers a better pay-off can be removed, and a criterion reflecting the appropriate attitude to risk can be applied to determine the best option. Chapman (1980) contains a useful introduction to pay-off matrices.

## 10.5.4 DECISION TREES

This decision analysis technique is appropriate to a sequence of inter-related decisions in the context of uncertainty. The analysis can be displayed in the form of branches stemming either from decision nodes, in which case the branches represent the options available at that stage, or from chance nodes, in which case the branches represent external events which the decision-maker does not control. Depending on how the future unfolds and the choices made at early stages, the decision-maker may then have a new set of options or the final outcome or pay-off at the end of a branch. Probabilities have to be assigned to the event branches. The average pay-offs associated with the chance nodes at the tips of the tree can then be calculated and the tree 'folded back' to the preceding decision node by selecting the option with the best expected pay-off. This process of folding back is continued until the first decision node is reached. Where the probabilities associated with events, especially those near the tips of the trees, are not known, subjective probabilities can be assigned and sensitivity analysis conducted to assess the implications of varying them. Greater certainty may obtain as time passes. Decision trees can be used to handle multiple-objective problems but only if explicit weights are attached to the objectives. Chapman (1981) contains a useful introduction to decision trees, and Behn and Vaupel (1982) make a strong case for their practical application in government decision-making.

## 10.5.5 RISK ANALYSIS

Risk analysis can be envisaged as a decision tree consisting only of chance nodes. The risk of a particular event occurring can be calculated by multiplying the probabilities of the sequence of events which would be necessary for it to occur. Unfortunately, risk analysis is least applicable in circumstances where it would be most useful—large, complex, innovatory projects with small but uncertain probabilities of catastrophic consequences—since there is unlikely to be a sufficient run of past data about possible events and their interaction to calculate objective probabilities. For a useful review article see Hadden and Hazelton (1980).

### 10.5.6 QUEUING THEORY

This is a set of procedures, rather than a theory as such, for solving queuing problems, which arise whenever a facility is too limited to provide instantaneous service to all customers on all occasions when those customers present themselves. Public policy examples of such problems include hospital waiting lists and queues in social security offices. The solving of such problems involves trading off the costs of waiting against the cost of providing facilities to meet what in some cases may be occasional peaks of demand. Where customers arrive to use a facility at regular and predictable rates, relatively simple deterministic models can be used; where, as is often the case, customers arrive at irregular rates, more complex probabilistic models are required. For a very basic introduction to queuing models see Stokey and Zeckhauser (1978, ch. 5).

### 10.5.7 INVENTORY MODELS

Inventory models are normally in the form of equations and enable the analysis of the appropriate amount of a commodity to keep in stock. The relevant considerations which have to be built into the model are: (1) the commodity has to be supplied on demand immediately or with a maximum specified delay to a specified level of probability; (2) as a result triggers are established below which a stock is not allowed to fall without reordering; (3) considerations of probable lags and delays in securing replenishment orders can be built into the model; (4) subject to these constraints, the cost of maintaining the stock should be minimized (i.e. it is not permitted to maintain an excessively large stock simply to eliminate the danger of running out); (5) it is possible to add in additional complications such as cost penalties for delays in supplying from inventory or placing orders to restock at short notice. A public policy example of the potential application of inventory models is defence supplies, where running out of ammunition or spare parts could have drastic consequences, yet the cost of maintaining stocks is high. The general principles behind inventory models are similar to those in queuing theory.

## 10.6 Economic, financial, and budgetary analysis

The techniques we have been discussing so far can be used, or ignored, at the discretion of policy-makers and their advisers. However, budgetary and related processes are inescapable in an organization of any complexity since they deal with basic questions about who gets what, how much, and at whose expense. Budgeting is a political as well as an administrative activity since it often involves choices among, or the ranking of, competing objectives or the choices may be among different means to an agreed end. In either case, budgetary processes are inextricably entwined with those of defining, comparing, and appraising options.

Thus decisions must be taken about the allocation of funds among policies and programmes. There is, however, room for discretion when it comes to deciding *how* to decide, or determining what approaches, methods, and techniques will be adopted within the budgetary process. In the 1960s and 1970s there was considerable interest in budget-making and attempts were made to introduce more systematic methods and analytical techniques and we now consider the main improvements which were sought.

### 10.6.1 NEED FOR A LONGER TIME PERSPECTIVE

In 1958, a parliamentary report (Select Committee on Estimates, 1958) was very critical of the system of public expenditure appraisal and control as it then existed in Britain. As a result of this and other criticisms, the Plowden Committee was set up and reported in 1961 (Plowden Report, 1961). The Plowden Report has claims to be regarded as the seminal document of the administrative reform movement of the 1960s. It was a 'managerialist' report, in that it emphasized government's need to emulate the business world's (alleged) grasp of the techniques and skills of modern management; and it also emphasized the need for 'planning' and was thus part of a larger planning mood which developed in the closing years of the Macmillan Cabinet. With regard to control of public expenditure, Plowden sought to extend the time-scale and context within which spending programmes would be assessed, by 'regular surveys . . . of public expenditure as a whole, over a period of years ahead, and in relation to prospective resources'.

The appropriate 'period of years' was seen for most purposes as being five, rather than the short-term (one or two years) perspective on public spending which had prevailed in the 1950s. Thus a 'public expenditure survey' should be conducted each year which, among other things, would update a five-year 'rolling estimate' or 'forward look'. The PES system was quickly set up and put in the hands of a major inter-departmental committee (PESC). The role of PESC at the end of the 1960s was described in a Treasury memorandum (Select Committee on Procedure, 1969) as confining itself to 'the task of agreeing a factual report showing where present policies are likely to lead in terms of public expenditure . . . if they remain unchanged over the ensuing five years, and what would be implied by a range of possible alternative policies'.

The PESC system has enduring many vicissitudes since the 1960s but the concept of a multi-year 'forward look' at expenditure still attracts lip-service, at least, within Whitehall. It is not, of course, a 'technique' but rather an approach to the budgetary process in government.

### 10.6.2 NEED TO RELATE SPENDING TO OBJECTIVES

In 1970 the newly elected Heath Government produced a White Paper, *The Reorganization of Central Government* (HMSO, 1970), which gave top-level endorsement to another criticism of traditional practices in the public sector, namely, the use of 'input budgeting'. The problem was plainly expressed by an MP (William Fife, a Chairman of the former Estimates Committee) who once complained that the Defence Estimates allowed his committee to know that it cost £1000 per annum to keep a guard-dog in Singapore but not how much the taxpayer was spending to maintain Singapore as a military base. Without such data, how could any informed assessment be made of the case for staying in Singapore?

Traditional public sector budgets are classified by 'inputs': that is, (a) by departments, and (b) by 'items of expenditure' such as salaries, rents, equipment purchases, etc. These do provide a convenient basis for controlling and accounting for public spending and even perhaps for identifying possible economies (e.g. reductions in the cost of staff phone calls).

For more sophisticated analysis a different approach appears to be required, and it takes the form of 'output budgeting'. An output budget is one in which the classification of spending proposals is (a) by broad functions or programmes as well as by departments or sub-departments, and (b) by purposes of expenditure (or objectives). Thus it can, for example, combine and cost all the inputs from various departments of government to the maintenance of an overseas base or the pursuit of a major policy such as protecting the security of Northern Ireland. Moreover, where a policy or objective can be given specific targets to achieve, it is possible to build in 'performance review' to output budgeting. Several Whitehall departments had been developing output budgets before the 1970 White Paper adopted the concept, notably Defence, and Home Office (for police services) and the Department of Education and Science.

### 10.6.3 THE NEED TO SET PRIORITIES BY COMPARING ALL COSTS AND BENEFITS

We have already discussed the problems of establishing priorities in 9.5. If there is a single technique which might claim to be relevant, it is cost-benefit analysis (CBA), which involves comparing options in terms of all their costs and benefits, both direct and indirect, both financial and social (see Peters, 1973; Sugden and Williams, 1978). As far as possible, these costs and benefits are quantified.

Quantification in the *economists' version* of CBA is usually in terms of money. The first step in evaluating a proposal, say, to build a new motorway, is to identify all 'relevant' costs and benefits, including indirect and social costs and benefits. In practice, there has to be a 'cut-off point' in terms of the number that can actually be considered, and this immediately introduces an element of subjective judgement. Then the relevant costs and benefits are evaluated in cash terms as far as possible, although certain 'intangibles' (such as the beauty of a threatened landscape) may be described only in words, with no cash value attributed, in a residual category of important but non-quantifiable considerations. The problems of attributing a financial value to benefits such as the saving of a life are obviously enormous and again the necessary element of subjectivity makes CBA vulnerable to its critics. The attraction of reducing as many costs and benefits as possible to a cash value is, of course, that it allows of commensurability (i.e. measurement on a single standard). However, cash costs which need not be incurred until several years hence do not have the same value as those which must be met immediately. Benefits, too, are affected by their incidence over time. Thus to achieve true commensurability the future costs and benefits must be 'discounted' to their present worth and the choice of an appropriate 'discount rate' is yet another controversial aspect of the procedure.

The *index approach* to CBA tries to avoid the apparent absurdities of seeking to reduce everything to money terms by giving a score out of, say, 100 to each of the relevant considerations. But the process of quantification is no less arbitrary.

Finally, the *balance sheet* approach evades the problem of trying to measure all aspects of costs and benefits on a common basis by simply setting out in semi-list form how a proposed undertaking fares in relation to a range of criteria. Where market prices are available, these are used, and wherever possible quantitative measures are employed, though without attempting to reduce them to financial terms. In some cases the information may be purely verbal. Difficulties with this approach include the burden on the decision-maker of having to weigh up a large amount of information expressed in different forms, but it could be argued that he would have to do this anyway and that the balance sheet procedure simply requires him to do so in as systematic and specific a manner as possible.

The economists' mode of analysis which is usually regarded as intrinsic to CBA does have the great virtue of encouraging decision-makers to consider 'opportunity cost'. Williams (1973), for example, argues that implicit in a decision to build a hospital is a decision *not* to use the same resources on, say, a school or the improvement of a stretch of roadway. Yet 'it might be discovered that the last £1m put into medical services reduced [the] death rate by 5 people per annum, whereas a similar extra sum spent on road improvements could be expected to reduce deaths by 10 people per annum' (Williams, 1973). This might suggest that priority decisions about health vs. roads vs. schools vs. armaments (etc.) could be simplified by calculating and comparing their respective cost-benefit ratios. Within health services, moreover, it might be possible to offer quite convincing evidence that resources committed to certain medical programmes could save more lives if redirected to other medical programmes.

From the reservations we have already expressed about the subjective, even arbitrary, aspects of CBA procedures and calculations, it will be obvious that we regard the claims of some of its early advocates as overstated. Critics such as Self (1970 and 1975) have attacked the pretentions of the 'econocrats' in much more extreme terms. The reasoned responses of a moderate CBA exponent such as Williams (1973) should also be read.

CBA is perhaps the best example of a technique which can *assist* decision-makers (by asking relevant questions and structuring discussions about priorities) but must not be allowed to *make* policy, since the seeming objectivity and precision of quantified 'answers' may conceal highly arguable predictions, assumptions, and attributions of value.

### 10.6.4 NEED TO ACHIEVE OBJECTIVES COST-EFFECTIVELY

A rather narrower but complementary concern to those of CBA is to find for each given objective the means which will be both effective (i.e. produce the desired output) and efficient (i.e. with the most favourable ratio of output to inputs of resources). The most obviously relevant technique is 'cost-effectivess analysis' (CEA), which is concerned with finding the cheapest means of accomplishing a defined objective *or* the maximum value from a given expenditure. In contrast to the economists' version of CBA, the benefits may be expressed in physical rather than monetary units, but otherwise many of the procedures are similar.

### 10.6.5 NEED FOR A MORE DELIBERATE SEARCH FOR ALTERNATIVES

One important meaning of 'options' is as alternatives, including radical alternatives to existing policies or ways of achieving them. One important budgetary technique which attempted to focus on options in this sense was Planning, Programming, and Budgeting Systems (PPBS), originally introduced in the US Department of Defense in the early 1960s. PPBS was described by its arch-exponent Charles Schultze (1968):

PPB calls for careful identification and examination of goals and objectives in each major area of governmental activity . . .
    Another crucial aim of the PPB system is the analysis of alternatives to find the most effective means of reaching basic program objectives, and to achieve these objectives for the least cost. The goal is to force agencies to consider particular programs not as ends in themselves—to be perpetuated without challenge or question—but as means to objectives, subject to the competition of alternative and perhaps more effective or efficient programs.

As Else (1970) noted, PPBS and related approaches involved a shift from viewing the budget as an instrument of *legal control* (i.e. money has to be spent as intended), via *managerial control* (cost-effectiveness, etc.), to playing a key role in *strategic planning*.

In 1965 President Johnson attempted to extend PPBS throughout the Federal Government. The story of how that attempt largely failed and of the very limited extent to which PPBS 'took root' when transplanted to British government (mainly local government) has been told at length elsewhere and need not be repeated here, although some more general lessons will be drawn at the end of this chapter. (On the rise and fall of PPBS see Schultze, 1968; Schick, 1973; Wildavsky, 1974, ch. 6; 1975, chs. 13–18.)

In British central government a highly selective form of PPBS was adopted in the 1970s, in the form of PAR (Programme Analysis and Review). The Heath Government, elected in 1970, had indicated that it saw PAR as a necessary supplement to PESC, since the latter 'does not call for explicit statements of the objectives of expenditure . . . nor can it regularly embody detailed analysis of existing programmes and of major policy options on them'. A team of businessmen was set up within the Civil Service Department to develop 'a system of regular reviews . . . designed to provide Ministers with an opportunity to identify and discuss alternative policy options'. The decision to adopt a less comprehensive approach than that of American PPBS was a sensible one and the intention was each year to select a few 'key areas' of government policy for intensive reappraisal, with a view to reviewing basic objectives, adjusting priorities between policy areas, and searching for more cost-effective means of achieving policies. From 1970 to 1973 the PARs carried out in Whitehall did have something of the 'cutting edge' which had been intended, mainly because they had some high-level political and administrative support, but thereafter they had less impact and PAR was abandoned by the incoming 1979 Conservative Government (Gray and Jenkins, 1983).

The fact that PARs fell into political and administrative disfavour does not mean that they were pointless. Indeed, of all the approaches that we have outlined, PAR has some claims to be among the most practical and, potentially at least, the most valuable. Some defensiveness in Whitehall about PAR's demise can perhaps be seen in the suggestion made to us by senior civil servants that 'programme analysis and review' is what they do all the time anyway. We are sceptical about that claim and frankly dismissive of the more political suggestion that Rayner-type studies are the natural successor or 'son of PAR', since merely to cut public expenditure is not even the same thing as achieving cost-effectiveness, let alone a reasoned set of priorities. The PAR type of approach may well have to be reinvented by a future central government and, in the meantime, it is to be hoped that some local authorities will persist with the closely-related 'key issue analysis' (Greenwood *et al.*, 1980).

## 10.6.6 NEED TO CHALLENGE INERTIA AND INCREMENTALISM

'Incrementalism' describes something about decision-making—and especially about budget-making—which practitioners recognize as readily as do theorists. In the short run at least, the 'base' budget is not to be seriously questioned and adjustments to it are made in terms only of relatively small increments—or, should public sector cutbacks take effect, small decrements.

How might these features of budgeting behaviour be challenged? The answer emerging from the United States in the 1970s appeared to be zero-base budgeting (ZBB). The essential steps of ZBB have been described (Phare, 1979) as. (1) designation of decision units, (2) formulation of decision packages for each decision unit, and (3) the ranking of decision packages in order of priority. 'Decision units' refer to the loci of decision-making about budgets within organizations. These may simply be the existing divisions of, say, a local authority, such as departments organized along professional or 'input' lines; or they may be defined in programmatic or 'output' terms, cutting across existing departmental and intra-departmental boundaries. Where output budgeting has already taken root, one would expect to find programmes used as the criterion for identifying decision units. 'Decision packages' refer to the way in which departmental or programme managers present their spending proposals for the next financial year. Ideally, this should be in the form of a statement of objectives to be achieved, levels of service performance associated with achieving such objectives, and the resources required to provide such services. Less ambitiously, packages may be presented simply in terms of the cost of resources necessary to provide stated levels of service.

So far, then, ZBB appears to involve little more than a variation on output budgeting and PPBS. The distinctive element arrives when the managers of decision units are required to justify in some detail not only what *existing* levels of spending should be maintained and, no doubt, incrementally added to in the next financial year, but why *any* spending on particular 'packages' (services, programmes, or objectives) should be continued for a further year. In other words, the budgetary 'base' is no longer unchallenged and the unthinkable alternative of a 'zero base' has to be contemplated. Finally, the managers of decision units are required to rank in order of priority the various packages they are proposing for funding. This, too, is an unusual requirement in budgeting and one which most departmental or programme heads particularly dislike. From the perspective of the central budget-makers, however, the full application of ZBB should supply them with much fuller data from the spending departments, including detailed arguments for the continuation of programmes and services (preferably with statements of the objectives to which these contribute), justifications for various levels of spending above 'zero' and indications of the priority attached to the various 'packages' by the 'unit' managers. The central finance division (or budget bureau, in American parlance) is then in a much better position to attempt a broad overview of spending proposals from all sections of the organization, to arrive at its own view of overall priorities and, in theory at least, to reallocate resources on a scale significantly greater than that of normal incremental or decremental adjustments.

The contrast between ambitious theory and limited practice is, however, particularly striking in the case of ZBB. President Carter failed to 'transplant' ZBB from the state of Georgia to Washington DC, but ZBB had changed budgeting practices in state governments only to a very partial extent in any case (Clynch, 1979).

### 10.6.7 LIMITS TO CHANGE IN BUDGETARY PRACTICE

To the extent that reforms in financial and budgetary methods were intended to achieve more 'rational' decision-making about the use of resources, we have already indicated (in 4.3) some of the limits which were always likely to apply, under the broad headings of cognitive, economic, organizational, and contextual factors.

Procedures such as 'forward looks' (PESC, etc.), PPBS, CBA, and ZBB place enormous strains upon the cognitive capacities of decision-makers. They lack reliable means of assessing future spending requirements. Particular problems arise in costing programmes or 'outputs', especially in attributing an appropriate share of indirect or overhead costs to a particular programme. Predicting the outcome of spending programmes is very difficult—indeed even after the event there will be room for debate about who has benefited and to what extent. There is scope for arbitrariness in determining 'cut-off points' in the listing of costs and benefits, in deciding what value to attach to the saving of lives, in the choice of a discount rate, and much else. The problems are not only, or even mainly, those of establishing the 'facts', since even greater potential for disagreement and allegations of arbitrariness attach to the choice of relevant 'values' and criteria to be applied.

In theory, some of these cognitive limits could be reduced, by increasing the staff and other resources committed to budget-making. However, any such increase would raise practical questions about the economics of achieving greater rationality. Since it is difficult to provide convincing proof that one method of budgeting is superior to another, it is particularly difficult to justify major increases in the costs associated with the budgeting process. Some of the procedures involved in output budgeting, PPBS, or ZBB are undoubtedly expensive in terms of staff time and tend to produce an infuriating amount of paper. The benefits which they offer are likely to be in the relatively long term whereas their cumbersomeness and costliness are all too evident in the short term which tends to preoccupy administrators as well as politicians. While it may be difficult to defend budget calculations which take the existing spending 'base' as given and tend to result only in incremental adjustments, it cannot be doubted that these are time-saving devices which also seem better suited to the limited cognitive powers of decision-makers.

'Organizational' factors include the problems of taking a corporate or synoptic view of budget-making, when central decision-makers are faced by the established interests, expertise, and influence of departmental heads, who in turn are under pressure from the spokesmen of sub-departmental groupings. Even the information systems of organizations tend to be locked into the 'verticalism' of spending departments and there are problems in developing new systems to support the 'lateralism' of comprehensive or programme-related budgeting.

Under 'contextual' factors we noted the importance of understanding the processual nature of decision-making and, especially, of budget-making. That is, it is an activity which can only be understood in terms of the influence of the past (which has determined the present 'base' budget) and of people's expectations of the future (expectations which do not normally extend to the possibility of a 'zero base' or of any significant cut in present levels of, say, old-age pensions or unemployment benefits). Those involved in current budget-making will be under enormous political pressures, not just from party political considerations but from 'politics' in the more general sense of intra-organizational and inter-organizational struggle for control over resources. Budgeting and politics have both been described in terms of 'who gets what, how much, and at whose expense'. Thus attempts to reform budgeting will either succeed and, by succeeding, alter the balance of power within and between organizations—for example, by strengthening the centre at the expense of departments—or, more probably, the reform attempts will be frustrated by the political reality of entrenched interests and an existing distribution of power and resources.

## 10.7 Presenting options to the client

So far we have discussed the ways in which options are identified and generated, categorized and defined, and appraised and compared. Several approaches, procedures, and techniques have been examined in relation to each of these activities. There is, then, a technical dimension to options appraisal and the skills of analysis would seem particularly relevant to this aspect of the policy process. We have also noted, however, the importance of the political dimension at every stage. Sometimes it will be evident from the beginning that political considerations are going to be so crucial that it is pointless even to attempt analysis. In other cases, analysis may be undertaken but the results will still have to be 'consumed' by the politicians with whom the final decision lies.

Writers such as Meltsner (1976) have therefore emphasized the need for the analyst to develop political as well as technical skills. The analyst should certainly have given some thought to the identity of the 'client' or consumer of the results of his analysis, to the other sources of information and advice upon which the client will draw, to the sorts of considerations and arguments which are likely to carry weight, and to the best way in which to present an options appraisal to this particular client or collective clientele. His experience may, for example, have taught him that the client does not wish to be burdened with too many arguments and data, will only consider a few options, and may even prefer a straight recommendation.

A very different picture of the client's requirements would probably be offered by most politicians. One of the most frequently recurring criticisms made by former cabinet ministers in Britain is that they were told too little about the options facing them or that a single recommendation was pressed on them. It must also be accepted that between ministers as clients and analysts (or advisers) as producers of options there will usually have been a Whitehall 'middle man' in the form of a senior (but generalist) administrator who prepared the final brief for the minister and, perhaps, reduced the range of options passed on to him. Politicians who genuinely wish to have several options presented to them, plus accompanying evidence and arguments for and against each option, should perhaps give more encouragement to the development of policy analysis techniques and personnel than they have given in the recent past, while also insisting on more direct access to such personnel (see e.g. Jenkins, 1971).

However, to have more options to consider will not greatly assist politicians if they have too little time for careful consideration because of the stage at which they are presented with the options. The comments of George Cardona (1981) who was a political adviser at the Treasury from May 1979 to November 1981, are revealing on this point:

There is, however, one serious shortcoming in the way the Treasury treats ministers and advisers. It is reluctant to let them become involved in issues at an early stage. It likes to present ministers with a fully worked-out set of options that have been discussed exhaustively at official level. By the time this process is completed, there can be too little time left for ministerial consideration of the options: ministers have to take a decision, and advisers have to advise, without having had the opportunity to watch the argument develop.

The inference to be drawn is that politicians should seek to become involved not only at every sub-stage of options identification and appraisal but also in earlier policy stages such as issue definition and objective-setting.

However, attempts by British ministers to become involved at earlier stages, though they will not be met with outright rejection, do seem likely to encounter cultural resistance, as Cardona points out:

On the few occasions when a minister tried to intervene in policy formulation at an early stage, the official reaction was rather like what would happen if a diner at a smart restaurant were to get up and serve himself: no one would actually stop him, but six waiters would rush forward to do it for him.

The question of the range of options relates to a theme which has been recurring since our initial consideration of models of policy-making in chapter 4. On the one hand, a consideration of a range of options is desirable, but on the other we are talking about extremely busy decision-makers who will not wish to read a full-length academic analysis of an issue, nor to be told that they have to read through twenty different options before making a decision.

Decision-makers will be concerned with the practical problem facing them as real decision-makers (not 'policy analysts') in a specific political setting. Briefs coming up to them, whether setting out a single recommendation or a number of options which list only purportedly 'objective' costs and benefits and fail to take into account the political consequences of options may be ignored or, if accepted, may turn out to have political repercussions which wreck the proposal. 'Political' is used here not in its narrow party sense (though this may be very important) but in the wider sense which includes the reaction of the public, affected interest groups, or implementing authorities. In 10.6.3 we referred to the application of cost-benefit analysis techniques, but many policy decisions do not lend themselves to this sort of approach, since there are important considerations which cannot be reduced to a calculus of pounds. An example would be the ending of religious segregation in Scottish schools, since to ignore the political consequences of options in such a case would be an act of culpable folly.

There is no easy way of resolving the tensions between the danger of neglecting possible consequences of a given option and the danger of flooding a decision-maker with too much material. The most effective compromise is probably a brief in the form of an 'options paper'. The first part of such a paper would be a brief summary of the problem to which the decision is addressed. A wide range of options should be listed, perhaps including an 'unthinkable' one. However, only a limited number of options (say, between three and five) within that range should be considered in detail; if there are significant policy differences possible under each option, these could be presented as sub-options. Each option should be described briefly in terms of (a) the course of action involved; (b) the costs and benefits in summary form. Among the costs and benefits which might be included are financial implications, manpower implications, social impact, likely reaction by groups and organizations to selection of that option, and (if appropriate, given the brief) the party and electoral implications. If appropriate given the respective roles of the analyst and the decision-maker, a recommendation about selecting one or more options might be made at the end of the paper. Above all, it is essential to keep such a paper to a readable length for a busy person, yet provide relevant information.

Our experience has been that setting an 'options paper' as an exercise can help the student or trainee to develop the skills both of analysis and of presenting the results of analysis to the political client. Whether the politician-client could benefit from training in the commissioning and utilization of options analysis is an interesting question which we have not had a comparable opportunity to pursue.

# 11

# Implementation

## 11.1 Implementation as part of policy-making

It is only in the past dozen years that social scientists, especially political scientists, have taken an interest in the process of implementation or accepted that it is part of the larger process of policy-making. We have already noted (see chapter 2) that previous studies tended to be of decisions rather than policies and that, in either case, the focus was upon the 'moment of choice' at which a decision was 'taken' or a policy 'made'. What happened thereafter was apparently of little interest to political scientists or, more accurately, it was the concern of a different group of specialists in fields such as public administration or management in the public sector. Since the publication of Pressman and Wildavsky's *Implementation* in 1973, however, there has been a surge of books and articles dealing with implementation as a key element in the study of public policy.

One reason for the refocusing of interest was the realization, especially in the United States, that many of the measures introduced by liberal administrations of the 1960s had in practice brought about relatively little by way of fundamental or lasting change. In Britain, too, there had been disappointments for Labour goverments in their reforming attempts, and in the early 1970s the Heath Government had first to abandon its policy of 'disengagement' of government from industry and then encountered enormous problems in seeking to bring government, including the judiciary, into the field of industrial relations and regulation of the trade unions. Specific 'failures' of implementation were observed, or alleged, in such fields as urban regeneration, land development, employment, control of pollution, and industrial restructuring. It seemed increasingly clear that governments were better at legislating than at effecting desired changes and the search was soon on for explanations of what Dunsire (1978) was to call 'the implementation gap'.

If the 'problem' is defined as policy 'failure', what are we to understand by this term? And if we understand 'what' has gone wrong, can we then explain 'why'?

In seeking to understand what is meant by policy failure, it is useful to distinguish between *non-implementation* and *unsuccessful implementation*. In the former case, a policy is not put into effect as intended, perhaps because those involved in its execution have been unco-operative and/or inefficient, or because their best efforts could not overcome obstacles to effective implementation over which they had little or no control. Unsuccessful implementation, on the other hand, occurs when a policy is carried out in full, and external circumstances are not unfavourable but, none the less, the policy fails to produce the intended results (or outcomes). In some cases, of course, a policy can fail on all dimensions, as when attempts were made to improve the competitiveness in world markets of selected British technologies by making available to private industry certain government-funded civil development contracts. The scheme was not carried through very imaginatively by the government agencies concerned, industrialists in any case showed little interest, partly because the economic climate was not such as to encourage enterprise, the take-up of contracts was well below the level of funding available, and the results in terms of greater competitiveness were disappointing even when funds were spent as intended. A similar multifaceted example of policy failure in the USA was the basis of Pressman and Wildavsky's pioneering study in 1973.

The reasons for failure appear to follow naturally from such studies. In plain terms, a policy is usually seen as being put at risk because of one or more of the following three causes: bad execution, bad policy, or bad luck. Thus the policy may be ineffectively implemented, which will be viewed by the initiators of the policy as bad execution. Or both policy initiators and those charged with its implementation may agree that external circumstances were so adverse that it was no one's fault— 'just bad luck'—that the policy failed. The reason which is less commonly —or at least less openly—offered in explanation of policy failure is that the policy itself was 'bad', in the sense of being based upon inadequate information, defective reasoning, or hopelessly unrealistic assumptions.

Simple as this level of analysis undoubtedly is, it does at least make the point that there is no sharp divide between (a) formulating a policy and (b) implementing that policy. What happens at the so-called 'implementation' stage will influence the actual policy outcome. Conversely, the probability of a successful outcome (which we define for the moment as that outcome desired by the initiators of the policy) will be increased if thought is given at the policy design stage to potential problems of implementation.

We shall return later in this chapter to the relationship between what Barrett and Fudge (1981) have called 'policy and action' and to their criticisms of what they describe as the 'top-down' perspective. For the moment, however, let us stay with the 'top-down' language of 'policy failure' and further explore why, in the real world, some degree of such failure is almost inevitable.

## 11.2 Why 'perfect implementation' is unattainable

In chapter 4 we followed Herbert Simon in approaching the study of how policies are made by first constructing an ideal-type model of 'perfect rationality' and then describing the many constraints (or 'bounds' in Simon's language) which tend to impede rational policy-making in practice. In other words, the descriptive model of policy-making was developed in terms of observed deviations from the ideal-type model of rationality. In our study of how policies are implemented, too, we shall initially proceed in the same way. In this case, we shall be following Christoper Hood's example in his valuable study of *The Limits of Administration* (1976) and borrowing his useful analytical concept of 'perfect administration'. In an article entitled 'Why Is Implementation So Difficult?', Gunn (1978) drew upon Hood's analysis and those of Pressman and Wildavsky (1973), Etzioni (1976), Kaufman (1971), Bardach (1977), Van Meter and Van Horn (1975) and King (1975 and 1976), to provide for civil servants a short guide to some of the reasons why, according to these pioneering writers, any state of 'perfect implementation' was likely to be virtually unattainable in practice. Like Hood again, Gunn emphasized that 'perfection' in this context was an analytical concept or 'idea' and not, in the colloquial sense of the term, an 'ideal' to be achieved. In other words, no prescriptive model was offered and, indeed, several of the logical preconditions of perfect implementation—such as 'perfect obedience' or 'perfect control'— were identified as being morally and politically quite unacceptable as well as unattainable in a pluralist democracy.

What, then, are these preconditions which would have to be satisfied if perfect implementation were to be achieved and why are they unlikely to be achieved in practice?

### 11.2.1 THE CIRCUMSTANCES EXTERNAL TO THE IMPLEMENTING AGENCY DO NOT IMPOSE CRIPPLING CONSTRAINTS

Some obstacles to implementation are outside the control of administrators because they are external to the policy and the implementing agency. Such obstacles may be physical, as when an agricultural programme is set back by drought or disease. Or they may be political, in that either the policy or the measures needed to achieve it are unacceptable to interests (such as party activists, trade unions, or, in some societies, the military) which have the power to veto them. These constraints are obvious and there is little that administrators can do to overcome them except in their capacity as advisers, by ensuring that such possibilities are borne in mind during the policy-making stage.

### 11.2.2 THAT ADEQUATE TIME AND SUFFICIENT RESOURCES ARE MADE AVAILABLE TO THE PROGRAMME

This condition partly overlaps the first, in that it often comes within the category of external constraints. However, policies which are physically or politically feasible may still fail to achieve stated intentions. A common reason is that too much is expected too soon, especially when attitudes or behaviour are involved (as, for example, in attempts to alter discriminatory attitudes towards the physically or mentally disabled). Another reason is that politicians sometimes will the policy 'end' but not the 'means', so that expenditure restrictions may starve a statutory programme of adequate resources. This happened in the case of the 1974 Control of Pollution Act, since it coincided with cutbacks in the public sector which denied local authorities sufficient funds to appoint the additional staff needed to implement the Act. A more unusual problem arises when special funds are made available, as in the Urban Programme, but have to be spent within an unrealistically short time, faster than the programme can effectively absorb them. It is important to realize that money is not a resource in itself but only a 'ticket' with which to purchase real resources, and there may be delays in this conversion process. The fear of having to return the 'unspent portion' of funding at the end of the financial year often leads public agencies into a flurry of expenditure, sometimes on relatively trivial items. Attempts to persuade finance officers to allow the carry-over of unspent funds to the next financial year are usually in vain, so that administrators are again quite limited in what they can do to overcome these constraints upon effective implementation. They can only advise politicians about the lead times which may be involved before a programme produces results, plan the annual cash flow to avoid any unspent portion, and seek to anticipate any blockages in converting cash into real resources.

### 11.2.3 THAT THE REQUIRED COMBINATION OF RESOURCES IS ACTUALLY AVAILABLE

The third condition follows on naturally from the second, namely that there must not only be constraints in terms of overall resources but also that, at each stage in the implementation process, the appropriate combination of resources must actually be available. In practice, there is often a 'bottleneck' which occurs when, say, a combination of money, manpower, land, equipment, and building material has to come together to construct an emergency landing-strip for the RAF, but one or more of these is delayed and as a result the project as a whole is set back by several months. As noted in 11.2.2, a temporary shortage of cash may be less serious in such circumstances than a blockage in the supply of some 'real' resource. The flow of additional funding for a programme can be swiftly increased, given political assent, by a turn of the fiscal 'tap', but there can be no guarantee that money can be converted into land, materials, or manpower within the time-scale of the programme. Thus a shortage in, say, the stock of seasoned timber can hold up a building programme for months. Or a dearth of skilled carpenters may seriously constrain a housing rehabilitation programme. In other words, particularly severe disruptions threaten when scarce resources are in the nature of a relatively fixed *stock* rather than a *flow*. The length of a delay in making good a deficiency in the supply of trained manpower, for example, will be determined by the minimum length of the training period involved. The main responsibility for such crises in implementation properly lies with administrative staff, including programme designers and managers, since they now have available to them a battery of techniques (often with attendant technology) such as network planning and control, manpower forecasting, and inventory control, which should help them to anticipate potential bottlenecks and take appropriate action in terms of generating or redistributing resources within the programme.

## 11.2.4 THAT THE POLICY TO BE IMPLEMENTED IS BASED UPON A VALID THEORY OF CAUSE AND EFFECT

Policies are sometimes ineffective not because they are badly implemented, but because they are bad policies. That is, the policy may be based upon an inadequate understanding of a problem to be solved, its causes and cure; or of an opportunity, its nature, and what is needed to exploit it. Pressman and Wildavsky (1973) describe any policy as a 'hypothesis containing initial conditions and predicted consequences'. That is, the typical reasoning of the policy-maker is along the lines of 'if x is done at time t(1) then Y will result at time t(2)'. Thus every policy incorporates a theory of cause and effect (normally unstated in practice) and, if the policy fails, it may be the underlying theory that is at fault rather than the execution of the policy.

Pressman and Wildavsky developed their argument from a detailed case-study of the failure of a programme in the late 1960s aimed at creating employment for members of minority groups in the Californian city of Oakland. The programme provided funds for public works and for making building and other loans available to private firms, in hopes that (a) resulting business opportunities would be taken up by investors and (b) result in the creation of new jobs which would (c) be filled by Blacks and Mexicans. Despite much initial goodwill the programme achieved very little. Few loans were taken up by firms and some proposals for public works came to nothing. Even when funds were spent as intended, the net increase in employment of members of minority groups was disappointingly small. One of Pressman and Wildavsky's conclusions was that the programme was based upon an inadequate theory of work-creation: this seeming failure of implementation was, at least in part, a failure of policy-making. A similar point is made by Bardach (1977, 251–2): 'If this theory is fundamentally incorrect, the policy will fail no matter how well it is implemented. Indeed, it is not exactly clear what "good" implementation of a basically misconceived policy would mean'.

Here, then, is one seeming problem of implementation which can only be tackled by better analysis at the issue definition and options analysis stages of the policy-making process. The difficulties of such analysis should not be underestimated, given the limits of our ability to understand and 'solve' complex social and economic problems, especially since, as Bardach (1977) reminds us, government tends to get landed with the most difficult problems with which no one else has been able to cope. However, we can attempt to improve issue definition (see Chapter 7); we can try to test the 'hypotheses' underlying various policy options; we may be able to learn something from foreign experience (although there is little evidence that we in Britain have learned anything from the policy failures described by Pressman and Wildavsky and other American writers); and finally, we must remember that the 'moment of choice' is not the end of the policy-making process and be prepared constantly to test underlying theory against problems of practice observed at later stages in the process.

### 11.2.5 THAT THE RELATIONSHIP BETWEEN CAUSE AND EFFECT IS DIRECT AND THAT THERE ARE FEW IF ANY, INTERVENING LINKS

Even from the very broad outline of the Oakland programme at 11.2.4, it will be seen that the theory underlying the policy was more complex than a simple 'if X, then Y' and extended the causal chain to 'if X, then Y, and if Y, then Z'. Pressman and Wildavsky argue that policies which depend upon a long sequence of cause and effect relationships have a particular tendency to break down, since 'the longer the chain of causality, the more numerous the reciprocal relationships among the links and the more complex implementation becomes'. In other words, the more links in the chain, the greater the risk that some of them will prove to be poorly conceived or badly executed. In the case of the Oakland programme a cruder but also more direct approach to work-creation might have had greater success. However, given the complexity of some recent British programmes—not least our own attempts to improve the employment prospects of minority groups or to regenerate our declining inner cities—we should not be too critical about American practice.

### 11.2.6 THAT DEPENDENCY RELATIONSHIPS ARE MINIMAL

This condition of 'perfect implementation' requires that there is a single implementing agency which need not depend on other agencies for success, or if other agencies must be involved, that the dependency relationships are minimal in number and importance. Where, as is often the case in practice, implementation requires not only a complex series of events and linkages (see 11.2.5) but also agreement at each event among a large number of participants, then the probability of a successful or even a predictable outcome must be further reduced. Pressman and Wildavsky argue that' 'Adding the number of necessary clearances involved in decision points throughout the history of the program will give an idea of the task involved in securing implementation.' (A *decision point* will be reached each time an act of agreement has to be registered for the programme to continue, and *clearance* is the name given to each instance in which a separate participant is required to give his consent.) By a process of simple arithmetical calculation, Pressman and Wildavsky show that, even if there is a high chance of obtaining a clearance from a single participant at a given decision point, when all the probabilities are multiplied together the overall chances of success are extremely slender.

Such calculations are a little misleading since, as Bowen (1982) points out, the chances of success are considerably improved if there are repeated attempts at securing agreement at tricky decision points, concentration of resources on difficult clearances, parallel attempts to achieve similar results by different routes, and the beginning of a 'bandwagon' effect (see also Bardach, 1977, 242–3). Further, Pressman and Wildavsky's calculation was based on an 'all-or-nothing' concept of a favourable outcome at each decision point, whereas the chances of partial success might well be higher. That being said, it still seems likely that the greater the number of clearances required among other bodies involved in implementation, the lower will be the chances of full implementation.

It is not only in a federal system such as the USA that programmes can become overextended in terms both of causal chains and numbers of participating agencies. Anthony King (1976) argues that the capacity of British government to deal with its problems is diminishing because 'the number of dependency relationships in which government is involved has increased substantially'. Thus it is nowadays relatively rare for implementation of a public programme to involve only a government department on the one hand and a group of affected citizens on the other. Instead there is likely to be an intervening network of local authorities, boards and commissions, voluntary associations, and organized groups. An example of multi-stage, multi-agency implementation is the Glasgow Eastern Area Renewal (GEAR) project, involving as it does the Scottish Office, Scottish Development Agency, Scottish Special Housing Association, Manpower Services Commission, Strathclyde Regional Council, City of Glasgow District Council, and several other public bodies—as well as community groups, the inhabitants themselves, and the private businesses and investors who, it is hoped, will be attracted to the regenerated area. The question of whether

GEAR is a partial success story or a 'mutually non-effective group of organisations' (Booth, Pitt, and Money, 1982) is the subject of some debate in Scotland. At several points, impatience with the problems of working with so large a group of organizations has led to suggestions that an Urban Development Corporation (similar to those introduced to England) might provide a more effective basis for regenerating Glasgow's declining East End.

## 11.2.7 THAT THERE IS UNDERSTANDING OF, AND AGREEMENT ON, OBJECTIVES

The requirement here is that there should be complete understanding of, and agreement on, the objectives to be achieved, and that these conditions should persist throughout the implementation process. (We should perhaps repeat that this 'requirement' is only in terms of the ideal-type model of 'perfect implementation': no prescriptive—far less descriptive— model is offered at this point.)

. As we noted in chapter 9, the theory of planning is replete with references to objectives which, we are told by managerialist writers, should be clearly defined, specific, and preferably quantified, understood, and agreed throughout the organization, mutually compatible and supportive, and provide a blueprint against which actual programmes can be monitored. However, as chapter 9 also showed at some length, most research studies suggest that, in real life, the objectives of organizations or programmes are often difficult to identify or are couched in vague and evasive terms. Even 'official' objectives, where they exist, may not be compatible with one another, and the possibility of conflict or confusion is increased when professional or other groups proliferate their own 'unofficial' goals within a programme. Official objectives are often poorly understood, perhaps because communications downwards and outwards from headquarters are inadequate. Even if objectives have initially been understood and agreed, it does not follow that this state of affairs will persist throughout the lifetime of the programme, since goals are susceptible to succession, multiplication, expansion, and displacement. Any of these tendencies will complicate the implementation process and even—in the eyes of top management—'subvert' it. Again we see that apparent 'implementation failures' may stem from features of other stages in the policy process.

## 11.2.8 THAT TASKS ARE FULLY SPECIFIED IN CORRECT SEQUENCE

Here the condition is that in moving towards agreed objectives it is possible to specify, in complete detail and perfect sequence, the tasks to be performed by each participant. The difficulties of achieving this condition of perfect implementation are obvious. Also it is surely desirable as well as inevitable that there should be some room for discretion and improvisation in even the most carefully planned programme. But techniques such as network planning and control (discussed further in 11.4.2) can at least provide a framework within which projects can be planned and implementation controlled, by identifying the tasks to be accomplished, the relationships between these tasks and the logical sequence in which they should be performed. There remain, of course, the managerial problems of actually ensuring that tasks are performed correctly and on time and of taking appropriate remedial action if they are not.

## 11.2.9 THAT THERE IS PERFECT COMMUNICATION AND CO-ORDINATION

The precondition here is that there would have to be perfect communication among and co-ordination of the various elements or agencies involved in the programme. Hood (1976) argues that for perfect implementation to be achieved it would be necessary to have a completely unitary administrative system—'like a huge army with a single line of authority'—with no compartmentalism or conflict within. He is not, of course, advocating such a system. Even to state this condition of perfect co-ordination is to know that, leaving aside questions of desirability, its attainment would be all but impossible within and among real-life organizations which are characterized by departmentalism, professionalism, and the activities of many groups with their own values, goals, and interests to protect.

Communication has an important contribution to make to co-ordination and to implementation generally. However, perfect communication is as unattainable a condition as most of the others we have examined. While management information systems (MIS) can assist in matching information flow to needs, they cannot ensure that the resulting data, advice, and instructions are understood as intended by the senders, or indeed, understood at all. Co-ordination is not, of course, simply a matter of communicating information or of setting up suitable administrative structures, but involves the exercise of power, and this leads to the final condition for perfect implementation.

## 11.2.10 THAT THOSE IN AUTHORITY CAN DEMAND AND OBTAIN PERFECT COMPLIANCE

Hood's phrase is 'perfect obedience' and he expands it to mean 'no resistance to commands at any point in the administrative system'. If there were any potential for resistance it would be identified (in Hood's model of 'perfect administration') by the system's 'perfect information' and forestalled by its 'perfect control'. In other words, the final and perhaps least attainable condition of perfect implementation is that those 'in authority' are also those 'in power' and that they are able to secure total and immediate compliance from others (both internal and external to the agency) whose consent and co-operation are required for the success of the programme. In practice, within an agency there may be compartmentalism, between agencies there may be conflicts of interest and status disputes, and those with the formal authority to demand co-operation may lack the power to back up these demands or the will to exercise it. Every administrative practitioner knows how difficult it would be to achieve the condition of perfect compliance. Most of us would add that we would not want to live or work in such a system.

When implementation involves, as it sometimes does, innovation and the management of change—with major departures from previous policies and practices—there will be particularly high probability of suspicion, recalcitrance, or outright resistance from affected individuals, groups, and interests, especially if insufficient time has been allowed for explanation and consultation or if any previous experience of change has been unfortunate. We cannot (and should not) hope ever to be free from such resistance, but we can learn a good deal about its nature and about the responses open to administrators from the study of individual, group, organizational, and political behaviour. Thus the psychologist, sociologist, and political scientist have at least as much to contribute to our understanding of implementation as have the programme designer, network planner, and information systems analyst. The potential contributions of these and other approaches are assessed in section 11.4.

## 11.3 A 'top-down' perspective?

The language, concepts, and approach employed to this point would be regarded by some more recent writers on implementation—or, in their language, 'the policy—action relationship'—as biased and limiting. Barrett and Fudge (1981) argue that much of the literature to which we have so far made reference demonstrates a 'managerial' perspective, reflecting a 'policy-centred' or 'top-down' view in which implementers are seen as 'agents' of those who claim to make policy. They argue that:

rather than treating implementation as the transmission of policy into a series of consequential actions, the policy—action relationship needs to be regarded as a process of interaction and negotiation, taking place over time, between those seeking to put policy into effect and those upon whom action depends.

From our previous comments on the interdependence of policy-making and implementation, on the scope for officials to initiate and influence policy, and on the limits to centrally imposed objectives, co-ordination, and demands for compliance, it will be obvious that we can agree with much of the above statement as a *description* of what happens in real life. We also agree—indeed, is there anyone who does not?—on the importance of understanding the contribution to 'the complexity of the policy process' of 'environmental, political, and organizational' factors. Thus, in seeking to criticize some at least of the so-called 'top down' writers, Barrett and Fudge are creating a straw man and sometimes appear to confuse ideal-type models of perfect implementation with a normative or prescriptive model.

Barrett and Fudge themselves often seem to drift between descriptive and prescriptive styles of argument. Hierarchy and the 'chain of command' are clearly out of favour and the term 'top down' is used virtually as an epithet throughout. They appear not only to argue against but actively to dislike any suggestions that 'politics and administration' might be viewed as separate, though such an argument has the curious effect of not only politicizing administration, but also, more worryingly, of de-politicizing politics. There is, of course, an important area of overlap between politics and administration but there are also more substantial areas of relatively independent functioning which are worth preserving, both analytically and in practice.

If pressed, we must plead guilty to a measure of sympathy with the top down view, if only on the grounds that 'those seeking to put policy into effect' are usually elected while 'those upon whom action depends' are not, at least in the case of civil servants and the staff of health services, nationalized industries, etc. In the case of local authorities, of course, we have competing democratic legitimacies, since local councils, too, are elected and we need not elaborate upon the controversy which has been created in the early 1980s by central government's unusually assertive attitude towards, and attempts to exercise dominance over, local authorities. Even in the case of central–local relations, however, we find it difficult to see why the view from the top is necessarily less valid than that from other levels. Of course, anyone can think of favourite examples of national policies so misconceived that they deserved to be stifled at birth and we have already indicated our view that 'implementation failures' can often be traced to inadequate policies. Choose different examples, however, and the 'bottom up' view looks less attractive. If a Home Secretary is committed to better relations between policemen and black youths, should we view with equanimity the persistence of 'street level' police attitudes and actions which are openly racist? If the central health departments were to take a stronger line on the need for preventive medicine, would it not be a matter of legitimate concern if many clinicians and health authorities continued to direct resources towards 'heroic' medicine which, in terms of lives saved (and the quality of some of those lives), often seem less than good value? If Parliament decided to move from left-hand to right-hand drive on our roads, would we be happy to leave to 'negotiation' between road-users, local authorities, and the central government such questions as when, how, and whether the change-over should take effect?

We do not disagree with Barrett and Fudge when they argue that on many occasions 'lower level actors take decisions which effectively limit hierarchical influence, pre-empt top decision-making, or alter "policies"', but we find it difficult to agree with their ready acceptance of, let alone their seeming acquiescence in, all these aspects of the 'policy/action continuum'. Implementation must involve a process of interaction between organizations, the members of which may have different values, perspectives, and priorities from one another and from those advocating the policy. Much of this interaction can and should take place before policy formulation (e.g. in the form of consultation of local authority associations by central government departments), although there is no guarantee that such prior consultation will produce prior consent. While attempts will subsequently be made by unconvinced local authorities and others 'upon whom action depends' to modify and redirect the policy's thrust, there are surely limits—if only legal and constitutional limits—to how far such post-legislative guerrilla skirmishing should be taken. Finally, we would argue that the prescriptive aspects of policy analysis are concerned precisely with rescuing 'policy' from mere 'action'.

## 11.4 Approaches to implementation

In this section we examine some of the contributions from various social science disciplines to understanding implementation and, in incorrigibly 'top down' vein, to improving the effectiveness of implementation.

### 11.4.1 STRUCTURAL APPROACHES

Modern organizational analysis has a good deal to offer to the study of implementation, since policy design and organizational design should be considered together, wherever possible. However, the days when it was fashionable to believe in universal principles of 'good organization' are long behind us and emphasis is now laid on different organizational structures as being appropriate to different types of organizational tasks and environments. To simplify this large subject we shall draw a distinction between 'planning *of* change' and 'planning *for* change'. The former occurs when change is generated within the organization or is largely within the organization's control as to direction, pace, and timing. Here implementation is seen essentially as a technical or managerial problem. Planning *for* change, on the other hand, takes place either when change is externally imposed (by other organizations or by environmental forces) or when the change process is difficult to predict, control, or contain. In this case, implementation will require a more adaptive approach, the policy-making process as a whole will be iterative rather than linear, and the relationship between policy and implementation will be closer to Barrett and Fudge's policy–action– policy continuum.

The organizational forms appropriate to planning *of* change can be relatively bureaucratic, in the Weberian sense of clearly-defined tasks and relationships and a hierarchical structure. In the case of planning *for* change, on the other hand, a quite different organizational structure may be appropriate, with some at least of the 'organic' features described by Burns and Stalker (1961) and later writers, such as relatively unde- fined tasks and relationships and less emphasis upon hierarchy. Organic structures are seen as being appropriate in an uncertain or fast-changing environment. They adapt more speedily and effectively, partly because they have a greater capacity for information processing, especially when

compared with the shortcomings of the traditional bureaucratic organization with its insistence on 'official channels' and vertical communications. More broadly, the organic prescription seems relevant to those
implementation situations in which we are concerned to design structures
capable of implementing a sequence of changing policies over time
rather than to design a specific structure for a one-off programme.
This point will be developed further in chapter 13, when we examine
policy succession.

Prescriptions for organic structures are often uneasily received
within the public sector because of such considerations as the sheer
scale of many governmental agencies, the demands of accountability,
and the requirement to show consistency over time and equity between
comparable cases. A possible compromise is 'matrix structure', in which
the 'verticals' of departments are cross-hatched by the 'horizontals'
of interdepartmental project teams (or task forces, programme groups,
etc.) led by project leaders. This combination of bureaucracy and
'adhocracy' has its own problems, such as 'dual authority', but it does
add a more flexible dimension to the traditional structures of governmental machinery (see also 13.8.4).

### 11.4.2 PROCEDURAL AND MANAGERIAL APPROACHES

To have structures appropriate to implementation is perhaps less
important than to develop appropriate processes and procedures—
including managerial procedures incorporating relevant techniques.
Again a contrast can be drawn between planning *of* and *for* change.
In the former case, implementation is seen as a technical or managerial
problem. The procedures involved are those of scheduling, planning,
and control. Thus after problem identification and selection of the
most cost-effective policy response, the implementation stage would
involve such sequential steps as: (1) design a programme incorporating
task sequences and clear statements of objectives, performance standards,
cost, and timing; (2) execute the programme, by mobilizing appropriate
structures and staffing, funding and resources, procedures and methods;
(3) build in appropriate scheduling, monitoring, and control devices to
ensure that the programme proceeds as intended or, if deviation occurs,
that appropriate corrective action is quickly taken. However, this
approach does assume a very high degree of control over the programme
and its outcome and of insulation from the environment.

The managerial technique which sums up much of this approach is
network planning and control (NPC) which provides a framework

within which projects can be planned and implementation controlled, by identifying the tasks to be accomplished, the relationships between these tasks, and the logical sequence in which they should be performed (see Lang, 1977) Sophisticated forms of networking, such as Programme Evaluation and Review Technique (PERT) allow for probability estimates of the duration of each task, calculation of the 'critical path' along which any slippage would delay the whole project, monitoring of any 'slack' elsewhere in the network, and reallocation of resources to permit activities on the critical path to be completed on time.

One reason why PERT became so fashionable in both the public and private sectors from the mid-1960s was its apparent success in ensuring that the Polaris nuclear submarine programme in the USA was completed on time—unlike so many other defence projects. However, Sapolsky (1972) has argued that PERT as described had little to do with keeping the project on time, but was on the other hand very useful in convincing political superiors of managerial effectiveness and thus reducing their interference in the management of the project—such interference having been a major source of delays in other defence projects!

Network analysis is also used in government for more mundane tasks, such as scheduling building contracts by local authorities. Even here it should be noted that the causes of deviations from schedule thrown up by the network still have to be identified by managers (who are likely to be aware of the deviation before it appears on a computer print-out), who will also be responsible for devising remedies, often on the site rather than in the computer room. Reallocating resources from one task to another may be delayed by the need to negotiate changes with trade unions. It should also be borne in mind for all users of network analysis that it is very expensive in terms of both data preparation and computer time.

We would stress that we are not arguing against the employment of network analysis or other related techniques. Even when network analysis is not used in day-to-day management it can be very valuable at the planning stage since it draws attention to project interdependencies and future resource needs (Sapolsky, 1972, 125). However, such techniques are clearly not enough on their own. As Albanese (1975, 203) notes, 'if network is to be useful it has to be an actual guide to behaviour'. That is, its utility as a control device depends on the extent to which a network is communicable, acceptable, feasible, and credible. This involves a nice balance between flexibility (the network must be adjusted as the project develops in practice) and rigidity (an entirely flexible network would have little force as a means either of planning or control). '

So far we have been talking in terms of the assumption of a high degree of control over implementation and its outcome (though PERT is designed to cope with probabilities rather than simple certainties). The absence of certainty or control does not mean that procedures for implementation are impossible, but rather that they have to be imbedded in a broader approach to the policy process as a whole which would stress an iterative rather than a linear view of that process. In addition to iterative scanning of the changing environment and careful problem definition, such an approach would include: (1) forecasting, including 'wedge' projections and 'alternative futures' based on different assumptions (see chapter 8); (2) contingency planning; (3) where possible, carrying forward several options until firmer evidence is available (see 8.9); (4) tentative objectives and programmes; (5) constant monitoring, feedback, and adjustment of programmes; (6) more fundamental reviews of assumptions, objectives, and programmes. It can be seen that these procedures are similar to the discussions in several places throughout this book of how analysis can be applied in the context of uncertainty.

In practice, implementation rarely involves either complete certainty and control, or unpredictability and lack of control: typically a combination of these occurs so that all the above processes are relevant, although in different mixes depending on the degree of predictability and controllability present. Another important variable is the extent to which it is necessary to negotiate and maintain consensus (or at least compliance) among various interested parties. This leads on to the importance of behavioural and political analysis, to which we now turn.

## 11.4.3 BEHAVIOURAL APPROACHES

There are limits to what can be achieved by manipulating structures and procedures. Human behaviour and attitudes must also be influenced if policies are to be implemented. The behavioural approach begins by recognizing that there is often resistance to change. In fact, the alternatives are rarely as simple as acceptance or resistance, and there is a spectrum of possible reactions, from active acceptance, through passive acceptance, indifference, and passive resistance, to active resistance. However, we can generalize about some of the sources of resistance to change involved in implementing policies.

To start with, there may be fear of change *per se*, because change means uncertainty and some people have a very low 'tolerance for ambiguity'. In addition, there may be more specific fears, such as fears about the economic effects of change in terms of earnings, benefits, job security, career prospects, etc. Threats to personal security need not all be economic: people are often uneasy about having to learn new skills, assume different responsibilities, meet higher standards, or work with colleagues in a novel setting. Individuals or groups may have status fears about the effects of a proposed change, and the 'political' effects of change may be resisted (e.g. changes in relative power positions).

The organizational effects of implementing a new or altered policy may be resented, especially if anticipated effects include greater size, 'bureaucratic' structures, impersonality, reduced personal or agency autonomy, etc. The context of change is often important, especially where change is thought to imply serious failures or shortcomings in existing arrangements. There may be confusion about the nature of the policy to be implemented and the underlying objectives, creating an environment of rumour and suspicion. Where previous experience of the introduction of new policies has been unfortunate, because of inadequate consultation or serious disruption or redundancies, fears of a new policy will be greater. Finally, those involved in implementing the policy or who are targets of the policy may feel that they are being hustled into change because the transition period is too short or because consultation has been too hurried, and the natural reaction is to try to slow down the process by one means or another.

If the symptoms and causes of resistance are understood, the 'treatment' prescribed by the behavioural approach is obvious and fairly simple in theory, though often far from simple to achieve in practice. To avoid or minimize resistance, full information should be provided at an early stage about proposed or anticipated changes, including the reasons, objectives, and means involved. There should be extensive consultation with affected parties (inside and outside the organization), and participative decision-making where possible. Frankness about problems and dangers ('valid communication') is advocated, as are persuasion—or 'seeking to convince rather than to command'—and 'conversion' of informal leaders and group influentials.

The aim, according to this approach, would be to create an atmosphere of trust, mainly by management showing concern for people's interests—and for their less obvious feelings (about loss of workmates, personal insecurities, etc.). The climate should be one which will encourage people to express the fears which often underlie ostensible reasons for resistance. Assurances should be given that changes will not be rushed and that resources will be adequate, and also that the effects of change will be reviewed and that there is some flexibility in the plan.

  It is important to realize that the more serious writers on the behavioural approach do not make the argument for such 'employee-centred' and 'participative' management on moral grounds or because democratic is 'nicer' than autocratic management. The argument is that such approaches are more effective, particularly in modern conditions where there is less willingness to accept that 'management knows better and top management knows best'.

  The best known attempt to apply behavioural analysis to management is 'OD', meaning 'Organizational Development' (see Eddy, 1970; 1981; see also 13.8.2). OD is a process for bringing about needed changes in an organization through the application of the behavioural sciences. It is also a form of management consultancy, in which the consultant acts as a change agent to influence the entire culture of the organization, including the attitudes and behaviour of key personnel. He may use 'sensitivity training', or 'T-groups' to do so. The emphasis of OD consultancy is on analysing problem-solving processes (and blockages) rather than on suggesting specific solutions to problems. By improving the ways in which problems are defined and tackled, the hope is that better and more lasting solutions will be achieved by the organization itself. An OD input is often thought particularly appropriate when potentially divisive major changes are sought or anticipated.

  Management by Objectives (MbO) is an approach which combines elements of the procedural/management techniques with behavioural analysis. Clearly, MbO forms a bridge between the specification of objectives (see chapter 9) and their implementation. MbO is a label which covers a wide range of practices and procedures tried out in the private sector, and to a lesser extent in the public sector, since the mid-1950s. The first central element of MbO is that there must be a *hierarchy* of goals, so that the individual manager can see how his personal objectives, if achieved, will contribute to larger organizational aims. Secondly, the process of arriving at goals or objectives under MbO must be *interactive*, that is, based on consultation and, if possible, joint agreement. If objectives are simply imposed on managers from above, then the system is not one of MbO. Thirdly, there must be a system of *performance appraisal* involving a mixture of managerial self-monitoring and self-control and joint evaluations of progress by each manager and his superior.

Attempts have been made in the last couple of decades to transplant MbO from the private to the public sector. In the Civil Service, for example, the Fulton Report (1968) talked about the need for 'accountable management', a concept which is very closely linked to that of MbO (see also Expenditure Committee, 1977). However, it is open to discussion whether or not MbO can be widely applied in the public sector without major adaptations in approach. Among the problems are the multiplicity of objectives (often unquantified) which civil servants are asked to perform, their frequent lack of direct control over the resources necessary for implementation (though recent initiatives on financial management may improve this), and the inevitability (even desirability as shown in 11.4.4) of political intervention in implementation. Finally, there is the intergovernmental nature of much implementation, which frequently makes it inappropriate to think in terms of a simple hierarchy of objectives and lines of responsibility.

The appropriateness of different strategies derived from behavioural analysis will vary according to the type of policy change to be implemented: thus the task of socializing recruits into a completely new organization will differ substantially from that of reorienting the staff of an existing organization which is asked to implement a policy with different objectives in the same policy area (see chapter 13).

### 11.4.4 POLITICAL APPROACHES

So far, three levels of analysis have been identified: organizational, procedural, and behavioural. The fourth and perhaps most fundamental level is that of political analysis. The term 'political' includes but is certainly not limited to party politics: rather, it refers to patterns of power and influence between and within organizations. The argument quite simply is that the implementation of a policy may have been carefully planned in terms of appropriate organization, procedures, management, and influences on behaviour, but if it takes insufficient account of the realities of power (e.g. the ability of groups opposed to the policy to block the efforts of its supporters) then the policy is unlikely to succeed.

More fundamentally, a political approach may challenge the assumptions on which the other approaches—especially that of some behavioural analysts and OD consultants—are based. Specifically, the assumption that conflict is an aberration which can be cured by improved 'interpersonal competence' would be challenged by many social scientists. Conflict between and within many organizations and social groups is endemic rather than exceptional and cannot simply be 'communicated' or 'co-ordinated' away. Thus the success of a policy is likely to depend, in the last resort, on the willingness and ability of some dominant group (or coalition of groups) to impose its will. Where no such dominance exists, implementation of some approximation to desired policy may only be achieved through a long process of 'incrementalism' and 'partisan mutual adjustment' (see 4.3). In some circumstances the distribution of power may be such as to produce policy stalemate at the implementation stage, even when the policy has been formally authorized and legitimated.

Analysis of the politics of the *intergovernmental* aspects of implementation is particularly important given that many central government policies are not actually delivered by central government departments. Local authorities and other bodies also initiate policies which require clearances from other organizations.

When the whole range and variety of public sector bodies are considered—central government departments, local authorities and 'quangos' of various kinds—it can be seen that over-generalization about intergovernmental relationships should be avoided. The scope available to each body in dealing with other organizations will depend on its resources of different kinds, not just finance and legal powers, and on what it wants from other organizations (cf. Rhodes, 1979b, 1981). Resources differ considerably, implying different constraints on the various bodies.

Even when one government body is formally subordinate to another, they will often be *inter*dependent. For example, it is not simply a matter of government departments or local authorities deciding on their attitude to the Scottish Development Agency (SDA), but of SDA deciding its attitude to them. In any pair of public organizations each is likely to want something from the other. The implication is that each is likely to have at least some discretion over implementation and some bargaining power in its relationship with the other, either during implementation or when implementation implications are being discussed at earlier stages. Where more than two organizations are involved, the scope for discretion may be higher because, for example, alliances and understandings can be used as levers on others.

To stress interdependence is not to argue that all organizations have similar resources or are equally powerful (cf. Rhodes, 1981). The notion of interdependence is quite compatible with asymmetry in the resources available to organizations. For example, central government clearly has access to legislative resources not available to local authorities and can use these not only in relation to the implementation of a particular policy but to change the 'rules of the game' in which relationships are normally conducted (such as the right to be consulted, the basic grant structure) or even to change or abolish other political actors, as with the re-elected 1983 Conservative Government's plans to abolish the Greater London Council and the metropolitan counties. That said, the Conservative Government has nevertheless been unable to get local authority spending down in line with its targets. The fact that one organization in an implementation relationship has a preponderance of resources does not exclude the likelihood that it will still be dependent on other organizations for key aspects of implementation: e.g. the Government could not send in commissioners to every local authority to take over council house sales.

The discussion so far may seem to have placed undue emphasis on potential conflict in intergovernmental policy implementation. Certainly, many policies embody values shared among all the bodies concerned; there may be problems of implementation, but not those arising from intergovernmental differences. However, the normal condition of mutual interdependence means that where there are actual or potential differences of view the government body wishing to promote the implementation of a policy will have to exercise political judgement about which strategy is most likely to improve the chances of implementation.

The fact that implementation may be multi-organizational and involve political bargaining or conflict does not preclude a role for analysis, albeit such analysis should be concerned with anticipating political obstacles and where possible taking them into account *before* the formulation of objectives and the selection of an option (see our reference to the question of what is needed from other organizations in the checklist for objectives in 9.4.4). A political strategy for implementation need not and should not be seen as separate from consideration of other more 'technical' factors.

All points considered in this section reinforce the argument in 2.3.2 that policy formulation and policy implementation are interdependent and that analysts must consider them in combination at all times. Politicians, too, must accept the need for their continuing interest and involvement if they are to be sure of even partial implementation of legislation they have sponsored, and there may well be a need for follow-up legislation and regulations to cover loopholes and fill in details. This is not to say that administrative and managerial considerations of the type considered in 11.4.1–11.4.3 are not important for successful implementation, but that they will often be subordinate to more explicitly political strategies.

# 12

# Evaluation

## 12.1 The need for policy evaluation

If we lived in a world of complete certainty and perfect administration there would be no need for evaluation: having selected the best option and put it into operation we would know in advance what its effects would be. However, we rarely have such certainty. Our understanding of many issues, especially social problems, is imperfect or even contested (see chapter 7 on issue definition). Our understanding of how government intervention will work and what its effect will be is therefore also limited. Further, this government intervention is only one of many influences on the target problem, because unforeseen changes may arise, because this programme may interact with a number of other programmes, and because it may be difficult to separate out the effects of a 'new' programme from the long-term effects of programmes which it replaces. All these problems make it both necessary to monitor the delivery of a programme and evaluate its success, and very difficult to do so.

Although evaluation is concerned with what happens once a policy has been put into effect, it is important that we should not leave it until that stage before we consider how we might go about evaluating the policy. If we do so, we may find that evaluation is impracticable or produces inconclusive results. The time to consider evaluation is at the options selection and programme design stages. The type of information required can be specified in advance. More dramatically, the extent to which an option is capable of being evaluated can be made one of the criteria for selection. Finally, the policy analysis approach to evaluation is not simply concerned with carrying out technically correct evaluations; it has to be concerned with how evaluation results are consumed and utilized.

## 12.2 Monitoring

• A precondition of meaningful evaluation—and an essential element of successful implementation—is that the activities involved in delivering the policy should be specified and the outputs so far as possible identified. This is not simply a matter for prior specification but a matter for continuous monitoring. It is very easy for programme drift to set in, for public officials to carry out different activities from those orginally envisaged (or even not all), or for the programme to reach clients other than those originally intended. To evaluate the programme in terms of its original objectives might lead to a conclusion that the policy was a failure, yet this might be misleading since the policy as originally envisaged might not actually have been put into effect.

It is therefore important to distinguish between failures of implementation (which it is the purpose of monitoring to avoid) and failure of policy. Of course, the distinction is not complete. If it proves impracticable to implement the policy in the way originally envisaged then this, too, can be considered a failure of policy design (see 11.1).

Fully effective monitoring will require initial specification of what programme delivery should involve: one cannot measure deviations from standards which are not specified. This involves linking programme goals to the objectives of the policy. Programme goals cover such matters as the number and types of people it is intended to serve, the kinds of service which will be offered, and the types of staff to be employed (Weiss, 1972, 26). Further, the degree of tolerance in meeting these goals would have to be specified—how much deviation over how long a time would be acceptable overall and at the level of individual offices or depots? Clearly if broad objectives are vague or conflicting there will be a problem about determining what programme goals would be appropriate. Programme goals may become a substitute for policy objectives. Monitoring will be possible, but evaluation would be problematic.

Monitoring requires the collection of information about the extent to which programme goals are being met. This may require the design of special information collection procedures, since the administrative data which would otherwise be collected might not be appropriate for monitoring purposes (see also 5.6.2). In addition to administrative records, surveys of actual or potential clients, and observation (as by, e.g., education inspectors) are means of collecting information (see Rossi, Freeman and Wright, 1979, ch. 4).

However, monitoring is not just about information collection. It requires decisions about what *action* will be taken if performance deviates unduly from what is desired. Thus, monitoring is about *control* and the exercise of power. Those involved in programme delivery will be aware of this, and this may affect how information about programme delivery is passed up to superiors. For managerial and political reasons governments may be unwilling to take the action which the monitoring information would otherwise indicate (see Hogwood, 1976).

Bloody-minded insistence on rectifying deviations thrown up by monitoring information would often be inappropriate. Systematic failure to meet programme goals may indicate a need to redefine those goals (e.g. employ a different type of staff if insufficient numbers of the originally specified kind are unavailable) or even to indicate that an evaluation of the practicality of meeting policy objectives should be carried out. Further, overrigid enforcement of programme goals may actually be counter-productive if it eliminates creative initiatives to meet more effectively the overall objectives of the policy.

Frequently, new or replacement policies are carried out by multi-purpose local authorities, which may have considerable scope for defining specific programme goals, if indeed they engage in specific definition of any kind. From the perspective of central government this makes monitoring problematic. Further, a particular programme may be only one of many tasks to be carried out within a department and may not be allocated to a separate section within it. This may be true even at the level of the individual, say, social worker who will typically be expected to implement a wide range of specific policies. It may often be difficult to draw boundaries round a set of activities and outputs that constitute a programme, yet this is a necessary precondition for effective monitoring and evaluation. It would clearly be perverse to insist on rigid compartmentalization and allocation of staff to one programme exclusively, particularly where there are arguments for integrated delivery of a number of programmes (e.g. because they are all aimed at similar types of families).

Yet if policy-makers have no idea about what is 'going on out there' they are unable to judge whether anything relevant is happening at all. or to measure the costs of programme delivery relative to the outputs.

In such circumstances policies become hopeful signals sent out to the periphery of the policy delivery system which are incapable of being effectively monitored. Crude evaluation of whether the desired effects have been achieved may be possible, but it will not be possible to attribute those effects to the policy if the extent of implementation is not even known.

## 12.3 Problems of analysing the impact of public policy

### 12.3.1 OBJECTIVES

Nothing illustrates more clearly the interaction of stages of the policy process than the way in which objective-setting (see chapter 9) shapes evaluation. If objectives are unclear or are not specified in any measureable form, the criteria for success are unclear. If there has been goal shifting or goal creep, should success be measured against the original objectives or what now appear to be the real objectives?

Vagueness in goals or concentration on immediate operational goals can be a consequence of divergences in views about policy objectives—often support from many quarters is necessary to get a programme off the ground and this may be better met by vague statements on which all can agree.

It could be argued that the early stages of evaluation can be of benefit because they force disagreements out into the open and may point to the need to reconcile these if effective programme delivery is to be possible. On the other hand, such clarification may result in some loss of political support: there may be a dilemma between viability in the sense of implementability and viability in the sense of political support. The search for goal statements may also reveal discrepancies between the policy goals and administrative practice. This points to the desirability of adjusting either objectives or activities to bring them into line with each other.

Where those involved in policy-making or programme delivery are unable to agree on a statement of specific and meaningful objectives what can the evaluator do? A number of courses of action are possible (cf. Weiss, 1972, 28):

(1) The would-be evaluator could give up, on the grounds that it is not possible to evaluate a policy unless clear guidance is given as to what the policy is for. This is a purist response, but one wonders whether such a purist should have become engaged in the messy business of policy analysis in the first place.

(2) The evaluator can pose the question about the objectives of the policy and wait for personnel involved in delivering the programme to reach a consensus. However, the evaluator may have to wait for ever.

· (3) After reading everything available about the programme, talking to practitioners and observing the programme in action, the evaluator can draw up the statement of goals himself. This may seem reasonable but there are two dangers:

(a) the evaluator may read in his own personal or professional interests or preconceptions into goal statements.

(b) If the study when completed produces adverse findings, the practitioners may turn round and say 'But that's not what we were trying to achieve anyway'.

(4) The evaluator can set up a collaborative effort in formulating goals by sitting down with programme practitioners, offering them goal statements, and altering them in the light of comments of programme staff until agreement is reached. Weiss (1972) argues that this is probably the best approach, but offers no advice on what agreement-forcing mechanisms might be used.

(5) The question of goals can be left on one side and one would conduct not a formal evaluation but a more exploratory open-ended study. This may be all that can be done if there is little agreement about what would constitute success.

(6) The evaluator could ask members of the target group what they consider to be the objectives of the programme. However, apart from the possibility that this may not conform with what the programme staff see as the objectives, it has to be noted that it may not be appropriate to ask the target group for their particularistic perspective, especially when they are the target of regulatory policies.

Even when a statement of clear, specific, and reasonable goals is attained, there are still a number of problems. For example, how important relative to each other are goals where more than one is specified? (see also 9.5). The evaluator may run into difficulties if he relies on programme staff to state priorities, since they may emphasize innocuous goals or those on which the organization scores highly. How far should the evaluator go in explicitly assigning weights to goals?

Ideally, any contradictory objectives should have been ironed out at the objective-setting stage, but all too often the evaluator will be faced with what may have turned out to be incompatible objectives. Choice about which objective to evaluate is different from the situation where there are merely multiple and independent objectives.

The time available, evaluation budget, and access to data all form constraints on which goals can be evaluated. The temptation is to study what can be studied within these constraints. However, this may ignore key concerns about the programme (e.g. whether the study of long-term goals might reveal 'sleeper effects'). This raises almost ethical questions about whether policy analysts ought to undertake evaluation when these constraints preclude examination of key objectives in an appropriate manner.

## 12.3.2 DEFINING AND MEASURING THE CRITERIA FOR SUCCESS

Even an apparently clearly stated objective may leave open the question of how the success of the objective is to be judged or measured. A programme might have the stated objective: 'To produce a 25 per cent improvement within a six month period in primary school pupils' understanding of basic geometrical principles through the use of microcomputers operated by the pupils'. This is a very detailed and apparently specific formulation of an objective, but it still leaves open whether we are to judge success by enjoyment shown by pupils during teaching sessions involving microcomputers, greater interest shown by pupils in basic geometry, knowledge of geometrical principles, or ability to apply those principles to other problems, or a combination of these. Further, it will be necessary to operationalize these criteria in some measurable form. It may be impracticable to measure attainment of objectives directly, so a more or less indirect indicator or range of indicators may be employed. The danger, of course, is that relatively hard or measurable criteria may be used, at the expense of more qualitative indicators which may be more valid indicators of programme success.

In some cases there may be readily available indicators used in previous studies which can be pulled down 'off the shelf'. However, care should be taken to use such indicators only where they are valid indicators of policy objectives. There is no point in using a measure which is standard if it is a standard measure of something other than the objective which is the focus of concern.

Unfortunately, where the criterion of success is not adequately represented by a previously tested indicator it will be difficult to ensure that the indicator used will be a reliable measure. To some extent possible confounding factors can be anticipated and controlled for, but snags with a particular indicator may only emerge during the course of the study, even worse, may never be clearly identified at all. Even an apparently simple question may contain a word which will be interpreted differently by different groups of people, and the way options for answering a result are set out may produce spurious results. Impressionistic assessments (such as teachers' views about pupils' attitudes) may be biased or poorly based.

### 12.3.3 HOW MUCH IS ENOUGH?

Even when objectives have been specified and priorities among them established, the issues remain of what outcomes are seen as relevant to meeting those objectives and what level of achievement in meeting those objectives would constitute success: would any movement in the desired direction be enough? Would a specified once-and-for-all improvement constitute success or is a continuing improvement in performance expected?

It is important to try to establish the standards considered to constitute success before the data are collected and analysed. Otherwise, what Weiss (1972, 32) calls 'fully-only' standards of judgement will come into play:

Different people looking at the same data can come up with different conclusions in the tradition of the 'fully-only' school of analysis. 'Fully 25 per cent of the students . . .' boasts the promoter; 'only 25 per cent of the students . . .' sighs the detractor.

The specification of performance would have to include an indication of the relationship between costs and other indicators which would constitute success. This should include consideration of marginal costs and benefits, since the last additional units of benefit may have been obtained at disproportionately high cost (where there is a threshold effect, the relationship between cash costs and performances would be the reverse).

### 12.3.4 SIDE EFFECTS

There can be considerable practical difficulties in attempting to identify and measure side effects, but the damage they cause, or the spill-over benefits they provide may be more significant than the impact in terms of the original objective. Actual reverse consequences may be relatively easy to pick up (though see Sieber, 1980), but there is a problem of how other consequences (adverse and beneficial) should be brought into a statement of objectives and how much side effects should be weighted relative to the central objectives.

## 12.3.5 INFORMATION

Information necessary to assess impact may not be available or may be available in unsuitable form. Data collected in the course of policy delivery may tell us a lot about the characteristics of the people actually receiving the benefit but little about the target population as a whole or about the impact of receiving a benefit. Some information may be available at local level, but not at central level where there may be the concern for evaluating the overall success of a programme delivered through local authorities. Local authority recording procedures may also vary between authorities, making comparison impossible. Information where available (e.g. about crime rates) may actually be misleading (see 5.4).

## 12.3.6 SEPARATION OF PROGRAMME IMPACT FROM OTHER INFLUENCES

We have quite a wide range of data about social conditions, but it is frequently very difficult to separate out the effect of a particular programme from all the other influences on people's lives. For example, improved health indicators can reflect improved living conditions arising from greater affluence and better housing or from improved health education as well as from treatment by doctors and hospitals through the National Health Service. Programme impact and other influences may operate in opposite directions, producing apparent but spurious perverse results. Many of the techniques of systematic evaluation outlined below are designed to tackle this problem through experimental or quasi-experimental designs, but as we will see, there can be practical difficulties in implementing these methodologies.

## 12.3.7 MULTI-PROGRAMME TARGETS

It is common for a single problem or group of the population to be the target of several programmes with the same or related objectives (e.g. the poor). In such cases it is impossible or meaningless to assess the impact of a single programme. For example, if vandalism goes down, is this due to improved police methods, better education, better housing layout, etc.? Big problems tend to have a lot of 'solutions' thrown at them, making it difficult to assess which, if any, of them are producing an effect. On the other hand, some programmes may work *only* in conjunction with others, so a research strategy to try to determine the effects of such programmes in isolation would be counter-productive. Complications also arise when there is a rapid sequence over time of programmes directed at a problem and it is difficult to separate out the continuing effects of now withdrawn programmes from the effects of newly introduced ones.

## 12.3.8 DISTRIBUTION OF IMPACT

Presumably we are concerned not just with total or average impact but with how impact is distributed and whether it is actually going to the groups intended to benefit most. There is some evidence (see e.g. Le Grand, 1982) that the reverse happens because better educated people tend to be more knowledgeable about working the delivery system and have the resources which are sometimes required to take maximum advantage of policy benefits.

## 12.3.9 POLITICAL SENSITIVITY OF MONITORING AND EVALUATION

As Weiss (1972) puts it, evaluation takes place in an 'action setting'. What is being considered is the success or failure of a programme to which politicians have committed their reputations, to which public employees may have made a personal commitment as well as having careers at stake, and from which clients may be receiving benefits even if in terms of evaluation criteria the impact of these benefits does not constitute a success. It is not surprising, therefore, that evaluation may be seen as a threat to the continuation of a programme in which a number of people have an important stake. This will naturally affect how evaluation results are utilized (see 12.6), but it will also affect the ease with which evaluation research can be conducted, since the co-operation (rather than simply compliance) of public officials and clients is often required in the evaluation. One paradox of evaluation is that it may only be possible to carry out monitoring or evaluation by promising not to use its results.

## 12.3.10 COST

As the figure of 1 per cent of total programme cost for some very large programmes in the United States indicates, systematic evaluation can be very costly (see Aitkin and Salmon, 1983). Unfortunately this is particularly true of the most methodologically reputable methods, such as the experimental approach. Such costs are a diversion from substantive policy delivery. They can be justified as a means of eliminating failed policies (though we discuss the difficulties of termination in chapter 13) and of leading to improved policy design in future. However, this is true only if the results of evaluation are actually utilized. The costs of evaluation can be reduced and the value of evaluation substantially increased if policies are initially designed both for ease of evaluation and for ease of succession or termination following evaluation.

## 12.4 Techniques for systematic evaluation

It is arguable that the evaluation literature has become too obsessed with the finer details of methodological improvement at the expense of recalling the purposes of evaluation, the practical limitations on evaluation, and the political context of evaluation. It is, of course, important to know the characteristics of the available methodologies and these are set out briefly below with considerations of their technical advantages and disadvantages, as well as any ethical or political considerations involved in their use.

In considering these methodologies it should always be borne in mind that the appropriateness of a methodology is determined by the purpose for which the evaluation is required. If what is wanted is a quick assessment of the short-term impact of a programme in its early stages to enable consideration of its funding for the next financial year there is little point in commissioning a very expensive experimental approach, the results of which may not be available for several years. Accordingly, it is desirable that the purposes of evaluation should be made clear at the beginning, and any disagreements about those purposes resolved.

Similarly requiring consideration at this stage is the extent to which it is desired to produce generalizable results. If the purpose of an evaluation is to provide guidance about whether an initially limited programme is to be expanded, it will be necessary to ensure that the characteristics which would obtain in the expanded programme are identified and assessed. Ideally the limited programme should have been established specifically to match all relevant conditions (see the discussion of the experimental approach in 12.4.3). Otherwise it may be possible to come to a conclusion about the impact of a specific project but not possible to generalize those findings to the likely impact of similar projects aimed at different target groups or in different types of area.

### 12.4.1 BEFORE-AND-AFTER STUDIES

A common-sense approach might appear to be to compare the situation in terms of relevant outcomes after programme implementation with the situation before the programme was started. Such outcomes might be considered at the level of individual members of the target group or in terms of aggregate or average outcomes, with the latter being much less satisfactory because it may conceal important variations in impact on an individual or groups of individuals and movement of individuals into and out of the target group, perhaps as a result of the programme itself.

Despite their superficial attractiveness, simple before-and-after studies are likely to have a number of unsatisfactory features. First of all, changes in outcomes may be the lagged effect of previous and now-replaced policies or of the period of no-policy rather than the emerging impact of the programme which is being evaluated. Secondly, if other policies which also affect these outcomes have also been changed then the study will pick up this aggregate effect rather than the effect of the specific programme with which we are concerned. Thirdly, there may have been other important changes in the economic or social environment impacting on the outcomes being examined; for example, if a youth training programme is introduced during a period of increasing unemployment and it is found that youths trained under the programme had a lower chance of getting a job than they would have done before the introduction of the programme it would be spurious to attribute a perverse impact to the training itself.

If a longer run of before-and-after data is analysed, a shift at the time of programme introduction in an otherwise smooth trend may provide prima facie evidence of programme impact, However, it would be important to consider the possibility of extraneous and simultaneous influences before drawing firm conclusions about programme impact.

If no past data were collected before the introduction of the programme to be evaluated then even a simple before-and-after comparison is impracticable. In such circumstances, participants in the programme may be asked to recall their previous status. This adds the possibility of faulty recall to the problem of comparisons with actual past data, but if this approach is the only possibility the evaluator may judge that despite the snags it may generate useful findings which would be better than no evaluation at all. The absence of past data would tend to point to inadequate data collection at the issue definition stage and to failure to anticipate evaluation needs prior to evaluation. Again, this emphasizes that although evaluation is towards the end of the policy process its analytical implications have to be considered much earlier.

The potential value of before-and-after studies can be substantially increased if multiple time series for a number of areas can be compared. Multiple time-series analysis is clearly much more likely to eliminate spurious findings than simple before-and-after studies: if an effect occurs in more than one area it cannot be attributed to special factors applying to that area (providing that comparison areas are selected to avoid countervailing influences). Thus this approach can be considered a quasi-experimental one (see 12.4.4).

### 12.4.2 MODELLING

One can attempt to reduce or remove the problems of the crude before-and-after approach by constructing, perhaps in mathematical form, a model of the programme which incorporates programme outputs, lags, and changes in other possible influences on outcomes. The basic procedures are similar to those involved in modelling in forecasting (see 8.6), with the difference that the focus is entirely on the past. This approach has been used in practical applications, for example in evaluating British regional policy (see Ashcroft, 1978) but there can be problems which may prevent it from producing an entirely definitive or satisfactory result. First, the use of modelling involves a theory of cause and effect; if the model simply repeats the assumptions of the policy theory embodied in the original policy design it is an inadequate test of whether that theory stands up in practice: eroneous assumptions about causal relationships may be shown up, but this will not include all the relevant non-policy variables which may have an impact on outcomes. Lack of suitable data or inherently unknowable values (such as what the rate of change of employment in each industry in a region would have been in the absence of regional policy) may lead to rather tortuous methods of constructing missing data and injecting them into the model. In circumstances where policy was not designed for ready evaluability, modelling may be the most appropriate method (especially if only aggregate data are available) but its limitations should be borne in mind in qualifying its results.

### 12.4.3 EXPERIMENTAL METHOD

The experimental method is the methodologically most 'reputable' method since it relies on well-understood survey and statistical techniques which enable the isolation of specific effects from a complex and changing pattern of effects. Unfortunately, practical and political considerations may limit its use in practice. (For an overview of social experiments which have been conducted see Ferber and Hirsch, 1982;

for discussions of the experimental method see Weiss, 1972, 60–7; or Rossi *et al.*, 1979, ch. 6.)

The experimental method uses experimental and control groups. Randomly selected samples of the target population (whether individuals, classrooms, cities, etc.) are assigned to be in either the experimental group which receives the programme or the 'control group' which does not. Both groups are influenced by all the factors which we noted posed problems for crude before-and-after comparisons, so any difference in outcomes affecting the two groups can be inferred to be the result of the programme (providing care is taken to avoid the 'Hawthorne effect', which is a response due merely to the attention that programme recipients receive). Alternative programmes can be tested by setting up more than one experimental group.

It should be clear that the experimental method requires that programme delivery is focused entirely on evaluation considerations. It requires that the programme be designed from the start to utilize the method and cannot be properly conducted retrospectively. It is incompatible with uniform delivery of the programme to all the target population. This points to one set of ethical and political problems with the method. If the programme is believed in advance to be of potential benefit, the method requires that the programme be withheld from potential beneficiaries (just as drug testing may require that potentially beneficial drugs should be tested on only a limited sample). This raises the question of whether it is ethical to withhold such a benefit (especially if early evaluation results are favourable). Politicians who see benefits going to, say, one city but not their own may seek extension of the programme. Against that it can be argued that only proper evaluation can truly identify whether the programme really is beneficial and the degree of any benefit, which it is necessary to know if we are to determine that the programme is not merely beneficial but the most cost-effective way of meeting policy objectives. This argument may, however, be less politically persuasive.

There are a number of more technical problems with the experimental method in addition to the Hawthorne effect already mentioned. Members of the control group may be 'contaminated' if they become aware of the role they are playing. Given the multiplicity of often overlapping and frequently changing programmes in many policy areas members of control groups may receive benefits from other agencies which produce similar outcomes to the programme being studied. Careful experimental design can help to overcome these problems.

Two further considerations are likely to limit the use of the experimental method: time and cost. The final results of the evaluation study may not be available for several years after the experiment was started (though preliminary results may provide earlier feedback). Thus, universal coverage may be delayed for a politically unacceptable period (i.e. beyond the lifetime of a government). The experimental method does not come cheap. First there are the costs of delivering the programme to the experimental group, though this will be far less costly than universal coverage of an inadequate programme. Secondly, there are the research costs; for example, in the United States two-thirds of the $8m for the New Jersey negative income tax experiment was spent on research (Rutman, 1980, 75).

The conclusions drawn from an experiment are, of course, limited to the conditions under which the experiment is performed. Thus it may not be legitimate to generalize for an experiment conducted in a small town to a nationwide programme also covering rural and large urban areas. Similarly, modifications to the programme as actually delivered in the experiment may weaken (or strengthen) the results obtained from the experiment itself. The experimental method is well suited to test programme variation and a number of different sets of conditions, but this increases the number of experimental and control groups needed and therefore the expense involved.

Another possible snag with the experimental method lies in possible contaminating effects arising from the very fact that it is innovative and experimental. When the project is routinized and generalized the enthusiasm which underlay the experiment, and which might have been crucial to its success, may be absent.

### 12.4.4 QUASI-EXPERIMENTAL METHOD

The practical and political problems of using the experimental method have led to increases in 'quasi-experimental' methods, which attempt to separate out as much as possible of the extraneous effects which make assessment of impact difficult, though without providing the full protection which a properly conducted experiment would do. Of these methods, the closest to the experimental method is the non-equivalent control group, where, instead of random selection, individuals or groups with similar characteristics are assigned to a comparison group. The main problem is how to ensure that the comparison group is as similar as possible to the experimental group. Matching is difficult if we do not know the characteristics which will affect whether the person benefits from the programme or not. Matching on the basis of scores achieved before programme delivery can be unreliable because of the technical phenomenon known as 'regression to the mean'.

Another problem is 'self-selection', where people who choose to enter a programme are different from those who do not in characteristics which it may be difficult to pick up (e.g. motivation). Despite these difficulties it will be better to have a non-equivalent control group than no comparison group at all. The evaluator can note any differences between the groups and whether any bias is likely to understate or overstate programme effects.

Evaluators may be able to take advantage of 'natural experiments' to make comparisons which enable the effect of programme variations to be assessed. We discussed the use of multiple time-series analysis in this regard in 12.4.1 above. More generally, variations in how a programme is implemented by local authorities, while perhaps perceived as a problem from the perspective of how the centre would like the programme implemented, do provide an opportunity for assessing the effectiveness of particular programme components or alternative procedures for delivery. However, because such variations may not even all be identified, let alone controlled for, precise results from such comparisons should not be expected.

## 12.4.5 RETROSPECTIVE COST–BENEFIT ANALYSIS

We have already come across cost–benefit analysis (CBA) in its more traditional role as a methodology for determining whether a project should be carried out and, if so, which option is best (see 10.6.3). As we noted then, one of the major problems with CBA as an aid to decision-making is that its calculations depend on assumptions about future events. With retrospective CBA this problem is removed and retrospective CBA might also seem to avoid the need for prior statement of objectives and priorities and to handle the problem of side-effects since, in the economists' version at least, all of these are reduced to monetary equivalents. However, the other problems of CBA remain—how to measure costs and benefits in financial terms and the problem of intangibles. Further, CBA by itself cannot handle the problem of separating programme effects from other effects on relevant outcomes. Arguably the costs and benefits can only be quantified after information about programme results has been generated by a good evaluation study; that is, CBA is not a substitute for the evaluation methods listed above, but an extension.

The economists' version of CBA is also ill-suited to handling distributional aspects of impact, since it seeks to summarize all aspects of a single aggregate figure. Where the purpose of the programme was precisely to be distributional, e.g. to provide housing for those in need, it is important to include this objective in the assessment. One possibility is to weight the benefits of the main target group more heavily than others who benefit, but it is perhaps better just to display the distributional effects.

The planning balance sheet approach to CBA (referred to in 10.6.3), which sets out costs and benefits under a number of headings, quantifying where possible but not only in monetary terms, may be one method of displaying impacts when it proves impossible to secure agreement about relative priorities between multiple objectives. By its nature it cannot provide an unambiguous assessment and leaves scope for disagreement about overall success or failure, but at least it provides a more formal basis for 'political evaluation'.

## 12.5 Who should carry out evaluations?

Much of the literature on evaluation is abstracted from the respective institutional settings of the evaluator and the programme being evaluated. Some even goes so far as to assume implicitly that the policymaker and the evaluator are one and the same person, so that possible clashes of interest between evaluator, policy-maker and operating staff do not arise. Clearly, however, whether or not evaluations are carried out by those delivering the programme can have important implications both for the technical effectiveness of the evaluation and for its utilization.

### 12.5.1 EVALUATION BY THE OPERATING STAFF

A big advantage of insider evaluations is that insiders will have the detailed knowledge of just what is involved in delivering the programme and of any points not foreseen at the policy design stage. However, this understanding can also be achieved by an outsider if he has access to information and the co-operation of the operating staff. Indeed, one of the major problems of information flow is *within* an organization, a problem faced by both insiders and outsiders.

The operating divisions may lack the specialized skills for good evaluations (though there is a shortage of such skills all round in Britain). This is at least as much an argument for having people with policy analysis training in operating divisions rather than confining them to the ghettos of policy analysis units. However, it has to be recognized that the shortage of evaluation skills and a possibly intermittent workload within any one operating division militate against evaluation by operating staff.

Another disadvantage of evaluation within the operating division is that a number of different organizations may be involved in policy delivery so that a fully rounded evaluation cannot be obtained by looking at the results of the activity in one organization.

If the results of an evaluation are to be utilized, then if they involve changing the existing programme the adjustments will have to be carried out by the operating staff. If these staff have been actively involved in the evaluation effort the chances of willing implementation of the changes are increased. Against that insider evaluations may be less likely to imply threatening changes in the first place. Where an outside evaluator is involved, the chances of subsequent implementation of changes may be improved if the evaluator has involved the operating staff in discussions about objectives, criteria, etc.

## 12.5.2 SPECIALIZED EVALUATION STAFF WITHIN THE ORGANIZATION

Evaluation can be carried out by a separate unit concerned with evaluation and analysis rather than delivery, though still within the organization responsible for delivery. Particularly where the evaluation staff are concerned with a number of different activities within the organization, they do not have the same vested interests in the continuation of any given programme in the same way. The link is even weaker if staff are specially hired temporarily to carry out the evaluation. While the relationship between evaluators and operating staff should not be seen as necessarily a clash, given the potential unpredictability of evaluation and its results there is bound to be tension.

At the margins between inside staff and commissioning an outside body is the use of paid consultants (including academics) either to advise the evaluators in the organization or to carry out some of the evaluation in co-operation with organization staff.

A final consideration is whether it is proper for an organization to be solely responsible for its own evaluation. As Wildavsky (1972, 518) puts it: 'No matter how good its internal analysis, or how persuasively an organization justifies its programmes to itself, there is something unsatisfactory about allowing it to judge its own case.' Periodically, therefore, even a self-evaluating organization should be subject to audits of the methods used in its evaluations or to independently conducted evaluation studies.

### 12.5.3 EXTERNAL EVALUATION COMMISSIONED BY THE DELIVERY ORGANIZATION

There is a wide range of bodies which can in principle carry out commissioned evaluation research (and do in practice in the United States): academic groups, not-for-profit organizations, and commercial firms, especially management consultants. Such an outside evaluator may have an opportunity to negotiate the purpose and focus of the study, but it should always be remembered that the commissioned evaluator is responsible to the organization (and the level within the organization) which commissioned the study.

Delivery staff may actually prefer evaluations to be commissioned from outsiders because of greater confidence in the credentials of academics or consultants (perhaps overrating the skills of such outsiders and underrating the skills of those who are already on the staff or could be hired). An outside organization may be commissioned to ensure greater public confidence in the evaluation results, either for reasons of expertise, or because a report from outsiders might appear to be more objective. However, apart from the fact that much high quality (and alas, in Britain often unpublished) evaluation has been done by insiders, there are two reasons for questioning whether reports commissioned by the delivery organization are necessarily 'objective'.

First, the commissioning organization may specify a set of guidelines to be used in the evaluation (objectives to be assessed, criteria to be used, levels to be judged as 'success') which will tend to predetermine the result, with the report essentially being used as an apparently external legitimation of the organization's viewpoint. Management consultants may be particularly useful for carrying out this sort of legitimation exercise.

Secondly, Weiss (1972, 20) suggests that 'It even happens that an outside research firm will sweeten the interpretation of programme results (by choice of respondents, by types of statistical tests applied) in order to ingratiate itself with a programme and get further contracts.'

### 12.5.4 EVALUATION BY FUNDING OR LEGISLATIVE BODIES

Organizations directly involved in policy delivery are far from being the only bodies potentially interested in evaluation, and, indeed, we have suggested that they may have some cause to fear it. Legislative and executive bodies which originally authorized the policy are likely to be concerned with assessing success, either because of concern with substantive policy effectiveness or for the more negative reason of avoiding the political embarrassment of an unsuccessful programme being exposed by others. (Conversely, political opponents of those who promoted the policy may commission an evaluation precisely to secure such political embarrassment.)

Such evaluation may be directly conducted by the staff of the executive or legislative bodies concerned (they are in a position to maintain a permanent specialist staff) or by commissioning outside consultants.

The fact that an evaluation is sponsored by a body other than the delivery organization might appear to imply greater detachment, but, as we have already hinted, central executive or legislative bodies may have their own political axes to grind. Delivery organizations may find themselves being evaluated on the basis of objectives and criteria other than those they were originally asked to implement. This indicates that while clearly stated criteria for evaluation at the policy design stage may pose a threat if the programme turns out to be unsuccessful, they can also provide a protection against the 'retrofitting' of quite different criteria.

Given that the evaluation will still have to rely heavily on information provided by the delivery organization, it obviously makes sense for the evaluating organization to secure the co-operation of the delivery organization, other than by the implied threat of cutbacks of funding. This might be secured by actively involving the delivery organization in the selection of programmes to be evaluated and the objectives and criteria to be examined. However, as the fate of Programme Analysis and Review (PAR) within British central government indicates, the adoption of an overly consensual style may lead to the selection of relatively anodyne topics for evaluation (see Gray and Jenkins, 1983).

## 12.6 The consumption and utilization of evaluations

The newcomer to evaluation might assume that having carried out the necessary research and prepared a report on the findings, the implications of the report in terms of policy-making would immediately be taken up by decision-makers, especially if the evaluation had been commissioned by government. As a result the newcomer would be puzzled as to why in most cases nothing at all seemed to happen. Perhaps assuming that the problem was the poor quality of many evaluations, our newcomer would be further perturbed to find that quality of methodology does not appear to be a particularly important determinant of whether evaluation research will be utilized.

A first important consideration is that where an evaluation is carried out by someone with an academic background, they may not state explicitly the policy implications of research, considering that their appropriate role terminates with the summary of the findings of the research. However, if the policy implications are not obvious, 'The programme manager winds up complaining about the irrelevance of the evaluation for his programmatic concerns, and the evaluator returns to his office lamenting the neglect of his work by decision makers' (Weiss, 1972, 111–12). However, if the research findings are so ambiguous that the research is irrelevant the evaluator should have the courage to say so.

The results of formal evaluations do not by themselves determine the policy implications of evaluation. This requires the exercise of political judgements about acceptable levels of effectiveness stated either after or (to avoid retrospective adjustments of what is acceptable) before the evaluation research itself.

Even if explicit policy implications are set out, the research findings may be presented in a technical language which makes it difficult for decision-makers (or even those trained in other disciplines) to understand the methods or even the conceptual focus (such as focus on economic costs and benefits only), which may determine the findings. If evaluation research is to be utilized, it has to be communicated in a language comprehensible to those who have to make decisions on the basis of it.

Such communication must include an indication of the limitations of the findings, whether resulting from conceptual focus, measurement problems, quality of data collected, or method of analysis. Not surprisingly, some evaluators have found it difficult to avoid the temptation to defend their findings, regardless of the limitations of the research. It is important to avoid the taking of overrigid decisions on the basis of relatively tentative findings. Limitations of research may be seized on by opponents of the policy implications of the findings, but the political impact of this will be all the greater if there was less than total honesty about those limitations in the first place. As always, analysis is an input to the political process and to attempt to 'shield' analysis from political flak by supressing qualifications on findings only demeans the analysis, without necessarily providing a protection from politics.

Evaluation results may not be consumed because they do not fit in with the timetable for decision-making. An evaluation may have originally been commissioned with a view to using its results to assist decision-making but lack of foresight about the need for evaluation might have led to a late start, or a sudden crisis necessitating an early decision might have intervened. On the research side, delays resulting from underestimates of time needed for data collection and analysis or the tendency of researchers to explore interesting byways are common. Policy analysis must be concerned about planning for evaluation to try to avoid the mistiming problem and about avoiding slippage in the evaluation research, just as it is concerned to avoid slippage in substantive implementation of programmes.

An evaluation report may disappear without trace if there is organizational resistance to the implications of its findings. This is particularly likely to be successful if the report shows that while the programme is not cost-effective it is producing some good effects. Organizational members may be reluctant to undergo disruption to working practices and career structures and will always be able to point to the time and costs involved in changing policies (points which will be developed further in chapter 13). The organization may have its own 'hidden agenda' of objectives (see chapter 9) on which its own survival will be the top item. Particularly where the programme involves delivering a service (as opposed to paying out cash) there may be a professional ideology about the proper way to deliver the service and findings which threaten these methods of work will tend to be rejected. These factors will not only lead to resistance to any serious proposal to implement changes but may even prevent the evaluation findings being seriously considered.

Issues of acceptability apply not only to members of the delivery organization but also to acceptability to clients, community organizations, and those who fund the programme. It will be particularly difficult to persuade those who originally sponsored the programme which has been evaluated to give serious consideration to findings which might appear to cast doubt on their original judgement. Where there has been a change of office, adverse evaluation results may be more readily considered or even seized upon.

All these points may lead to a great deal of pessimism about the potential for the utilization of evaluation research. However, the evidence from the United States indicates that while only a small minority of evaluation reports have a directly traceable effect on specific decisions, the findings may in the somewhat longer run affect how policy-makers and their advisers perceive issues in that policy area (Davis and Salasin, 1979). This is similar to the 'appreciative' role which Vickers (1965, 50) describes Royal Commissions and similar bodies as having.

Related to this is the question of how widely the results of the evaluation should be disseminated. Should they go only to the organization which commissioned them or should they also be made available to parties, MPs and councillors, and clients? Decisions about dissemination may not be within the control of the researcher, but any researcher undertaking a commission to do an evaluation might like to ask at the very start about the dissemination and then consider whether he wishes to undertake research which will be made available only to the commissioning organization and may be suppressed if the findings are adverse.

While analytical rigour is always desirable, if not fully practicable, in the conduct of evaluation research, the consumption of evaluation is inevitably going to be a political process, both in terms of internal organizational politics and the broader political process.

# 13

# Policy Succession and Policy Termination

## 13.1 The end of the policy process

It might be thought that having gone through the various stages from issue search (chapter 5) to evaluation (chapter 12) we had reached the end of the policy process. However, this would be to neglect the consequences of evaluation and how the policy cycle is terminated or leads into a new policy cycle. The analytical implications of policy termination and succession (the replacement of one or more existing policies by one or more other policies) have only recently begun to be explored (see especially deLeon, 1978; Hogwood and Peters, 1983).

Since the mid-1970s interest has developed rapidly, mainly in the United States, in the analytical issues and practical problems involved in terminating programmes. This interest can be seen to have at least two strands: (a) the logical outcome of an adverse evaluation of a programme is that the programme ought to be abolished or replaced; (b) a political climate of budget retrenchment raises the possibility of government withdrawal from some existing activities, or alteration of those activities to a less costly form. One thing which does emerge from the termination literature is that complete terminations of programmes are rare; i.e. some replacement is normally provided.

Much of policy analysis has either been based on the mistaken assumption that policies come new into the world or fails to distinguish the important differences between genuine policy innovation and policy succession. Analysis is frequently based on the assumption that analysts and decision-makers can start with a clean slate. However, as we will show below, the policy succession process is affected at each stage by the previous policy, with the extent of this effect depending on the nature of the policy succession attempted. Hogwood and Peters (1983) suggest three reasons for expecting policy succession to be an increasingly common feature of policy formulation in contemporary Western political systems, and therefore for greater attention by analysts:

(1) Governments have over the years gradually expanded their activities in particular fields of policy, so that there are relatively few completely new activities in which they could be involved. Proposals for 'new' policies are likely to overlap at least in part with existing programmes.

(2) Existing policies themselves may create conditions requiring changes in policies or programmes because of inadequacies or adverse side effects.

(3) The relative rates of sustainable economic growth and the financial implications of existing policy commitments imply that the latitude for avoiding the problems of policy termination or policy succession by instituting a new programme without cutting the old is considerably reduced.

If neither succession nor termination takes place, then the existing policy will continue (policy maintenance). This can occur through inertia, through deliberate decision or through the failure of proposals for termination or succession. The difficulties of termination or succession may often make attempting them seem hardly worth the effort, but it should be remembered that the consequence may be the maintenance of an existing policy which is inadequate or otherwise unsatisfactory.

## 13.2 Varieties of succession and termination

Termination and succession can be considered in terms of a number of different aspects of organization and policy, though in practice they may be intertwined (see deLeon, 1978, 283–5).

(1) *Functional.* A function is a service such as 'health care' which transcends individual organizations and policies; a number of agencies and policies can all serve the same policy function. Cases of functional termination in modern Western states are rare (the termination of the colonial function is an exception), and a huge political effort would be necessary to achieve success.

The concept of functional succession does not appear meaningful, though a redefinition of a function may occur (e.g. from alleviation of poverty to income maintenance).

(2) *Organizational.* Organizational termination could be easier to achieve than functional termination, but organizations are designed to last, and evidence from both the United States and Britain suggests that most of them do just that (albeit undergoing considerable transformations in many cases). More common than outright termination are transformation, merging, and splitting. Organizations may survive the termination or replacement of policies and programmes they were responsible for delivering.

(3) *Policy termination or succession.* Policies are generalized approaches or strategies for solving a particular problem. We would expect that policies would be easier to terminate than the sponsoring organization for a number of reasons: (a) an organization will prefer to foresake some of its policies or programmes rather than have the organization itself terminated; (b) policies as such will have fewer political allies than organizations as such; (c) policies are easier to evaluate relative to a given objective than organizations with multiple objectives; (d) most policies will have critics. Policies are most vulnerable to termination if their underlying theory or approach is no longer considered legitimate or fashionable. A policy can survive a termination of a programme designed to pursue the policy if it is replaced by an alternative programme.

(4) *Programme termination or succession.* Programme here refers to the specific measures designed to carry out a policy (e.g. either tax allowances or investment grants can be used for a policy of encouraging industrial investment through financial incentives). Arguably, programmes are the most vulnerable aspect of policy liable to termination. On the one hand, they are closest to the problem and therefore their impact can be most directly measured and, if found inadequate, blame most easily affixed. Against that, there may be close client identification with the programme. Programme termination is, of course, likely to be much easier if an alternative programme is initiated at the same time, i.e. if it is in fact programme succession.

Policy succession can take many forms, and the form which finally emerges may not be the same as that proposed when the policy succession was first initiated. Policy successions vary in the extent to which they produce one-for-one replacement of existing policy. This occurs in two main ways:

(*a*) The 'coverage (e.g. in terms of clientele) of the replacement policies may not match that of the old. The replacement programme may not cover all of the clients of the old, but may provide for previously uncovered clients. Similarly, even if the coverage of the replacement policy is identical to that of the old, the objectives of the policy may vary.

(*b*) Policy succession may result in the same number of programmes, fewer or greater.

These two dimensions of succession have implications for the process of changing policy, or, to be more accurate, we must discuss policy succession in terms of a variety of processes. When a policy succession involves a reduction in the number of clients or organizations, or a shifting of the objectives of programmes, the process is likely to be more conflictual and the policy actors more defensive. These types of changes are 'minus-sum games', in which there will be more losses than gains. In general, the intensity of involvement of political actors will be related not only to the magnitude of change but also to its direction: potential losers will tend to fight harder than potential gainers. Thus, even where overall gains and losses balance out, there would be an asymmetry in the intensity of involvement of gainers and losers. More complex types of succession will be associated with more complex processes, with a greater number of policy actors, and greater variations in perceptions, interests, and opportunities for building up support for and opposition to proposals.

Different types of policy succession will have different types of problems associated with them which it would be sensible to take into account in considering alternative strategies for securing policy change. For example, consolidation of two or more programmes or organizations poses important *intra*organizational problems at the implementation stage, while splitting up an existing organization may pose *inter*organizational difficulties.

Care must be taken in generalizing about types of policy succession, since different political systems will have different balances of types of succession. For example, because of the structuring of British central government into departments, there will be a greater proportion of complex successions combining splitting and consolidation than is the case in US federal government with its more agency-oriented structure. The important point to note here is that these differences (quite apart from other systems-related variations) will have implications for the process of securing succession, since the politics of the process varies according to the succession type.

## 13.3 How succession differs from innovation

While changes involving a high degree of innovation and those involving a high degree of succession both go through a similar sequence of stages in the policy process, the nature of the activities within each stage differs according to whether succession or innovation is involved. If the distinguishing features of the policy succession process were to be summarized in one sentence, then we would point to the extent to which the policy actors, the process, and the substantive outcomes of the policy process are all shaped by the existing policies which succession is intended to replace (see also Wildavsky, 1980, ch. 3).

The effects of existing policies are evident at each stage of the policy succession process. At the agenda-setting stage, the range of issues considered is shaped by those which have already been considered. Once a particular type of policy has been treated by the political system, the political agenda has been expanded to include that issue, although the previous treatment(s) of the issue may lead to the assumption that the problem has already been solved, with the consequence that politicians and officials are less willing to take the role of advocates of policy change.

Policy succession will encounter more mobilized interests than will policy innovation. Both producers and consumers of policies will have been developed around a particular existing policy, so that an attempt at policy succession will challenge their interests. This may be contrasted with policy innovation, in which the absence of these interests permits the formation of a group of policy promoters with less direct involvement by affected interests. Also at this stage, the politicians must consider the political pay-offs to them for mobilizing a majority among their colleagues and, if in a minority, in the House of Commons or council. In general, they may have higher returns to their investments of time and energy when they can advocate a new policy rather than when they 'simply' try to modify an existing policy.

Implementing policy succession rather than innovation involves changing existing organizations rather than creating new organizations.

It also involves changing the attitudes and behaviour of existing organizational members rather than recruiting and training new members. Perhaps most importantly, implementing policy succession is more likely to involve greater interactive effects with other policies and programmes than is genuine policy innovation. Therefore, the interorganizational politics of accommodation and adjustment are likely to be more pronounced in policy succession than in policy innovation.

Finally the impact of policy-making upon clients and the policy environment is likely to be different depending on whether a policy innovation or policy succession is being adopted. In particular, once a policy area has been processed through the policy cycle, expectations of benefits from future policy changes tend to be diminished by the probable weakness of the initial policy. Policy areas would not be candidates for policy succession if the initial policy adopted were totally salutory in its effects and capable of solving the problem addressed. Initial failures breed disillusionment about subsequent changes, so that there is less idealism and (perhaps) more realism about the probability of significant improvements in the policy area.

On the other hand, however, it will be considerably easier to isolate the effects of the policy innovation compared to the policy succession. All the problems of repeated treatments in research design obtain in the real world of policy evaluation (see chapter 12), so that making definitive statements about the effectiveness of a particular policy change becomes increasingly difficult as the number of different policy successions increases.

In summary, both the policy innovation and policy succession processes have hurdles which present particular difficulty. For the policy innovation process, this is primarily placing the issue on the agenda and overcoming resistance to its consideration by government at all. The absence of organizations and clienteles receptive to the particular policy issue makes government relatively insensitive to that issue. Innovations will also normally face greater long-run additional resource cost implications than successions. For policy succession, however, the principal hurdles are overcoming the inertia and defensiveness of existing organizations and clientele groups, which, having identifiable benefits being provided to them, may fear and resist change and policy succession.

## 13.4 Difficulties in securing termination

There are a number of reasons why policy termination has been particularly difficult to plan and implement (see Bardach, 1976, 128–30; deLeon, 1978, 186–93). Many of them are also relevant to policy succession.

(1) *Intellectual reluctance.* People are unwilling to confront issues pertaining to death, even organizational death, particularly if the observer has a vested interest (professional, emotional, intellectual, etc.) that makes the exercise unpalatable. Reluctance to realize policy shortcomings is reinforced for the analyst because policies are typically designed to solve or at least reduce a specified problem; the options proposed and the programmes chosen were not originally selected with the thought that they would prove deficient.

(2) *Lack of political incentives.* On the one hand, there is a reluctance by politicians to admit past mistakes. On the other hand, political rewards appear to accrue to those promoting novelty and innovation. The beneficiaries of policy termination where, say, this accrues in the form of lower taxes or more all round for other programmes may be too dispersed or the benefits too small for there to be a clear 'constituency' for politicians to cultivate, though this may now be less true than it was following the greater citizen awareness of tax burdens which developed in both Britain and the United States in the late 1970s.

(3) *Institutional permanence.* Policies and especially organizations are designed to last. Organizations are created to perpetuate a service or relationship. The problem-solving, adaptive nature of organizations further immunizes them from easy termination. Organizations are designed to recognize, act upon, and reduce problems before the threat attains a magnitude which endangers the organization's existence, or at least its jurisdiction in dealing with such problems.

(4) *Dynamic conservatism.* Related to this are the consequences of the fact that organizations and policies are dynamic entities. The successful completion of a policy objective may not be sufficient grounds for disbanding the organization, since new objectives can be defined within the organization which require its continued existence. On the other hand, the inability of an organization to resolve a problem is similarly unlikely to result in its termination. If proponents of a policy find themselves lacking allies in one organization, they may move to another, more hospitable agency.

(5) *Anti-termination coalitions.* There are significant political groups both within and without the threatened agency that will be opposed to termination. Each group will have its own assets and tactics, but they are particularly likely to be successful when they form coalitions to block threatened termination. Case studies have shown that similar pressures and arguments often occur during the formative stage of a policy in creating and defining the initial demand. However, they apply more strongly to the politics of termination than initiation for two reasons: (a) the internal bureaucracy that would be opposed to termination actions is well entrenched; (b) external allies will be particularly purposeful since they will already have benefited from the threatened agency's service. (Similar considerations apply to policy succession, though in the case of policy succession there will be an opposing pro-succession coalition.)

(6) *Legal obstacles.* In the United States the Federal Government has to operate under the constraints of 'due process'. In Britain there are also less significant legal constraints on the ability of central government to terminate abruptly its own programmes and those run by local authorities.

(7) *High start-up costs.* Considerable political resources have to be mobilized to counter anti-termination coalitions and organizational reluctance to terminate. Further, it may be possible to gain support for the termination only if alternative programmes are offered (i.e. policy succession rather than policy termination); however, attractive alternatives may not be available, and termination may therefore fail.

(8) *Adverse consequences.* Concern about the adverse consequences of termination for staff or clientele who may suffer 'through no fault of their own' may be a focus both of genuine concern and political opposition.

(9) *Procrastination and refusal.* Even when authorized, a termination decision may not be fully implemented (or implemented at all) as a result of delays in phasing out or the exploitation of ambiguities in the wording of the decision to the extent that this amounts to a refusal to obey it.

### 13.5 Aids to securing succession and termination

In section 13.8 we discuss how in designing policies and policy-making systems now we can do so in such a way as to make future changes to or terminations of those policies easier. We cannot, however, reverse history and redesign programmes and organizations which are already in operation without such built-in evaluation or termination triggers. In such cases the analyst or practitioner of policy succession or termination must therefore be prepared to intervene in an existing organization to bring about a smooth transition from one policy to another.

There is no ready technology for implementing a policy succession but only rather ill defined ideas about what must be understood and what needs to be avoided. As far as policy termination is concerned, since it is rarely attempted and even more rarely successful, the relatively limited number of successful examples makes it difficult to draw out analytical generalizations and the lessons in terms of strategies for successful implementation. However, based on our understanding of succession and termination, the following strategies can be suggested as worth considering.

(1) Attention should be paid to the 'political context' and 'natural points' for succession and termination (e.g. a change of administration following an election or an economic crisis) (see deLeon, 1978, 295).

(2) Thought should be given to the time horizon of succession and termination and whether the change should be a gradual process or an immediate and total action (see deLeon, 1978, 295). The first is more likely to be successful in minimizing opposition to the decision, but is also more vulnerable to procrastination and deflection.

(3) If agencies were allowed to retain some or all of the money saved from terminating or cutting back a policy or programme or even carry it over to the following financial year, they would have a greater incentive to cancel or change questionable programmes (see Biller, 1976, 144–5). This would, of course, reduce the savings from termination or succession.

(4) Arrangements could be made to ease adverse transitional or distributional impacts of succession or termination among staff, clients, and the localities of any facilities (see Behn, 1978, 407–8). Such arrangements might include redundancy payments or guaranteed redeployment for employees, alternative uses of facilities so that closure would not have an adverse impact on the locality, or help to localities where facilities are phased out.

Again, such arrangements would reduce any financial benefits of succession or termination.

(5) An important, perhaps necessary, strategy for policy succession or termination is the *delegitimation* of the theory or assumptions underlying the existing policy (e.g. the institutionalization of the mentally ill, pupil selection at 11+) (see Behn, 1978, 399–400).

Although these strategies can be suggested as potentially useful, it is important that the individual circumstances of each proposed succession and termination are considered. It is important to take account of the characteristics of the existing policy, those of the proposed replacement policy (if any), and any special characteristics of the process of transition (for more detailed discussion of these characteristics see Hogwood and Peters, 1983, especially 224–39).

### 13.6 The need for design for future succession or termination

In section 13.5, we examined the perspective of the advocate of policy succession or termination faced with a set of existing policies, and attempting to find ways of changing those policies. This is all that can be expected, given that existing policies have not been designed for ready change. However, on a practical level, it would be advisable for those who advocate solutions to the problems faced by society to begin to design their policies with a greater sensitivity to the problems which future generations of policy-makers will have when they will almost inevitably attempt to alter the policy. It is only human to want to leave a monument of some sort to one's work, but one generation's monuments may be the next generation's mausoleums. Even policies which are generally regarded as successes may contain such rigidities that they inhibit even greater success.

There are a number of factors which together indicate that policy succession (and more occasionally, policy termination) should be considered as the 'norm' for the future.

#### 13.6.1 CHANGING PROBLEMS

A first factor influencing the need to design for policy succession is that the problems that society is encountering will change. A policy-maker in any one time is rarely so well informed or perceptive as to be able to ensure that the manner in which he or she perceives a problem will be enduring and consequently should design in flexibility when devising solutions.

This is by no means a plea for incrementalism, as it may be interpreted to be. Small steps may promote as much inflexibility as major overhauls of a policy area. Indeed, rather paradoxically, it could be argued that incremental decision-making tends to build in more inflexibility than does more synoptic decision-making. An incremental solution for an existing problem—which may be the policy itself—tends to imply that the basic framework of policy delivery is adequate and that only minor adjustments need to be made in order to make the programme function well (Dror, 1968). The more incremental changes there are, the longer there is an apparent acceptance of the underlying paradigm, the more rigidities are likely to be built into the service delivery system, and the less amenable to change clients and organization members will become. On the other hand, a major policy change may be necessary to instill a new paradigmatic structure for the policy, and may imply greater flexibility than adjustments to established policy.

Rather than being a plea for incrementalism, this is a plea for strategic thought in the design of new policies, or the redesign of existing policies. There is a need to understand the essential elements of the services to be provided, the organizations which will deliver those services, and the clients who will benefit from them. With those elements fully understood, and the need for flexibility also understood, the policy-maker has some hope for designing policies which, if not successful, will be amenable to change.

## 13.6.2 CHANGES IN THE PREVAILING WISDOM ABOUT SOLUTIONS

As well as the nature of the problems changing, the conventional wisdom about how to address the problems also changes. For example, the conventional wisdom about harsh punishment for prisoners changed in the 1960s to a more lenient and 'rehabilitative' approach. Prison programmes, and even the physical structure of the prisons themselves, designed under one of these conceptions of the appropriate manner of handling criminals may be useless under other definitions of the appropriate solution.

These types of sea changes in the conception of the appropriate 'technology' for 'solving' problems have occurred numerous times in education, and in social policy, where the technology for producing desired results is less certain. The certainty which surrounded economic policy in the 1950s and 1960s, when it was assumed that the Keynesian system allowed 'fine-tuning' of the economy, has now been shattered by events and the growth of monetarism. Perhaps especially in policy areas such as these care should be exercised when designing a policy to make policy succession an easier goal to attain.

### 13.6.3 CHANGES IN THE RESOURCE BASE

In addition, the resources available for confronting the problems of society also change. The experience of most Western industrialized nations following the oil price rises in 1973–4, and continuing into the 1980s, is that policies built on the premiss of affluence have to be re-examined. It is not just the reduction of financial resources which can present problems for government, but the exhaustion of real resources as well. Policies built on the assumption of permanently cheap energy, or cheap natural resources more generally, simply make no sense any more.

From the strategic perspective, governments may face at least two types of strains on resources which will influence their ability to pursue certain types of policies. One is a strain on governmental resources, without any strain on real economic or natural resources. This was the case of Proposition 13 in California; here there was continued availability of resources in the economy, but the voters acted to deny those resources to government. In anticipation of situations such as this, policies could be designed so as to be able to transfer clients and functions to the private sector. This might be done through attempts to co-ordinate public and private programmes even during times of affluence, and the development of flexible organizational relationships that would facilitate the 'privatization' of certain activities. In this case, the total use of resources might be changed very little; the difference would be in who was spending the resources. In Britain, such developments would inevitably become embroiled in a highly ideological party political debate.

The second and more severe problem arises when there is a reduction, or at least a slowing of growth, of real resources. In this instance, mechanisms may have to be found which use less to perform the relevant activity, as in perhaps switching from the direct delivery of a service to the use of incentives to those who might want to provide it by voluntary means, or the use of suasion. There may be a need to design programmes in a modular structure, not dissimilar to that implied in zero-based budgeting, in order to be able to de-escalate efficiently the level of service delivery. However, the advocate of succession should not assume that those resisting a succession are fools. Those opponents will resist the development of the modular structure, understanding its implications for partial termination and succession. Thus, perhaps the most crucial fight in a succession campaign will be over procedure and organization rather than substance.

### 13.6.4 CHANGES IN DEMAND

Finally, demand for certain types of policy may change (see also section 5.5.1). The policy problem may be defined as the same, but the number of citizens demanding the service may decline. A change in demand is especially important when the service in question is relatively capital intensive and an increase in demand for a service of this type will take a long time to implement, since the additional capital stock has to be produced. But even for labour-intensive services there may be a large number of individuals who may be trained to deliver a certain type of service and whose jobs may be threatened by a reduction in service, or who must be trained if there is an increase in demand.

If the demand for a service is increased or reduced significantly, there may also be a significant modification not only in the *volume* of service provided but also in the type of service provided. For example, at a low volume of service, it may be possible to deliver services directly, whereas when volume increases government may choose to change to a cash transfer programme to achieve the same goal. Similarly, if a transfer or incentive programme experiences a reduction in demand, there may be pressure to switch to more labour-intensive direct delivery of service. This may be justified in terms of providing superior services to the clients, but in reality it may be a means of protecting the jobs of those already working on the programme.

Clearly, if one is planning ahead for succession, it may be easier to design programmes such as transfers or incentives that do not employ either large numbers of specialized employees or large capital plants. By reducing these fixed costs (fixed politically if not legally) any changes in the programme can be effectuated much more easily. Of course, some programmes must be delivered by public employees directly, and still others are better delivered by public employees. But if succession is considered as a primary design element in a programme, and if there is known to be fluctuation in demand, consideration should be given to designing programmes that do not require large cadres of public employees, especially those with specialized training. Again, such developments would inevitably have ideological connotations in Britain.

### 13.7 Problems of designing for future succession and termination

Some definite problems arise when a policy is designed for ease in future successions or terminations. Neither public employees nor clients are prone to appreciate a programme which is perceived by those making the policy decisions as only a temporary measure to meet the problem. No matter how loosely the legislation for a programme is written, both public employees and clients will attempt to solidify their positions and create permanence, or at least the illusion of permanence. Public officials will seek to gain tenure and will attempt to make some aspects of their programme essential for the functioning of other programmes. Clients will organize and attempt to develop an entitlement ethos about their programme. In addition to the understandable attempts of individuals to protect themselves, other problems will arise when legislation and organizations are designed explicitly to make future policy successions easier to implement.

One of the design problems associated with planning for policy succession is balancing the enforceability of a programme during its current cycle against the ability to produce effectively a policy succession in future cycles. The more enforceable a piece of legislation is during the current cycle, the clearer will be the guidelines for action and the greater will be the precision of the training of the employees. The members of the organization responsible for implementing the legislation will be trained to carry out their tasks in certain ways, and clients would come to expect certain types of benefits and behaviours from the organization. But the precision that would assist in implementation of one programme would also make succession that much more difficult to bring about in the future.

Another interesting aspect of the trade-off between enforceability and policy succession concerns the choice of instruments to implement the policy. As we noted above, policy instruments which involve hiring large numbers of personnel are more difficult to modify later. However, where there is a staff charged with implementing the programme it is likely that this method of service delivery would produce greater compliance with the laws than other methods of service delivery. Contracting out may be the most flexible means of providing a service, although control over the provision is weakened substantially. A contract can be terminated much more readily than a tenured civil servant, and the provision of the service by a contract agency may make it appear less of an entitlement. However, although change is possible, the direction of that change is less amenable to direct control by government than a change within its own organizations

## 13.8 Design strategies for easing future succession and termination

A number of writers have suggested ways in which future successions and terminations might be eased, and a number of techniques from the literature on organizational development are potentially relevant. Many of these suggested solutions themselves have problems, and none provide panaceas. However, given the importance of avoiding becoming 'locked in' to the existing pattern of policies, it is worth drawing on all available means.

### 13.8.1 CHANGING PERCEPTIONS

Ideally, policy succession and even termination should be regarded as an integral and beneficial part of the policy process (see deLeon, 1978, 194–5). The possibility of inadequacies or failure or even just changing circumstances should be realized right from the start of the policy process at the stage when the original policy alternatives are considered. Special attention should be paid to the evaluation stage, since it provides the measures relative to the policy objectives that determine if the succession or termination options need to be exercised.

One of the barriers which must be overcome if policy succession is to be a more acceptable outcome for the policy process is largely psychological. Both employees and clients have come to regard any public programme as virtually permanent. Consequently, any attempt to alter or terminate an existing policy in favour of an alternative will be greeted with apprehension or hostility. There is a need, therefore, to teach both sets of people that change is a natural component of the policy life-cycle, and further that many changes may be positive. Change through policy succession may make the work of employees easier or more effective, and may improve the quality of services delivered to clients. Of course, it will be difficult to convince members of both groups of the efficacy of changes being proposed.

One means of changing perceptions is to be completely honest with those whom the change may affect. There has been a tendency in government to attempt to restrict information and to 'doctor' the news in order to prevent adverse reactions. This has by now become so common that few official pronouncements of good news are likely to be accepted at face value. Being truthful has obvious moral benefits, but may have the effect of co-opting those whom organizational leaders wish to influence. By telling clients or employees the truth, and asking them how to respond to the change, the leadership of the organization can effectively involve them in change.

There may also need to be some change in the macroclimate of policy-making. The leadership of an organization may have as much difficulty in adjusting to change as do the members of the organization or its clients. Any change in a programme, especially one initiated from outside the organization, may be perceived as a failure of the leaders of the organization. To save face, the leadership may resist change rather than co-operating with the changes and attempting to make them more effective. In the world of the public bureaucracy, bigger is generally perceived as better than smaller, and stability is generally better than change. Until some of these perceptions can be altered, it may be difficult to obtain the type of leadership for policy succession which will be required.

## 13.8.2 INTERNAL MOTIVATIONS FOR POLICY SUCCESSION

Another approach to reducing resistance to policy succession is to develop stronger internal motivations for the succession. This will, of course, involve overcoming the apprehensions which change, and especially change affecting people's livelihood, is likely to engender. One means of overcoming the resistance to change is through training and socialization. However, to use training to promote policy succession would require altering the manner in which training in organizations has traditionally been conducted. Most training in organizations tends to preach that there is one proper way of achieving the goals of the organization. It may be possible to teach instead, if not cynicism, at least some scepticism about the manner in which the organization functions. This is, of course, more easily done in the upper echelons of the organization, where, through better education and greater security, greater detachment and scepticism may already exist. Also, we would expect younger employees, who have not yet invested many years of their lives in the organization, to be more willing to question the traditional approach of the organization to its problems and to accept policy successions.

A number of approaches have been advanced for promoting policy succession and organizational change (see also 11.4.3). For example, there is the use of consultants as 'change agents' who would go into an organization to aid the organization in identifying its own need for change and to assist in developing the mechanisms for change (Lippitt, Watson and Westley, 1958). Group-oriented approaches to organizational change, largely referred to as 'sensitivity training' (Schein and Bennis, 1965), concentrate attention on the internal dynamics of small groups, but then help the members extrapolate from that experience to the larger organizational setting. A more extensive approach to these problems within organizations goes under the label of 'organizational development', or 'OD' (Eddy, 1970). This approach 'goes beyond traditional training and consulting projects and attempts to help an organization establish and conduct a long-range process of self-evaluation and constructive change and renewal' (Eddy, 1981, 184).

As this array of suggested methods exists for changing the internal dynamics of an organization, it would appear logical that they could be applied to the problem of changing the policies which the organization administers. Changing the goals of the organization is a fundamental form of organizational change and if the above methods (among others) have proved useful in the pursuit of changing behaviour within an organization with (relatively) stable goals, they may be applicable to the more difficult problem of goal change. To the critics of these approaches, they are more theology than scientific methods of approaching the problems of organizational change, but they do offer some promise if used appropriately and with awareness of their limitations.

These strategies appear most appropriate in organizations which have an external reference group that can inform them that their performance is no longer adequate. Professional organizations may serve this purpose for some organizations, while clients or suppliers may do so for others. Relatedly, organizations in which the relevant technology or ideas of best practice change rapidly may have to undergo re-examination of objectives and planned change more often than others. Finally, more integrated and homogenous organizations can undertake this type of change more readily than can more conflictual organizations.

### 13.8.3 CHANGING INCENTIVES

We have already noted in 13.5 the possibility of easing successions and terminations by reducing the financial and other penalties suffered as a result of change. For these to be fully effective as incentives, however, they will have to be routinized rather than used on an *ad hoc* basis once change has been proposed. As most political systems function, there are few incentives for an organization to engage in policy succession, especially if that policy succession may result in less money or fewer staff. Any money which an agency is able to save in a given year is not retained by the agency but reverts to the general fund. If agencies were allowed to retain at least a proportion of the money saved from terminating a policy or programme, or even carry it over to the following financial year, they would have some positive incentive to cancel or replace questionable programmes. This might reduce the cost savings from such policy successions, but would certainly ease the transition from one policy to another. More generally, arrangements could be standardized to ease the adverse transitional or distributional impacts of termination among staff, clients, and the localities of any facilities.

Such a restructuring of incentives would at least make the incentives offered to a policy-maker more neutral when considering whether to engage in a policy succession, so that the case may be decided on the merits of the issues rather than the difficulties which a succession might present for organizational members and clients. Even more positive incentives, such as promoting officials who are effective at succession or termination may change the balance of incentives in favour of change, at least for senior administrators.

### 13.8.4 CHANGING THE NATURE OF INSTITUTIONS

The manner in which organizations in the public sector are designed can also facilitate policy succession. There is a tendency to assign individuals to one post in an organization, to train them for that post only, and to maintain a relatively rigid structure within the organization. Organizations should be designed, however, with the possibility of succession in mind. Consideration might be given to a greater use of internal matrix designs for organizations. This can ensure that members have continuing positions in the organization but have the flexibility to establish (and terminate) project teams or task forces (Davis and Lawrence, 1977; Biller, 1976, 139–44).

Although such an internal organizational form may be desirable from the perspective of policy succession, it is not clear how many policy problems could be tackled by such means, nor how the problems it might have for accountability could be overcome. The matrix form of organization might be quite appropriate for innovative or project-based policy-making (Peters, 1983) but not for more routine policies cerving large numbers of clients. But paradoxically it is just the latter type of policy which may be most in need of policy succession. Further, it is only human to advocate a flexible matrix structure for everyone else's policy areas, but to want a more institutionalized and permanent organizational structure for your own pet policy.

An alternative to the matrix form of organization is to develop a staff of 'salvage specialists' who are trained in reallocating resources freed by policy successions or terminations to other positions where they can do the most good (Biller, 1976, 146–7). This may alleviate some staff reluctance and uncertainty engendered by the succession process and can help to overcome internal resistance.

### 13.8.5 PROMOTING SUCCESSION AND TERMINATION THROUGH BUDGETING

A fully executed system of zero-based budgeting (ZBB), if such a thing is possible, should throw up opportunities for termination (see also 10.6.6). This is not the place for a full consideration of ZBB (see the papers on ZBB in Kramer, 1979), but it is worth noting the formidable analytical requirements of ZBB and the fact that the bulk of the analysis is carried out by the agencies concerned (see Brewer, 1978, 341–2). The introduction of ZBB into the US Federal Government under President Carter made no noticeable difference to the rate of policy termination.

### 13.8.6 'SUNSET' LAWS AS POLICY SUCCESSION AND TERMINATION TRIGGERS

There has been considerable interest in the United States in the idea of 'sunset laws'. Programmes would only be given legislative and budget authority for a period of, say, five years and would automatically terminate unless relegislated. (This is, of course, already common for individual pieces of British legislation, but is not applied to all programmes.) Such relegislation would only occur after a favourable evaluation. Problems with the idea include the formidable review requirements and legislative burden (Brewer, 1978, 342–3). These problems might be reduced if only agencies falling below a 'success threshold' of standards set in the legislation were subject to 'sunset', but there would be problems in setting useful operational standards. Other problems are that an organization which has to defend its existence may devote a sizeable amount of its resources to that task, or it could obscure its activities in such a way that effective evaluation would he impossible (deLeon, 1978). Because of the threatening elements of sunset legislation in the USA, its provisions are rarely applied vigorously in the states which have introduced it. Removal of the automatic termination provision would reduce this threatening element, but would also reduce pressure for serious re-examination of programmes.

The basic idea of sunset laws has been a periodic review of all organizations and their programmes, but it may be worthwhile to build in less periodic triggers as well. Several factors might be considered as means of selecting organizations for review. If we are concerned with making changes which may improve the efficiency of government or reduce its costs, then one obvious criterion for choice is the size of the budget and the staff. Secondly, *change* in the size of the budget is an obvious criterion; if a budget is increasing rapidly, this may be a sign of the success of the programme or it may be an indication of a poorly designed programme taking on too many clients or spending money ineffectively. It is also important to note not only changes in the budget which enables delivery of a policy, but also the changing environment within which the policy functions. Although the social indicators movement has not developed to the level once anticipated, changes in major indicators of demand for services can be used as triggers for reviews of programmes (see sections 5.6.3 and 5.6.4).

## 13.9 A cautionary note

Although in this chapter we have stressed the importance of planning ahead for the possibility of succession and termination, it is important to conclude by placing this emphasis in perspective. If termination or succession is to be a major consideration of agencies, these may become the major agenda items of the organization and it cannot fulfil its real goals. Change is important, but excessive emphasis on change may make it, or termination, appear inevitable.

# Part III
# Conclusion

# 14

# Policy Analysis for the Real World

## 14.1 The analysis of policy

In this book we have attempted to present a process-focused rather than a technique-oriented approach to policy analysis. Analysis, in our view, is primarily about determing the characteristics of the issue being analysed and the organizational and political setting of the issue, with the actual mechanics of particular techniques being secondary and consequential. To ignore the process context in promoting the use of techniques or, even worse, to assume that the process can simply be adjusted to fit round particular favoured techniques is a guarantee of the dismissive reaction to the advocacy of a more analytical approach which is already all too common in Britain.

Definition of the characteristics of the analytical problem, such as the degree of uncertainty about the future and the extent to which a final commitment has to be made in the immediate future, is a precondition of the selection of the appropriate technique or techniques— if indeed any are applicable. Training in the process of selecting the analytical techniques appropriate to a particular stage in the policy process and to a particular problem has, in our view, been grossly neglected in policy analysis training relative both to grand theorizing and the mechanics of the techniques themselves. One of our major aims in this book has been to go some way towards remedying this imbalance.

Policy analysis cannot provide a quick fix for intractable problems. Indeed, if a problem is really intractable then all good policy analysis can do is point out that there is no solution to the problem as defined, or that the resources required would be enormous in relation to the scale of the problem. Should policy analysis become more widespread there would be an irony if it became fallaciously associated with reduced policy efficacy, since arguably many of the 'easy' problems are already the subject of government policies, and what politics and analysis are now asked to resolve are the difficult problems together with the policy failures and resource implications of existing policies. However, even this apparently negative role for analysis in drawing attention to intractabilities is a highly worthwhile one, since it would help to reduce the waste of resources involved in kamikaze policy attacks on societal brick walls.

There is, however, no need to be apologetic about the limitations of policy analysis. While policy analysis cannot of itself resolve value conflicts or determine political priorities, analysis can inform choices even about high-level strategic decisions such as the relative priority to be accorded to cash income maintenance or provision in kind through health care and social work.

The potential contribution of policy analysis is probably greatest at the middle level of analysis, where a problem is currently ill-defined or poorly measured, where there are a number of actual or potential policy interests, and where the issue does not fit neatly into a single organizational responsibility. An example of such a middle-level problem is road safety, which was in fact the subject of a PAR (Programme Analysis and Review) in British government in the early 1970s.

Above all, it is important that policy analysis does not aim too low. If analysis deals with purely technical issues it evades the 'policy' part of the analysis.

## 14.2 The political setting of analysis

Policy analysis cannot make politically difficult decisions any easier and, indeed, by laying out the implications of options more explicitly may make it more difficult to achieve the types of fudge and compromise which produce coalitions of decision-makers or placate losers. However, the fact that (in some, but certainly not all cases) decisions may be politically easier in the absence of analysis which points up dilemmas and long-run costs and uncertainties does not thereby mean that the adverse consequences of poorly thought out policies are avoided. Unless the promotion of easy agreements is to be regarded as the sole end of politics, the substantive policy consequences of decisions must receive equal attention to the maintenance of an acceptable system for taking those decisions.

However, to assume that policy analysis can only make the task of politicians more difficult is unduly pessimistic. Even where policy analysis does produce evidence about the unpalatable nature of all available options, this evidence can be used to make the selection of one of those options (rather than an unrealistic 'easy' option) more acceptable to those who have to take the decision and to those who are affected by it. To suppress or fail to collect evidence about the difficulty of the policy choices it is facing can only weaken both the decision-making capacity of government and the trust which the governed place in the political system.

Politics and analysis should not be seen as necessarily incompatible, any more than secret internal analysis precludes political embarrassment. In Autumn 1982 selective leaks of a report by the now defunct Central Policy Review Staff (CPRS) in Britain led to the Cabinet disowning (but not publishing!) the report, which had looked at long-term trends in public expenditure, discussing what might need to be cut on the basis of various assumptions about economic growth if expenditure was to be contained within specified ceilings. The Government's rather hasty backing away from the poisoned chalice offered by the CPRS report did not, of course, remove the underlying issues, and following the June 1983 election, it became clear that the future of welfare expenditure into the 1990s was again receiving Cabinet attention.

A *Times* leader proposed a model for handling this issue, based in part on the experience of the Beveridge Report in 1942–3 and the 1978 review of supplementary benefit expenditure under the then Labour Government, which we believe constitutes a sensible marriage between politics and analysis, while being realistic about the political constraints: 'thought, research, publication of background information, debate, action' (*The Times*, 9 August 1983). The first stage was that 'The Cabinet must agree a set of clear objectives, then commission research and the preparation of options.' Although government departments had a monopoly of much of the detailed information, this did not preclude outsiders with fresh or alternative perspectives. The Government could commission studies from research institutes such as the Policy Studies Institute or from the Economic and Social Research Council (formerly the Social Science Research Council).

High quality research leading to openness, a Green Paper containing models of the welfare state and its finances in the 1990s built on a variety of economic assumptions, buttressed by background papers and a set of choices for reform will not guarantee rational discussion or a happy outcome. British politics is too polarized and the bulk of the British press too trivial for that . . . Yet coming clean with the public at least offers policy-makers a fighting chance, since they must win the argument. Open government may mean more argument, but it can also mean better government (*The Times*, 8 August 1983).

Such a process would provide no panacea—let alone remove the need for awkward political decisions if the projected paths of expenditure and existing commitments are incompatible—but even less so do politics or analysis on their own.

## 14.3 Politics and analysis

Decisions by politicians are given a role to play by virtually all writers on policy analysis, from the most rationalist to the most incrementalist, though much of the writing in the rationalist tradition assumes its politicians to be highly depoliticized animals. Since rational models have no internal mechanisms for determining values and objectives and priorities among them, these have to be injected by a decision-maker. However, a unitary decision-maker is normally assumed, and the whole political process by which the decision is arrived at is ignored. Politicians are viewed as necessary, but the political process is subordinated to the requirements of analysis.

In his recent writing, Simon (1983) has gone rather further than this, stressing the important role of political mechanisms in a democracy and envisaging circumstances in which debate and confrontation may be the only appropriate mechanisms for handling issues:

When an issue becomes highly controversial—when it is surrounded by uncertainties and conflicting values—then expertness is very hard to come by, and it is no longer easy to legitimate the experts. In the circumstances, we find that there are experts for the affirmative and experts for the negative. We cannot settle such issues by turning them over to particular groups of experts. At best, we may convert the controversy into an adversary proceeding in which we, the laymen, listen to the experts but have to judge between them. [Simon, 1983, 97].

For writers such as Lindblom and Wildavsky, on the other hand, politics (though seen as having disadvantages compared to market mechanisms) is more than just a means of injecting values into rational choice, but is elevated into a mechanism of analytical significance itself.

A multiplicity of participants in the political process reduces the chance of a feature being overlooked because of the way the issue had been defined in the minds of proposers of a decision. This benevolent, perhaps (as the later Lindblom would accept) complacent, view of the political process is perhaps based largely on the more open US system and may not apply in the same way to the largely non parliamentary process in Britain, involving in most cases confidential discussions between recognized groups and government departments.

Our own view is that to postulate politics as the means by which values or objectives can be injected into analysis at the beginning of the policy process, with the decision naturally emerging from the analysis, is to get the role of analysis in the policy process at least partly back-to-front. A piece of analysis once completed is consumed and (if utilized at all) injected into the political process, from which a decision will then emerge. This is both inevitable, in the sense that it is unrealistic to expect all the policy implications of analysis to be accepted without political question, and is in some ways analytically desirable—the exposure of analysis to critical appraisal can itself be of analytical value.

The relationship between politics and analysis at its best is iterative. In the chapters in part II we have pointed to the importance of the political setting and the consumption of analysis at all stages of the policy process from agenda-setting onwards. Even after an option has been selected, the role of policy analysis—and politics— is far from over.

Analysis, then, is seen as supplementing the more overtly political aspects of the policy process rather than replacing them. The relationship between analysis and politics will often be a tense one, but to treat politics as a residual is to doom analysis, not politics, to irrelevance.

## 14.4 The politics of analysis

There is no such thing as totally 'neutral' analysis. Values are at the centre of policy-making, and we have argued in this chapter that it is not practicable or even desirable to insulate analysis from political debate by attempting to specify values and objectives and leaving it to 'value free' analysis to produce the 'optimal' solution (see also 7.3).

There are, however, a number of more subtle ways in which analysis could be said to have political implications. In the previous section we noted that different prescriptive models of decision-making have profound implications for the nature of the political process. This applies also to the advocacy of the use of particular analytical techniques.

The training of policy analysts must incorporate what we called in section 2.5.8 the 'analysis of analysis'. This includes both the appraisal of the assumptions about facts and values built into definitions of a problem and proposed solutions to it, and the ability to analyse critically the often implicit assumptions associated with particular techniques, both about criteria for desirable policies (e.g. the use of approximations to market prices) and about the processes by which decisions are made. Sensitivity to value issues and questions of distribution of policy rather than simply global policy impact would also form an appropriate part of a policy analyst's training.

The use of analysis can be seen as having implications for political power. Because expertise is often concentrated in a particular government agency, its analysis, even when published, may be very difficult to challenge. Further, as we have pointed out on many occasions, many analytical techniques are very costly, so their use may be confined to affluent agencies and groups. Against that, the costs of the critical appraisal of analysis are relatively cheap, even if a full 'counter-analysis' is too costly.

For those who see analysis as resulting in the reinforcement of the existing distribution of political and economic resources, a potential solution is that policy analysis resources should be widely available to all existing (and potential) organized and unorganized groups or that policy analysts can act as disinterested 'friends of the court'. However, this begs the question of how total policy analysis resources and their distribution are to be determined. The point is not to oppose such a use of policy analysts, but to suggest that policy analysis itself has no 'rational' means for determining such a distribution, and thus the issue is inevitably one for political determination.

We recognize that who uses analysis and how it is used have an important political dimension. However, policy analysis as such cannot be expected to shoulder all the burden of issues of access to political and economic resources which politicians and political and social theorists have failed to resolve.

## 14.5 Practical policy analysis

If we are interested in the role of policy analysis in the policy process rather than simply the academic study of the policy process, then there are a number of obvious, perhaps trite, but often overlooked guidelines which have to be followed. First of all, if analysis is to be undertaken, let alone consumed and utilized, it must be of practical advantage to one or more decision-makers who are either interested in the substance of the issue or see how the analysis can be used as political justification for their position. Alternatively, analysis may enter into the policy process because it has been used to embarrass the Government by, say, an interest group drawing attention to the Government's neglect of an issue or the poor quality of the analysis underlying the Government's treatment of an issue.

If the results of analysis are to be of practical use, they have to be both comprehensible and timely. From the perspective of an analyst, the use to which his analysis is put may amount to abuse. However, it is no use policy analysts cringing and whinging about simplifications and distortion in the way the results are misused. This is (a) inevitable, (b) much more likely if neither the original analyst nor some 'translator' has taken the trouble to set out key conclusions and important caveats in readily comprehensible form. Deliberate distortions are much more likely to be exposed, either by the analyst (or by his surreptious briefing of the press or other political participants) or opponents of those abusing the analysis in this way.

In any practical use of policy analysis there is unlikely to be any one single type of analyst. Indeed, our own preference is not to see analysts solely as a breed apart. Hogwood (1984) suggests that what should be hoped for is:

a range of different types of analysts, some specialists in particular techniques; others specialising in particular policy areas, all (I hope) with at least some ability to communicate their findings to decision-makers and some awareness about how their specialism fits into the policy process as a whole. Others may be closer to the traditional idea of a political adviser, but specialise in interpreting the results of policy analysis for specific political masters. At least some, however, must be jacks-of-all-trades, perhaps master of none, but with an ability to identify potentially relevant techniques, if not the ability to carry them out, an awareness of their strengths and weaknesses, and a strong emphasis on the problems of decision-makers.

To revert back to the opening of this chapter, our concern is with a process approach to analysis rather than with analysis as little dollops of output from mathematical models which are produced by analysts and handed over to decision-makers. This process approach, and the lessons of the fate of policy analysis initiatives in British central government, emphasize the importance of perception by decision-makers of of the usefulness of analysis in general and of its application to specific issues. It also stresses a consumption-focused rather than a technique-focused approach to presenting the output of analysis.

The ultimate success of policy analysis would be achieved if it became so routinized that it was not seen as an activity separate and distinct from decision-making. But to return to the real world, the scope for more analytical thinking in public decision-making is so vast that separate training in the role of analysis is essential for further progress. The approach presented in this book cannot resolve all the policy problems facing governments any more than it has been able to resolve the disputes among writers on policy analysis. We hope, however, that we have made the case that analysis is not simply something which it would be nice to have in an ideal world but a way of thinking which is practicable in the real world.

# References

Aguilar, F. J. (1967), *Scanning the Business Environment*. New York: Collier-Macmillan.

Aitken, M. C. and L. G. Salmon (eds.) (1983), *The Costs of Evaluation*. Beverley Hills, Calif.: Sage.

Albanese, R. (1975), *Management: Towards Accountability for Performance*. Homewood, Ill.: Irwin.

Allison, G. T. (1971), *Essence of Decision*. Boston: Little, Brown.

Anderson, J. E. (1975), *Public Policy Making*. London: Nelson.

Ansoff, H. I. (1975), Managing strategic surprise by reference to weak signals, *California Management Review*, 18(2), 21–33.

Argenti, J. (1969), *Management Techniques*. London: Allen & Unwin.

―――― (1974), *Systematic Corporate Planning*. London: Nelson.

Arrow, K. J. (1954), *Social Choice and Individual Values*, 2nd ed. New York: Wiley.

Ashcroft, B. (1978), The evaluation of regional policy, *Studies in Public Policy*, No. 12. Glasgow: Centre for the Study of Public Policy, University of Glasgow.

Ashford, D. (1981), *Policy and Politics in Britain*. Oxford: Blackwell.

Bachrach, P. and M. S. Baratz (1962), Two faces of power, *American Political Science Review*, 56, 947–52.

Baker, J. I. H. (1977), CPRS, the car industry, and Chrysler: a case of 'misframing'? Unpublished paper: London Business School.

Bardach, E. (1976), Policy termination as a political process, *Policy Sciences*, 7, 123–31.

―――― (1977), *The Implementation Game*. Cambridge, Mass.: MIT Press.

―――― (1978), Subformal warning systems in the species *Homo politicus*, *Policy Sciences*, 9, 415–39.

Barker, A. (ed.) (1982), *Quangos in Britain*. London: Macmillan.

Barrett, S. and C. Fudge (1981), *Policy and Action*. London: Methuen.

Barron, I. and R. Curnow (1979), *The Future with Microelectronics*. London: Francis Pinter.

Behn, R. D. (1978), How to terminate public policy: a dozen hints for the would-be terminator, *Policy Analysis*, 4, 393–413.

Behn, R. D. and J. W. Vaupel (1982), *Quick Analysis for Busy Decision-Makers*. New York: Basic Books.

Biller, R. P. (1976), On tolerating policy and organisational termination: some design considerations, *Policy Sciences*, 7, 133–49.

Boaden, N. (1971), *Urban Policy Making: Influences on County Boroughs in England and Wales*. Cambridge: Cambridge University Press.

Booth, S. A. S., D. C. Pitt and W. J. Money (1982), Organizational redundancy? A critical appraisal of the GEAR project, *Public Administration*, 60, 56–72.

Bowen, E. R. (1982), The Pressman–Wildavsky paradox: Four addenda or why models based on probability theory can predict implementation success and suggest useful tactical advice for implementers, *Journal of Public Policy*, 2, 1–22.

Braybrooke, D. and C. E. Lindblom (1963), *The Strategy of Decision*. New York: Free Press.

Brewer, G. D. (1978), Termination: hard choices, harder questions, *Public Administration Review*, 38, 338–44.

Brookes, S. K., A. G. Jordan, R. H. Kimber and J. J. Richardson (1976) The growth of the environment as a political issue, *British Journal of Political Science*, 6, 245–55.

Bruce-Gardyne, J. and N. Lawson (1976), *The Power Game*. London: Macmillan.

Bullock, A. and O. Stallybrass (1977), *The Fontana Dictionary of Modern Thought*. London: Fontana/Collins.

Burch, M. and B. Wood (1983), *Public Policy in Britain*. Oxford: Martin Robertson.

Burns, T. and G. M. Stalker (1961), *The Management of Innovation*. London: Tavistock.

Cardona, G. (1981), One step ahead of 'Yes Minister', *The Times*, 11 December, 9.

Carley, M. (1980), *Rational Techniques in Policy Analysis*. London: Heinemann.

Castles, F. G., D. J. Murray and D. C. Potter (eds.) (1971), *Decisions, Organizations and Society*. Harmondsworth, Middlesex: Penguin.

Chapman, M. (1981), *Decision Analysis*, Civil Service College Handbook No. 21. London: HMSO.

Clarke, R. V. G. (ed.) (1978), *Tackling Vandalism*, Home Office Research Study No. 47. London: HMSO.

Clynch, Edward J. (1979), Zero-Base Budgeting in Practice, *International Journal of Public Administration*, 1, 43–64.

Cobb, R. W. and C. D. Elder (1972), *Participation in American Politics: The Dynamics of Agenda Building*. Boston: Allyn and Bacon.

CPRS (Central Review Staff) (1975), *The Future of the British Car Industry*. London: HMSO.

——— (1977), *Population and the Social Services*. London: HMSO.

Dahl, R. (1970), *Modern Political Analysis*, 2nd ed. Englewood Cliffs, NJ: Prentice Hall.

Davis, H. and S. Salasin (1979), Evaluation and change. In L. E. Datta and R. Perloff (eds.), *Improving Evaluations*. Beverley Hills, Calif.: Sage, 257–71.

Davis, S. and P. Lawrence (1977), *Matrix*. Reading, Mass.: Addison-Wesley.

deLeon, P. (1978), A theory of policy termination. In J. V. May and A. Wildavsky (eds), *The Policy Cycle*. Beverley Hills, Calif.: Sage, 279–300.

Dexter, I., A. (1981), Undesigned consequences of purposive legislative action: alternatives to implementation, *Journal of Public Policy*, 1, 413–31.

DHSS (Department of Health and Social Security) (1976), *Sharing Resources for Health in England · Report of the Resource Allocation Working Party*. London: HMSO.

Downs, A. (1972), Up and down with ecology–the 'issue-attention cycle', *The Public Interest*, 28, 38–50.

Dror, Y. (1964), Muddling through–science or interia?, *Public Administration Review*, 24, 153–7.

––––– (1968), *Public Policymaking Reexamined*. Scranton, Pa: Chandler.

––––– (1971), *Ventures in Policy Sciences*. New York: Elsevier.

Dunsire, A. (1978), *Implementation in a Bureaucracy*. Oxford: Martin Robertson.

Dye, T. (1972), *Understanding Public Policy*. Englewood Cliffs, NJ: Prentice-Hall.

Easton, D. (1979), *A Systems Analysis of Political Life*, rev. ed. Chicago: University of Chicago Press.

Eddy, W. B. (1970), Beyond behaviouralism?: organization development in public management, *Public Personnel Review*, 22, 169–74.

––––– (1981), *Public Organization: Behaviour and Development*. Cambridge, Mass.: Winthrop.

Else, P. (1970), *Public Expenditure, Parliament and PPB*. London: Political and Economic Planning (PEP).

Encel, S., P. K. Marstrand and W. Page (1975), *The Art of Anticipation*, Oxford: Martin Robertson.

Etzioni, A. (1964), *Modern Organizations*. Englewood Cliffs, NJ: Prentice-Hall.

––––– (1967), Mixed scanning: a 'third' approach to decision-making, *Public Administration Review*, 27, 385–92.

––––– (1976), *Social Problems*. Englewood Cliffs, NJ: Prentice-Hall.

Expenditure Committee (1977), *The Civil Service*, Eleventh Report from the Expenditure Committee, HC535, Session 1976–7. London: HMSO.

Ferber, R. and W. Z. Hirsch (1982), *Social Experimentation and Economic Policy*. Cambridge: Cambridge University Press.

Forrester, J. (1971), *World Dynamics*. Cambridge, Mass.: Wright-Allen Press.

––––– (1982), Global modelling revisited, *Futures*, 14, 95–110.

Fulton Report (1968), *Civil Service*, Cmnd 3638. London: HMSO.
Galbraith, J. K. (1969), *The New Industrial State*. Harmondsworth, Middlesex: Penguin.
Gershuny, J. (1978), Transport forecasting: fixing the future, *Policy and Politics*, 6, 373–402.
Glennerster, H. (1981), Social service spending in a hostile environment. In C. Hood and M. Wright (eds.), *Big Government in Hard Times*. Oxford: Martin Robertson, 174–96.
Gordon, I., J. Lewis and K. Young (1977), Perspectives on policy analysis, *Public Administration Bulletin*, No. 25, 26–35.
Gray, A. and W. I. Jenkins (1983), Policy analysis in British central government: The experience of PAR, *Public Administration*, 61, 429–50.
Greenberger, M., M. A. Crenson and B. L. Crissey (1976), *Models in the Policy Process*. New York: Russell Sage Foundation.
Greenwood, R., C. R. Hinings, S. Ranson and K. Walsh (1980) Incremental budgeting and the assumption of growth. In M. Wright (ed.), *Public Spending Decisions: Growth and Restraint in the 1970s*, London: Allen & Unwin, 49–67.
Gross, E. (1969), The definition of organizational goals, *British Journal of Sociology*, 20, 277–94.
Gunn, L. A. (1966), *The Role of Government in the Allocation of Resources to Science*. Paris: OECD.
—— (1976), Policy analysis in central government. Paper prepared for SSRC meeting on central government reserach.
—— (1978), Why is implementation so difficult? *Management Services in Government*, 33, 169–76.
—— (1980), Policy and the policy analyst. Paper delivered to Public Administration Committee (PAC) Annual Conference, University of York, September 1980.
—— and P. Lindley (1977), Devolution: Origins, events and issues, *Public Administration Bulletin*, 25, 36–54.
Hadden, S. G. and J. Hazelton (1980), Public policies toward risk, *Policy Studies Journal*, 9, 109–17.
Hansen, S. B. (1983), Public policy analysis: some recent developments and current problems, *Policy Studies Journal*, 12, 14–42.
Harrison, E. F. (1975), *The Managerial Decision-Making Process*. Boston: Houghton Mifflin.
Haywood, S. C. and H. J. Elcock (1982), Regional Health Authorities: Regional government or central agencies? In B. W. Hogwood and M. Keating (eds.), *Regional Government in England*, Oxford: Oxford University Press, 119–42.
Headey, B. (1974), *British Cabinet Ministers*. London: Allen & Unwin.
Heclo, H. (1972), Policy analysis, *British Journal of Political Science*, 2, 83–108.
—— and Wildavsky (1974), *The Private Government of Public Money*. London: Macmillan.

Heidenheimer, A, J., H. Heclo and C. T. Adams (1975), *Comparative Public Policy: The Politics of Social Choice in Europe and America*. New York: St Martins Press

Hellriegel, D. and J. Slocum (1974), *Management: A Contingency Approach*. Reading, Mass.: Addison-Wesley,

Helmer, O. (1977), Problems in futures research: Delphi and causal cross-impact analysis, *Futures*, 9, 17–31.

—— (1981), Reassessment of cross-impact analysis, *Futures*, 13, 389–400.

Hirschman, A. O. and C. E. Lindblom (1962), Economic development, research and development, policy making: Some converging views, *Behavioural Science*, 7, 211–22.

HMSO (1970), *The Reorganization of Central Government*, Cmnd 4506. London: HMSO.

Hogwood, B. W. (1976), Monitoring of government involvement in industry: The case of shipbuilding, *Public Administration*, 54, 409–24.

—— (1984), Policy analysis: the dangers of oversophistication, *Public Administration Bulletin*, 44, 19–28.

—— and B. G. Peters (1983), *Policy Dynamics*. Brighton: Wheatsheaf and New York: St Martins Press.

Hood, C. C. (1976), *The Limits of Administration*. London: Wiley.

—— and M. W. Wright (eds.) (1981), *Big Government in Hard Times*. Oxford: Martin Robertson.

Jenkins, R. (1971), On being a minister, *Sunday Times*, 17 January 1971. Reprinted in V. Herman and J. E. Alt (eds.), *Cabinet Studies: A Reader*, London: Macmillan.

Jenkins, W. I. (1978), *Policy Analysis*. Oxford: Martin Robertson.

Jones, G. (ed.) (1980), *New Approaches to the Study of Central–Local Government Relationships*. Farnborough, Hants.: Gower/SSRC.

Jones, M. (1982), Family embrace from Thatcher, *The Sunday Times*, 22 August 1982.

Jordan, A. G. (1981), Iron triangles, woolly corporatism, or elastic nets: images of the policy process, *Journal of Public Policy*, 1, 95–123.

Kaufman, H. (1971), *The Limits of Organizational Change*. Alabama: University of Alabama Press.

Keeling, D. (1972), *Management in Government*. London: Allen & Unwin.

Kerr, S. (1976), Overcoming the dysfunctions of MbO, *Management by Objectives*, 6(1), 13–19.

Keynes, J. M. (1936), *The General Theory of Employment, Interest and Money*. London: Macmillan.

Kimber, R. *et al.* (1974), The Deposit of Poisonous Waste Act 1972: a case of government by reaction? *Public Law*, Autumn 1974, 148–219.

King, A. (1975), Overload: Problems of governing in the 1970s *Political Studies*, 23, 284–96.

King, A. (1976), The problem of overload. In A. King (ed.), *Why is Britain Becoming Harder to Govern?*, London: BBC Publications, 8–30.

Klein, R. (1980), Creating problems (Review of Aaron Wildavsky, *The Art and Craft of Policy Analysis*), *New Society*, 53, 141.

Kogan, M. (1975), *The Politics of Education: Edward Boyle and Anthony Crosland in Conversation with Maurice Kogan*. Harmondsworth, Middlesex: Penguin.

Kramer, Fred A. (ed.) (1979), *Contemporary Approaches to Public Budgeting*. Cambridge, Mass.: Winthrop.

Lang, D. W. (1977), *Critical Path Analysis*, 2nd edn. London: Hodder and Stoughton.

Lasswell, H. (1970), The emerging conception of the policy sciences, *Policy Sciences*, 1, 3–14.

Le Grand, J. (1982), *The Strategy of Equality: Redistribution and the Social Services*. London: Allen & Unwin.

—— and R. Robinson (1976), *The Economics of Social Problems*. London: Macmillan.

Lerner, D. and H. Lasswell (1951), *Policy Sciences*. Stanford: Stanford University Press.

Lind, G. and C. Wiseman (1978), Setting health priorities: A review of concepts and approaches, *Journal of Social Policy*, 7, 411–40.

Lindblom, C. E. (1959), The science of muddling through, *Public Administration Review*, 19, 79–88.

—— (1965), *The Intelligence of Democracy*. New York: Free Press.

—— (1968), *The Policy Making Process*. Englewood Cliffs, NJ: Prentice-Hall.

—— (1979), Still muddling, not yet through, *Public Administration Review*, 39, 517–26.

—— and D. K. Cohen (1979), *Usable Knowledge: Social Science and Social Problem Solving*. New Haven: Yale University Press.

Linestone, H. and M. Turoff (1975), *The Delphi Method: Techniques and Application*. Reading, Mass.: Addison-Wesley.

Lippitt, R., J. Watson and G. Westley (1958),*The Dynamics of Planned Change*. New York: Jarcourt, Brace & World.

Lodge, P. and T. Blackstone (1982),*Educational Policy and Educational Inequality*. Oxford: Martin Robertson.

Lonsdale, A. J. (1978), Judgement research in policy analysis, *Futures*, 10, 213–26.

Lukes, S. (1974),*Power: A Radical View*. London: Macmillan.

Macdonald, J. and G. K. Fry (1980), Policy planning units—Ten years on,*Public Administration*, 58, 421–37.

McKay, D. I. and A. W. Cox (1978), *The Politics of Urban Change*. London: Croom Helm.

McLean, M. (1976), Does cross-impact analysis have a future?, *Futures*, 8, 163–9.

March, J. G. and H. A. Simon (1958), *Organisations*. London: John Wiley.

Meadows, D. II., D. L. Meadows, J. Randers and W. W. Behrens (1972), *The Limits to Growth*. Washington DC: Potomac Books.

Meltsner, A. (1976), *Policy Analysts in the Bureaucracy*. Berkeley: University of California Press.

Mohr, L. B. (1973), The concept of organizational goal, *American Political Science Review*, 67, 470–81.

Moser, Sir Claus (1980), Statistics and public policy, *Journal of the Royal Statistical Society, Series A*, 143(1), 1–31.

Newland, C. A. (1976), Policy/program objectives and federal management—The search for government effectiveness, *Public Administration Review*, 36, 17–20.

Newton, K. and L. J. Sharpe (1977), Local outputs research: some reflections and proposals, *Policy and Politics*, 5, 61–82.

Norman, J. M. (1975), *Elementary Dynamic Programming*. London: Edward Arnold.

Paterson Report (1973), *The New Scottish Local Authorities: Organisation and Management Structures*, Report of a Working Group (Chairman: I. V. Paterson). Edinburgh: HMSO.

Perrow, C. (1961), The analysis of goals in complex organisations, *American Sociological Review*, 26, 854–66.

—— (1970), *Organisational Analysis: A Sociological View*. London: Tavistock.

Peters, B. G. (1983), *Public Policy in America: Process and Performance*. New York: Franklin Watts.

Peters, G. H. (1973), *Cost-Benefit Analysis and Public Expenditure*. London: Institute of Economic Affairs.

Phare, G. Rowland (1979), Beyond Zero-Base Budgeting, *Managerial Planning*, July–August, 18–23.

Pinkus, C. E. and A. Dixon (1981), *Solving Local Government Problems: Practical Applications of Operations Research in Cities and Regions*. London: Allen & Unwin.

Plowden, W. (1981), The British Central Policy Review Staff. In P. R. Baehr and Björn Wittrock (eds.), *Policy Analysis and Policy Innovation*. London and Beverley Hills, Calif.: Sage.

Plowden Report (1961), *The Control of Public Expenditure*, Cmnd 1432. London: HMSO.

Pollitt, C., J. Negro, L. Lewis and J. Patten (eds.) (1979), *Public Policy in Theory and Practice*. London: Hodder and Stoughton.

Polsby, N. (1980), *Community Power and Political Theory*, 2nd edn. New Haven: Yale University Press.

Pressman, J. I. and A. Wildavsky (1973), *Implementation*. Berkeley: University of California Press.

Prince, M. J. (1983), *Policy Advice and Organisational Survival*. Aldershot, Hants.: Gower.

Ramsey, J. B. (1977), *Economic Forecasting: Models or Markets?* London: Institute of Economic Affairs.

Rawlinson, J. G. (1981), *Creative Thinking and Brainstorming*. Farnborough, Hants.: Gower.

Rees, T. B. (1981), Research, Statistics and policy making. Paper to the Royal Institute of Public Administration Conference on Public Influence and Public Policy, 10–11 April 1981.

Rhodes, R. A. W. (1979a), *Public Administration and Policy Analysis: Recent Developments in Britain and America.* Farnborough, Hants.: Saxon House.

—— (1979b), Research into central–local relations: A framework for analysis. In Social Science Research Council, *Central–Local Government Relationships.* London: SSRC, Appendix 1.

—— (1981), *Control and Power in Central–Local Government Relationships.* Farnborough, Hants.: Gower/SSRC.

Richardson, J. J. (ed.) (1982), *Policy Styles in Western Europe.* London: Allen and Unwin.

—— and A. G. Jordan (1979), *Governing Under Pressure: The Policy Process in a Post-Parliamentary Democracy.* Oxford: Martin Robertson.

Rose, R. (1973), Comparing public policy: An overview, *European Journal of Political Research*, 1, 67–94.

—— (1976a), *The Dynamics of Public Policy.* Beverley Hills, Calif.: Sage.

—— (1976b), *Managing Presidential Objectives.* London: Macmillan.

—— (1976c), Disciplined research and undisciplined problems, *International Social Science Journal*, 28, 99–121.

—— (1976d), *Northern Ireland: A Time of Choice.* London: Macmillan.

Rossi, P. H., H. E. Freeman and S. R. Wright (1979), *Evaluation: A Systematic Approach.* Beverley Hills, Calif.: Sage.

Rothschild Report (1971), Report on the Organisation and Management of Government R & D. In *A Framework for Government Research and Development*, Cmnd 4814. London: HMSO.

Rutman, L. (1980), *Planning Useful Evaluations: Evaluability Assessment.* Beverley Hills, Calif.: Sage.

Sackman, H. (1975), *Delphi Critique.* Lexington, Mass.: Lexington Books.

Sandbach, F. (1980), *Environment, Ideology and Policy.* Oxford: Basil Blackwell.

Sapolsky, H. M. (1972), *The Polaris System Development: Bureaucratic and Programmatic Success in Government.* Cambridge, Mass.: Harvard University Press.

Schein, H. and W. G. Bennis (1965), *Personal and Organizational Change through Group Methods.* New York: John Wiley.

Schick, A. (1973), A death in the bureaucracy: The demise of federal PPB, *Public Administration Review*, 33, 146–56.

Schulman, P. R. (1980), *Large-scale Policy Making.* New York: Elsevier.

Schultze, C. (1968), *The Politics and Economics of Public Spending.* Washington DC: The Brookings Institution.

Select Committee on Estimates (1958), *Treasury Control of Expenditure*, HC 254, Session 1957–8. London: HMSO.

Select Committee on Procedure (1969), *First Report from the Select Committee on Procedure*, HC 410, Session 1968–9. London: HMSO.

Self, P. (1970), 'Nonsense on stilts': Cost-benefit analysis and the Roskill Commission, *Political Quarterly*, 41, 249–60.

—— (1975), *Econocrats and the Policy Process: The Politics and Philosophy of Cost-Benefit Analysis*. London: Macmillan.

Sharpe, L. J. (1975), Social scientists and policy-making: Some cautionary thoughts and transatlantic reflections, *Policy and Politics*, 4, 7–34.

SHHD (1977), *Scottish Health Authorities Revenue Equalisation: Report of the Working Party on Revenue Resource Allocation*. Edinburgh: HMSO.

Shils, E. and H. A. Finch (trs. and eds.) (1949), *Max Weber on the Methodology of the Social Sciences*. New York: Free Press.

Sieber, S, D. (1980), *Fatal Remedies*. New York: Plenum.

Silverman, D. (1970), *The Theory of Organisations*. London: Heinemann.

Simon, H. A. (1947), *Administrative Behaviour*, 1st edn. London: Macmillan.

—— (1957a), *Administrative Behaviour*, 2nd edn. London: Macmillan.

—— (1957b), *Models of Man*. London: John Wiley.

—— (1960), *The New Science of Management Decision*. Englewood Cliffs, NJ: Prentice Hall. (A second version, with additional chapters, was published in 1965 as *The Shape of Automation*. A revised edition was published in 1977 under the original title.)

—— (1976), *Administrative Behaviour*, 3rd edn. New York: Free Press.

—— (1983), *Reason in Human Affairs*. Oxford: Blackwell.

Solesbury, W. (1976), The environmental agenda, *Public Administration*, 54, 379–97.

Steiner, G. A. and J. B. Miner (1982), *Management Policy and Strategy*. London: Macmillan.

Steiss, A. W. and G. A. Daneke (1980), *Performance Administration*. Lexington, Mass.: Lexington Books.

Stewart, J. D. (1974), *The Responsive Local Authority*. Croydon: C. Knight.

Stokey, E. and R. Zeckhauser (1978), *A Primer for Policy Analysis*. New York: Norton.

Stringer, J. K. and J. J. Richardson (1980), Managing the political agenda: Problem definition and policy making in Britain, *Parliamentary Affairs*, 23, 23–39.

Study Commission on the Family (1983), *Families in the Future: A Policy Agenda for the '80s*. London: Study Commission on the Family.

Sugden, R. and A. Williams (1978), *The Principles of Practical Cost-Benefit Analysis*. Oxford: Oxford University Press.

Thomas, R. (1980), *Do Statistics Influence Policy?* Milton Keynes: The Open University Press.

Thompson, J. D. (1967), *Organisations in Action*. New York: McGraw-Hill.

Tribe, L. H. (1972), Policy science: analysis or ideology? *Philosophy and Public Affairs*, 2, 66–110.

Van Meter, D. and C. E. Van Horn (1975), The policy implementation process: A conceptual framework, *Administration and Society*, 6, 445–88.

Vickers, Sir G. (1965), *The Art of Judgment: A Study of Policy Making*. London: Chapman & Hall.

Weinberg, A. M. (1963), Criteria for scientific choice, *Minerva*, 1, 159–71.

Weiner, L. (1976), Future scanning for trade groups and companies, *Harvard Business Review*, September/October, pp. 14 and 174–6.

Weiss, C. H. (1972), *Evaluation Research: Methods of Assessing Program Effectiveness*. Englewood Cliffs, NJ: Prentice-Hall.

White, D. (1979), How polluted are we—and how polluted do we want to be? *New Society*, 11 January 1979, 63–6.

Wildavsky, A. (1962), *Dixon–Yates: A Study in Power Politics*. New Haven: Yale University Press.

—— (1969), Rescuing policy analysis from PPBS, *Public Administration Review*, 29, 189–201.

—— (1971), Does planning work? *The Public Interest*, Summer 1971, 24, 95–104.

—— (1972), The self-evaluating organization, *Public Administration Review*, 32, 509–20.

—— (1973), If planning is everything, maybe it's nothing, *Policy Sciences*, 4, 127–53.

—— (1974), *The Politics of the Budgetary Process*, 2nd edn. Boston: Little, Brown.

—— (1975), *Budgeting: A Comparative Theory of Budgetary Processes*. Boston: Little, Brown.

—— (1980), *The Art and Craft of Policy Analysis*. London: Macmillan. (Published in the USA as *Speaking Truth to Power*, Boston: Little Brown.)

Williams, A. (1973), C.B.A.: Bastard science and/or insidious poison in the body politik? In J. N. Wolfe (ed.), *Cost-Benefit and Cost-Effectiveness Analysis*, London: Allen & Unwin, 30–63.

Wiseman, C. (1978), Selection of major planning issues, *Policy Sciences*, 9, 71–86.

Wolman, H. (1981), The determinants of program success and failure, *Journal of Public Policy*, 1, 433–64.

Wright, M. W. (ed.) (1980), *Public Spending Decisions: Growth and Restraint in the 1970s*. London: Allen & Unwin.

Young, K. (1977), Values in the policy process, *Policy and Politics*, 5, 1–22.

# Index

see also inter-organizational
interaction
descriptive:
analysis, 45, 207
models, 3, 43, 49–53, 70–1
design, see policy design
deviance, 117
Dexter, L. A., 123–4
disaggregation, 76, 80, 120–1
see also aggregation
discounting, 98, 185–6, 190
distribution of impact, 227, 234,
249, 258
Dixon, A., 177
Dror, Y., 6, 29, 55–7, 62, 88, 166,
172, 173, 251
Dunsire, A., 197
Dye, T., 28
dynamic programming, 54, 177–80

Easton, D., 25
econometrics, 140–2
economic data, 74, 81, 130
economically rational model, 6, 56,
62
economics, 35, 44, 45, 140–2, 143,
185–7, 233–4, 251–2
Eddy, W. B., 257
education policy, 148–9, 159–60,
173, 194, 224
Elcock, H. J., 165
Elder, C. D., 67
elite theory, 71
Else, P., 187
employees, see public employees
Encel, S., 137–8, 142, 143
envelope curve, 135
environmental policy, 68
ethical considerations, 228, 231, 240
Etzioni, A., 60–1, 89, 119, 156, 198·
evaluation, 4, 5, 9–10, 24–5, 27, 33,
219–40
and implementation, 212, 215
and issue definition, 110, 126–7
and issue search, 84–5
and monitoring, 212, 215, 220–2
and objectives, 152, 158, 162–3,
164, 222–4, 233–4, 235,
236, 237, 239
and policy succession and policy
termination, 241, 243, 246,
249, 259–60
techniques, 228–34

utilization, 237–40
Expenditure Committee, 215
experimental method, 230–2
see also quasi-experimental
method
experimental programme, 126
extrapolation, 133–5, 136, 139–40

family policy, 115–16
feasibility, 174–5, 177, 211
feedback, 25, 105, 126, 143, 173,
232
Ferber, R., 230
Finch, H. A., 43
forecasting, 4, 5, 8, 24, 62–3, 73,
79–80, 82–3, 110, 125–6,
128–49, 151, 212
Forrester, J., 141–2, 145–6
frame analysis, 109, 119–20
see also policy frames
Freeman, H. E., 125, 221, 231
Fry, G. K., 38
Fudge, D., 198, 207–9
Fulton Report, 153, 215
functional termination, 242–3
see also policy termination

Galbraith, J. K., 98
gap analysis, 160
Gershuny, J., 129
Glennerster, H., 49
goal displacement, 156
goals, see objectives
Gordon, I., 26–8
Gray, A., 38, 188, 237
Greenberger, M., 143
Greenwood, R., 189
Gross, E., 156
Gunn, L. A., 24, 26, 167, 174, 198

Hadden, S. G., 182
Hansen, S. B., 34
Harrison, E. F., 151
Hawthorne effect, 231
Haywood, S. C., 165
Hazelton, J., 182
health policy, 17, 89, 154, 165,
166–8, 170, 174, 186, 208
Heclo, H., 13, 19, 21–2
Heidenheimer, A. J., 13
Hellriegel, J., 73, 78
Helmer, O., 138
heuristic problem-solving, 54